Western Europeans were among the first, if not the first, to invent mechanical clocks, geometrically precise maps, double-entry bookkeeping, exact algebraic and musical notations, and perspective painting. By the sixteenth century more people were thinking quantitatively in Western Europe than in any other part of the world. They thus became world leaders in science, technology, armaments, navigation, business practice, and bureaucracy, and created many of the greatest masterpieces of Western music and painting.

The Measure of Reality discusses the epochal shift from qualitative to quantitative perception in Western Europe during the late Middle Ages and Renaissance. This shift made modern science, technology, business practice, and bureaucracy possible. It affected not only the obvious – such as measurements of time and space and mathematical technique – but, equally and simultaneously, music and painting, thus proving that the shift was even more profound than once thought.

The Measure of Reality

BOOKS BY ALFRED W. CROSBY

America, Russia, Hemp and Napoleon: American Trade with Russia and the Baltic, 1783–1812 (1965)

The Columbian Exchange: Biological and Cultural Consequences of 1492 (1972)

Epidemic and Peace, 1918 (1976)

Ecological Imperialism: The Biological Expansion of Europe, 900–1900 (1986)

Germs, Seeds, and Animals: Studies in Ecological History (1994)

The Measure of Reality

QUANTIFICATION
AND WESTERN
SOCIETY,
1250–1600

Alfred W. Crosby

CAMBRIDGE
UNIVERSITY PRESS

Published by the Press Syndicate of the University of Cambridge
The Pitt Building, Trumpington Street, Cambridge CB2 1RP
40 West 20th Street, New York, NY 10011-4211, USA
10 Stamford Road, Oakleigh, Melbourne 3166, Australia

First published 1997

Printed in the United States of America

Library of Congress Cataloging-in-Publication Data
Crosby, Alfred W.
The measure of reality : quantification and Western society,
1250–1600 / Alfred W. Crosby.

p.   cm.

Includes index.

ISBN 0-521-55427-6

1. Europe – History – 476–1492.   2. Europe – History – 1492–1648.
3. Historiometry.   4. History – Methodology.   I. Title.
D202.C76   1997
940 – dc20   96-3092
                                                                         CIP

A catalog record for this book is available from the British Library.

ISBN 0-521-55427-6 hardback

Take away number in all things and all things perish. Take calculation from the world and all is enveloped in dark ignorance, nor can he who does not know the way to reckon be distinguished from the rest of the animals.

St. Isidore of Seville (c. 600)

And still they come, new from those nations to which the study of that which can be weighed and measured is a consuming love.

W. H. Auden (1935)

Contents

Preface

This is the third book I have written in my lifelong search for explanations for the amazing success of European imperialism. Europeans were not the cruelest and not the kindest imperialists, not the earliest and not the latest. They were unique in the degree of their success. They may retain that distinction forever, because it is unlikely that one division of the world's inhabitants will ever again enjoy such extreme advantages over all the rest.

Cyrus the Great, Alexander the Great, Genghis Khan, and Huayna Capac were great conquerors, but they were all confined to no more than one continent and at best a wedge of a second. They were homebodies compared with Queen Victoria, on whose empire (to resuscitate a very old cliché) the sun literally never set. The sun also never set on the empires of France, Spain, Portugal, the Netherlands, and Germany in their heyday. The explanations for this triumph, popular in Europe circa 1900, were fueled by ethnocentrism and justified by Social Darwinism. They were, simply, that those members of the human species most subject to painful sunburns were the most recent, highest, and, in all likelihood, final twigs on the exfoliating tree of evolution. Pale people were the brightest, most energetic, most sensible, most aesthetically advanced, and most ethical humans. They conquered all because they deserved to.

That seems hilariously unlikely today, but what other explanations are there? I have written books about the biological advantages that the white imperialists enjoyed. Their diseases mowed down American Indians, Polynesians, and Australian Aborigines. Their animals and plants, cultivated and wild, helped them to "Europeanize" wide expanses of the world and make them comfortable homelands for Europeans.[1] But as I played out my role as a biological determinist, I was nagged by the impression that Europeans were incomparably successful at sending ships across oceans to predetermined destinations and at arriving at those destinations with superior weaponry – with, for instance, cannons superior to those of the Ottomans and the Chinese; that they were more efficient at operating joint-stock companies and empires of unprecedented extension and degree of activity than anyone else – that they were in general far more effective than they should have been, at least as judged by their own and others' precedents. Europeans were not as magnificent as they believed, but they were able to organize large collections of people and capital and to exploit physical reality for useful knowledge and for power more efficiently than any other people of the time. Why?

The textbook answer is, put simply, science and technology, and that was certainly true for generations and still is in large parts of the world. But if we gaze back through and beyond the nineteenth century to the beginnings of European imperialism, we see little of science and technology as such. Westerners' advantage,

---

[1] *Ecological Imperialism: The Biological Expansion of Europe, 900–1900* (Cambridge University Press, 1986); *The Columbian Exchange: Biological and Cultural Consequences of 1492* (Westport, Conn.: Greenwood Press, 1972); *Germs, Seeds, and Animals: Studies in Ecological History* (Armonk, N.Y.: Sharpe, 1994).

I believe, lay at first not in their science and technology, but in their utilization of habits of thought that would *in time* enable them to advance swiftly in science and technology and, in the meantime, gave them decisively important administrative, commercial, navigational, industrial, and military skills. The initial European advantage lay in what French historians have called *mentalité*.

During the late Middle Ages and Renaissance a new model of reality emerged in Europe. A quantitative model was just beginning to displace the ancient qualitative model. Copernicus and Galileo, the artisans who taught themselves to make one good cannon after another, the cartographers who mapped the coasts of newly contacted lands, the bureaucrats and entrepreneurs who managed the new empires and East and West India companies, the bankers who marshaled and controlled the streams of new wealth – these people were thinking of reality in quantitative terms with greater consistency than any other members of their species.

We look upon them as initiators of revolutionary change, which they certainly were, but they were also heirs of changes in *mentalité* that had been fermenting for centuries. This book is about those changes.

Writing this book has been a major battle for me, and I never would have completed it without my many allies. I owe the Guggenheim Foundation and the University of Texas for time and money, and I owe the Library of Congress for access to its stacks and the advice and counsel of its staff. I owe Brenda Preyer, Robin Doughty, James Koschoreck, and André Goddu for checking over the chapters pertaining to their respective specialties. Martha Newman and Eduardo Douglas waded through the entire manuscript and saved me many errors. I owe very special thanks to Robert Lerner, who read the whole manuscript carefully and long stretches of it meticulously, and pulled me back from many a precipice. Finally, there is my Cambridge editor, Frank Smith, who read my book as many times as I wrote and rewrote it, a Sisyphusian ordeal.

The Measure of Reality

PART ONE

Pantometry Achieved

Pantometry [f. Gr. $\pi\alpha\nu\tau o$- Panto-, all + Gr. -$\mu\epsilon\tau\rho\acute{\iota}\alpha$ measurement.]
1. Universal measurement: see quots. *Obs.* [1571 Diggs (*title*) A Geometrical Practice, named Pantometria, divided into three Bookes, Longimetra, Planimetra, and Steriometria.]

Oxford English Dictionary

CHAPTER ONE

Pantometry: An Introduction

Every culture lives within its dream.
Lewis Mumford (1934)[1]

In the mid-ninth century A.D. Ibn Khurradadhbeh described Western Europe as a source of "eunuchs, slave girls and boys, brocade, beaver skins, glue, sables, and swords," and not much more. A century later another Muslim geographer, the great Masudi, wrote that Europeans were dull in mind and heavy in speech, and the "farther they are to the north the more stupid, gross, and brutish they are."[2] This was what any Muslim sophisticate would have expected of Christians, particularly the "Franks," as Western Europeans were known in the Islamic world, because these people, barbarians most of them, lived at the remote Atlantic margin of Eurasia, far from the hearthlands of its high cultures.

---

[1] Lewis Mumford, *Technics and Civilization* (New York: Harcourt, Brace & World, 1962), 28.
[2] Bernard Lewis, *The Muslim Discovery of Europe* (New York: Norton, 1982), 138–9.

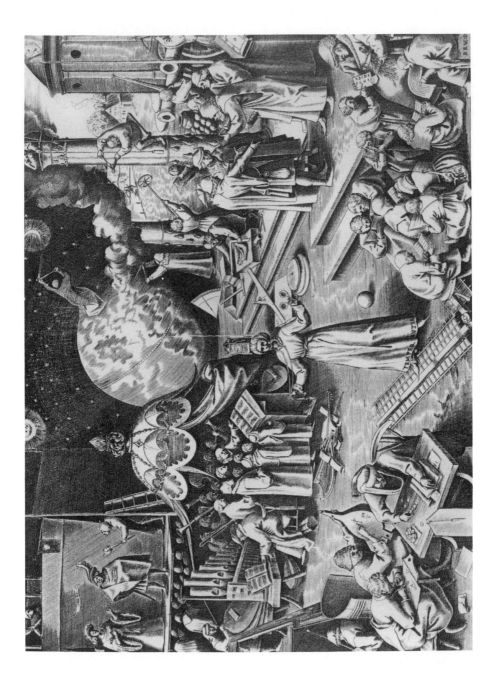

Six centuries later the Franks were at least equal to, and even ahead of, the Muslims and everyone else in the world in certain kinds of mathematics and mechanical innovation. They were in the first stage of developing science-cum-technology that would be the glory of their civilization and the edged weapon of their imperialistic expansion. How, between the ninth and the sixteenth centuries, had these bumpkins managed all that?

What was the nature of the change in what would be called in French their *mentalité*? As a necessary preliminary to any attempt to answer that, we should examine that *mentalité* in the 1500s. It is the effect, and knowing it, we will know better what to look for in the way of causes.

Kitsch is a peephole through which we may see samples if not always of a society's bromides, then of what it is thinking about with freshest intensity and even of *how* it is thinking. I offer in evidence Pieter Bruegel the Elder's 1560 print of Temperance[3] (Figure 1), then the most prestigious of the ancient Virtues. A Latin motto printed below the original is bromidic ("We must look to it that we do not give ourselves over to empty pleasures, extravagance, or lustful living; but also that we do not, because of miserly greed, live in filth and ignorance")[4] but the artist, aiming for sales, made sure that just about everything else in the print was

[3] My interpretation of this print is drawn largely from H. Arthur Klein and Mina C. Klein, *Peter Bruegel the Elder, Artist* (New York: Macmillan, 1968), 112–16.

[4] H. Arthur Klein, *Graphic Worlds of Peter Bruegel the Elder* (New York: Dover, 1963), 243–5.

Figure 1. Pieter Bruegel the Elder, *Temperance,* 1560. H. Arthur Klein, *Graphic Worlds of Peter Bruegel the Elder* (New York: Dover Publications, Inc., 1963), 245.

new or at least newly applauded. No one would or could have created such a picture five hundred years before or, in its entirety, even a hundred years before, no more than a map of America.

Progressive Westerners ply their crafts around the figure of Temperance. The sixteenth was a great century for astronomy and cartography – it was the century of Nicolaus Copernicus and Gerhardus Mercator – and so at the top and center a daredevil astronomer teetering on the North Pole measures the angular distance between the moon and some neighboring star. A colleague below takes a similar measurement of the distance between two locations on earth. Just below and to the right is a clutter of measuring devices – compasses, a mason's square, a plumb bob, among other things – and people using them. Bruegel obviously assumed that his contemporaries and prospective customers took pride in their ability to measure, to oblige a fluid reality to stand still and submit to the application of the quadrant and T square.

The upper right of the print is devoted to violence. There the people and devices – musket, crossbow, and artillery – are all associated with war, arguably the central occupation of Europeans in Bruegel's century. In the Middle Ages battles had been settled by the collision of aristocrats on horseback, but military technology had changed and now battles were dominated by the confrontations of great blocks of plebeian pedestrians armed with "standoff" weapons like pikes, crossbows, harquebuses, muskets, and artillery. Leading the new armies required more than courage and a solid seat on your charger.

Sixteenth century military textbooks commonly included tables of squares and square roots to guide officers in arranging hundreds and even thousands of men in the new battle formations of the Renaissance West: squares, triangles, shears, bastard squares, broad squares, and so on.[5] Officers, the good ones, now

---

[5] Bernabe Rich, *Path-Way to Military Practise (London 1587)* (Amsterdam: Da Capo Press, 1969).

had "to wade in the large sea of Algebra & numbers"[6] or to recruit mathematicians to help them. Iago, the old soldier and villain of Shakespeare's *Othello*, dismisses Cassio as an "Arithmetician," who had "never set a squadron in the field,"[7] but such number-smiths had become a military necessity.

The new kind of war had reduced foot soldiers to quanta. They, even more than the men of the Greek phalanx and Roman legion, learned to perform like automatons. They began to do something that we have considered characteristic of soldiers ever since: to march in step. Niccolò Machiavelli, military as well as political theorist, declared that "as a man that is dancing, and keeps time with the music, cannot make a false step; so an army that properly observes the beat of its drums cannot easily be disordered."[8] Textbooks and drillmasters reduced the foot soldiers' complicated manipulations of pike and firearm to series of distinct motions — twenty, thirty, forty — all requiring approximately the same concentration and duration. François Rabelais laughed at soldiers who peformed like "a perfect clockwork mechanism,"[9] a kind of machinery of which we will hear much more in Chapter 4.

In Breugel's print, just below the two cannons at the upper right, are five men, probably arguing about the contents of the large book beside them, most likely the Bible. It was such disputes that drove men to cast cannons and to turn foot soldiers into escapements and cogs. Below the debaters a teacher instructs chil-

[6] Thomas Digges, *An Arithmeticall Militaire Treatise Named Stratioticos (London 1571)* (Amsterdam: Da Capo Press, 1968), 70.

[7] William Shakespeare, *Othello,* act I, scene 1, lines 18–30.

[8] Niccolò Machiavelli, *The Art of War,* in *The Works of Nicholas Machiavel* (London: Thomas Davies et al., 1762), 44, 47, 54. See also William H. McNeill, *The Pursuit of Power: Technology, Armed Force, and Society since A.D. 1000* (Chicago: University of Chicago Press, 1982), 128–34.

[9] François Rabelais, *The Histories of Gargantua and Pantagruel,* trans. J. M. Cohen (Harmondsworth: Penguin Books, 1955), 141.

dren in reading letters. Literacy was increasingly important for the
ambitious. Even sergeants needed to be literate, "for it is harde by
Memorie to discharge so many things wel as he shal be charged
withall."[10]

Johannes Gutenberg a century before had standardized Gothic
letters, casting them onto the faces of small metal cubes of uniform
dimensions, excepting width ("M" being, after all, wider than
"I"). He lined these up on a block like ranks of soldiers on parade,
wedged them tight, and then pressed the block on paper, printing
a whole page at a time. His most famous product was the Mazarin
Bible: forty-two lines to the page of about 2,750 letters each, with
left and right margins justified.[11]

The lower left of the print is devoted to a tempest of calculation. A merchant counts his money, with which we measure all
things. An accountant calculates in Hindu-Arabic numerals, and
someone — a peasant? — seems to be jotting calculations on the
back of an old lute or bellows. What is the mark by his hand? It
looks like a drawn version of a tally stick, a piece of wood notched
to indicate numerical values: a broad notch for a guilder, a narrower one for divisions thereof.[12]

Next, moving clockwise, is a painter (Bruegel himself?), his
back turned to us, possibly in embarrassment. In this print Bruegel
violated the primary diktat of Renaissance perspective that a picture should be geometrically consistent and should include no
more than one point of view. He jammed several scenes together,
each with its own point of view. The people and objects on the
right side are spatially (if vaguely) related to steps that indicate

[10] Digges, *Stratioticos,* 87.
[11] Michael Clapham, "Printing," in *A History of Technology,* eds. Charles
Singer et al. (Oxford: Clarendon Press, 1957), 3: 386–8; Gutenberg Bible,
Humanities Research Center, University of Texas, Austin.
[12] Karl Menninger, *Number Words and Number Symbols: A Cultural History of Numbers,* trans. Paul Broneer (Cambridge, Mass.: MIT Press,
1969), 251.

third dimension by rising, that is, receding, toward the back (the top). In contrast, the lines of the organ on the left stretch straight back from the viewer toward an unseen but obviously lower horizon. The astronomer and cartographer bob autonomously in surrealistic space.

The effect is disjointed, but Bruegel knew full well what he was doing. He and his customers were familiar with the geometrical rules of Renaissance perspective, and by breaking them he was able to indicate the independence of the otherwise contiguous scenes by giving each an independent perspective. (Much more about Renaissance perspective in Chapter 9.)

Immediately above the artist are a number of musicians and one drudge pumping an organ. The singers are performing music from texts. They are children and adults of several ages, hence of several vocal ranges, and they are accompanied by the organ, a sackbut, a cornett, and other instruments. The likelihood is that they are singing polyphonically, and if so, they certainly need texts. The sixteenth was the century of Josquin de Prés and Thomas Tallis, the golden age of church polyphony, a kind of music so complicated that it could be performed best – perhaps can be performed only – with the aid of written notation. Renaissance music notation, like ours, its descendant, consisted of lines indicating, from top to bottom, the pitch of notes, and figures thereon indicating the order of the notes and rests, which in duration were all equal or exact multiples or fractions of each other. Tallis, one of Bruegel's contemporaries, will compose *Spem in alium*, in *forty* separate parts, possibly for Queen Elizabeth's fortieth birthday in 1573.[13] This motet is the ne plus ultra of the quantum approach to sound, not surpassed as a bravura display of counterpoint from that day to this.

To show that his age was not all war, work, and tricky tech-

[13] Paul Doe, "Tallis, Thomas," in *The New Grove Dictionary of Music and Musicians*, ed. Stanley Sadie (London: Macmillan, 1980), 18: 544.

nique, Bruegel included a reference to the contemporary theater, jester and all, in the upper left corner. This painter seems to have had a nose not only for current but for future trends as well. Lope de Vega will be born two years after Bruegel finishes this drawing, and Shakespeare two years after that.

Temperance herself occupies the center of the picture. In her left hand she holds spectacles, a symbol of sagacity, and in her right hand are reins that lead to a bit in her mouth, representing self-restraint. She wears spurs on her heels (control over great power) and a snake knotted around her waist as a belt (evil passions under control?). She stands on the vane of a post windmill, medieval Europe's greatest single contribution to power technology. At the dead center of the picture – surely not by accident – she wears on her head what was then the most distinctively Western of all contrivances for measuring quantity: the mechanical clock, whose titanic *TICK-TOCK* had already been thundering in Europe's ears for 250 years.[14]

Bruegel's print is a sort of potpourri of what quickened the attention of urban Western Europeans circa 1560, of what we might call the West's Renaissance dream. The collection is such a miscellany that it is not easy to put a name to that dream. No one was concerned with its internal consistency or even thought of it as a whole. It was a yearning, a demand, for order. Many of the people in Bruegel's picture are engaged in one way or another in visualizing the stuff of reality as aggregates of uniform units, as quanta: leagues, miles, degrees of angle, letters, guldens, hours, minutes, musical notes. The West was making up its mind (most of its mind, at least) to treat the universe in terms of quanta uniform in one or more characteristics, quanta that are often thought of as arranged in lines, squares, circles, and other symmetrical forms: music staffs, platoons, ledger columns, planetary or-

[14] Klein, *Graphic Worlds of Peter Bruegel the Elder*, 243–5.

bits. Painters were thinking of scenes as geometrically precise visual cones or pyramids focused on the observing eye. The Renaissance's unprecedented and, to this day, unmatched achievement in painting, the most purely visual of the arts and crafts, was, assuming that eras do have zeitgeists, predictable, even inevitable; but I am getting ahead of myself.

The choice of the Renaissance West was to perceive as much of reality as possible visually and all at once, a trait then and for centuries after the most distinctive of its culture. The choice extended even to what was least visual and most fleeting, that is to say, music. You can see on a page several minutes of music at once. You cannot hear it, of course, but you can *see* it, and instantly gain knowledge of its entire arc through time. The Renaissance choice in music was to limit variation, to reduce improvisation. It made the same choice in war, choreographing the actions of men lost in the cloudy terror of battle. The sixteenth seems to have been the first century in which Western European generals practiced tactics with lead soldiers on a table.[15]

What shall we call this devotion to breaking down things and energies and practices and perceptions into uniform parts and counting them? Reductionism? Yes, but that is a baggy category; it does not help us to place in relation to other developments Niccolò Tartaglia's answer in the 1530s to the question of how much a cannon should be tilted upward to fire a ball the farthest. He fired from a culverin two balls of equal weight with equal charges of powder, one at 30 and the other at 45 degrees of elevation. The first went 11,232 Veronese feet, the second 11,832.[16] This is quantification. This is how we reach out for

---

[15] J. B. Kist, *Jacob de Gheyn: The Exercise of Arms, A Commentary* (New York: McGraw-Hill, 1971), 6; J. R. Hale, *War and Society in Renaissance Europe, 1450–1620* (Baltimore: Johns Hopkins Press, 1985), 144–5.

[16] A. R. Hall, *Ballistics in the Seventeenth Century* (Cambridge University Press, 1952), 38–42.

physical reality, push aside its darling curls, and take it by the nape of the neck.

We, who, in W. H. Auden's words, live in societies "to which the study of that which can be weighed and measured is a consuming love,"[17] have difficulty imagining an alternative to our approach to reality. We need for purposes of comparison examples of another way of thinking. The writings of Plato and Aristotle celebrate an *un-*, an almost *anti*metrological approach and have the further advantage of being representative of our ancestral mode of thought at its best.

These two men thought more highly of human reason than we do, but they did not believe our five senses capable of accurate measurement of nature. Thus Plato wrote that when the soul depends on the senses for information, "it is drawn away by the body into the realm of the variable, and loses its way and becomes confused and dizzy."[18]

The two Greeks' criteria for dividing data into categories of what we can be pretty sure about and what we will never be sure about differ from ours. You and I are ready to agree that the raw data of everyday experience are variable and our senses frail, but we believe we have a category that the two philosophers did not think they had: a category of things that are sufficiently uniform to justify our measuring them, after which averages and means can be calculated. As for the dependability of our senses in making such measurements, we point to the achievements we have made on the basis of their dependability: power looms, spacecraft, actuarial tables, and so on. That is not a solid answer – our successes may be accidents – but it is an example of the way humans often

---

[17] W. H. Auden, *The English Auden: Poems, Essays and Dramatic Writings, 1927–1939* (London: Faber & Faber, 1986), 292.

[18] *The Collected Dialogues of Plato*, eds. Edith Hamilton and Huntington Cairns (Princeton, N.J.: Princeton University Press, 1961), 62.

assess their capabilities: that is, what works and what does not? Why did Plato and Aristotle, who were bright indeed, shy away from the category of the usefully quantifiable?

There are a minimum of two points to be made here. First, the ancients defined quantificational measurement much more narrowly than we do, and often rejected it for some more broadly applicable technique. Aristotle, for instance, stated that the mathematician measures dimensions only after he "strips off all the sensible qualities, e.g. weight and lightness, hardness and its contrary, and also heat and cold and other sensible contrarities."[19] Aristotle, "the Philosopher," as medieval Europe called him, found description and analysis more useful in qualitative terms than in quantitative ones.

We would claim that weight, hardness, and temperature "and other sensible contrarities" are quantifiable, but that is not implicit either in these qualities or in the nature of the human mind. Our child psychologists declare that humans, even in infancy, show indications that they are innately endowed with the ability to count discrete entities[20] (three cookies, six balls, eight pigs), but weight, hardness, and so on do not come to us as quantities of discrete entities. They are conditions, not collections; and, even worse, they are often flowing changes. We cannot count them as they are; we have to see them with our mind's eye, quantify them by fiat, and then count the quanta. That is easily done with measuring extension – for example, this lance is so many feet long, and we can count them by laying the lance on the ground and mincing along its length. But hardness, heat, speed, acceleration – how in the world would we quantify those?

---

[19] *The Works of Aristotle,* ed. W. D. Ross (Oxford: Clarendon Press, 1928), 8: 1061a.

[20] B. Bower, "Babies Add up Basic Arithmetic Skills," *Science News,* 142 (29 Aug. 1992), 132.

What can be measured in terms of quanta is not as simple as we, who have the ex post facto advantage of our ancestors' mistakes, think. For instance, when in the fourteenth century the scholars of Oxford's Merton College began to think about the benefits of measuring not only size, but also qualities as slippery as motion, light, heat, and color, they forged right on, jumped the fence, and talked about quantifying certitude, virtue, and grace.[21] Indeed, if you can manage to think of measuring heat before the invention of the thermometer, then why should you presumptively exclude certitude, virtue, and grace?

Second, unlike Plato and Aristotle, we, with few exceptions, embrace the assumption that mathematics and the material world are immediately and intimately related. We accept as self-explanatory the fact that physics, the science of palpable reality, should be intensely mathematical. But that proposition is not self-explanatory; it is a miracle about which many sages have had their doubts.

Mathematics-beyond-counting-fingers-and-toes probably originated in advances in such measurements as were required to weigh grain for sale and to count and record large numbers of sheep and other animals in such marketplaces as those along the Tigris and the Indus, to measure the march of the heavens in order to choose the proper day for planting, and to survey wet, featureless fields in Egypt after Nile floods. But then practical measurement and mathematics diverged and have tended to maintain that separation ever since. Weighing, counting, and surveying were worldly activities, but mathematics proved to have transcendental qualities that intoxicated those trying to reach through the scrim of mundanity for truth. Surveyors must have known the Pythagorean theorem (the square of the hypotenuse of a right

[21] J. A. Weisheipl, "Ockham and the Mertonians," in *The History of the University of Oxford*, ed. J. I. Catto (Oxford: Oxford University Press, 1984), 1: 639.

triangle is equal to the sum of the squares of the other two sides) for centuries before a member of their profession recognized its philosophical and mystical implications. The theorem, the surveyor decided, was evidence for the presence of the transcendental; it was abstract, perfect, and as eerily referential as the appearance of a rainbow out of mists and blowing rain. Then this proto-Pythagorean slogged out of the muddy fields and probably founded a religious order. Pure mathematics and metrology have been separate subjects from that day to this.

The former, said Plato, pertained to philosophy, by which one would "grasp true being." The latter pertained to ephemeralities: war, for instance, for which the soldier must know mathematics in order to deploy his troops properly; and commerce, for which shopkeepers must know arithmetic in order to keep track of buying and selling.[22]

Plato recommended turning away from the material world because it "is always becoming and never is" and turning toward "that which always is and has no becoming."[23] He directed our attention to absolute beauty, goodness, and righteousness, and to the ideal triangle, square, and circle, to abstractions that, he was sure, existed independent of the material world. He was certain that attaining knowledge of such entities could be accomplished only by "the unaided intellect." The intellect could begin its journey to the attainment of philosophical knowledge by the study of mathematics. He recommended that prospective philosopher-kings study mathematics "until, by the aid of pure thought, they come to see the real nature of number."[24]

It is difficult to know exactly what he meant by that, but we can illustrate it. Plato decided that the number of citizens in the

---

[22] *The Republic of Plato*, trans. Francis M. Cornford (New York: Oxford University Press, 1945), 242–3.
[23] *Collected Dialogues of Plato*, 1161.   [24] *Republic of Plato*, 242.

ideal state was 5,040. That number seems a sensible choice because it may represent about as many people as can hear one individual speak at a time without special amplification, but Plato did not select it for that reason. He chose it because it is the product of $7 \times 6 \times 5 \times 4 \times 3 \times 2 \times 1$.[25] This is mathematical mysticism, and the path from it to numerology is shorter than that to double-entry bookkeeping.

Aristotle was inclined to think that Platonism lacked ballast. In contrast to his great teacher, he honored those who kick boulders and, in their pain, insist that a broken toe is proof that boulders are real. He accepted sensory data – *but* he doubted that mathematics was of much use in interpreting those data. Geometry, for instance, was all well and good, but boulders were never perfectly spherical nor were pyramids perfectly pyramidal, so what was the use of treating them as such? The intelligent person would, of course, see that one boulder was bigger than another, more or less round than another, but would not waste time trying to measure exactly anything as variable as material reality.

Science (and a great deal else characteristic of modern societies) can be defined as the product of the application of mathematics, with its Platonic precision, to Aristotle's crude realities. But abstract mathematics and practical metrology repel as much as attract each other. Certain figures of classical Mediterranean civilization – Ptolemy, for instance – interwove them with great success, but they unraveled during the last centuries of the Western Roman Empire and fell apart in the early Middle Ages. Other geniuses of other civilizations – Mayan and Chinese, for example – achieved intellectual triumphs using mathematical techniques to analyze and manipulate measurements, but in these societies,

[25] Carl B. Boyer, *A History of Mathematics* (Princeton, N.J.: Princeton University Press, 1968), 96.

too, the theoretical and practical eventually diverged. When the Spaniards arrived on the coasts of Yucatán and Central America in the sixteenth century, the Maya were in the intellectual doldrums and were no longer refining their mathematics and calendar.[26] By the time the Spaniards and Portuguese arrived in Eastern Asia, the Chinese had forgotten the giant clocks of the Sung Dynasty, and their calendar was defective and stayed that way until the Jesuits helped them to fix it.[27]

The record indicates that cycles of advance and retreat, in this case of combining abstract mathematics and practical measurement, and then of nodding and napping and forgetting, is the norm of human history. The West's distinctive intellectual accomplishment was to bring mathematics and measurement together and to hold them to the task of making sense of a sensorially perceivable reality, which Westerners, in a flying leap of faith, assumed was temporally and spatially uniform and therefore susceptible to such examination. Why was the West successful in bringing off what was a shotgun marriage?

How, why, and when did Europeans move or begin to move from their mensuratively dubious beginnings to, or at least toward, the rigorous arts, sciences, techniques, and technologies Bruegel paraded before his customers in his *Temperance?* How, why, and when did Europeans get beyond simply heaping up sensory data like pack rats collecting shiny junk? How, why, and when did they save themselves from an eternity of baying at the moon of Platonic reality? "How" makes up the burden of this

---

[26] Alvin M. Josephy, *The Indian Heritage of America* (New York: Knopf, 1969), 209–12.

[27] Albert Chan, "Late Ming Society and the Jesuit Missionaries," in *East Meets West: The Jesuits in China, 1582–1773*, eds. Charles E. Ronan and Bonnie B. C. Oh (Chicago: Loyola University Press, 1988), 161–2.

book. "Why" is perhaps the chief mystery of Western civilization, a riddle engulfed in an enigma, and the subject of the last half of the book. "When" may be the easiest of the three questions, and we can try to answer it immediately.

Western civilization's acquaintance with quantification certainly dates at least as far back as the Neolithic (my herd has twelve goats and yours only seven), but millennia passed before it became a passion. Ptolemy, Euclid, and other mathematicians of Mediterranean antiquity had fruitfully devoted themselves to matters of measurement and mathematics, but few Western Europeans understood or even had access to their works in the early Middle Ages. Westerners believed in the Bible, wherein it was said that God "hast ordered all things by measure and number and weight" (Wisdom of Solomon 11: 20), but, as of 1200 or so, were paying little deliberate or deliberative attention to the concept of reality as quantifiable.

The master masons of the Gothic cathedrals, who raised up buildings of pleasing proportions that rarely fell down, were a sort of exception, but their geometry was purely practical. They did not know Euclid but, like good carpenters today, practiced geometry by manipulating, often literally, a few basic figures: triangles, squares, circles, and so on. Their tradition by and large was transmitted orally, and measurement on the job was a matter of the master's pointing to the stone with his rod of office and pronouncing, "Par cy me le taille" (Here's where you cut it for me).[28]

Then, between 1250 and 1350, there came, not so much in theory as in actual application, a marked shift. We can probably pare that century down to fifty years, 1275 to 1325. Someone

---

[28] Lon R. Shelby, "The Geometrical Knowledge of Mediaeval Master Masons," *Speculum*, 47 (July 1972), 397–8, 409; Erwin Panofsky, *Gothic Architecture and Scholasticism* (Latrobe, Pa.: Archabbey Press, 1956), 26, 93.

built Europe's first mechanical clock and cannon, devices that obliged Europeans to think in terms of quantified time and space. *Portolano* marine charts, perspective painting, and double-entry bookkeeping cannot be precisely dated because they were emerging techniques, not specific inventions, but we can say that the earliest surviving examples of all three date from that half century or immediately after.

Roger Bacon measured the angle of the rainbow, Giotto painted with geometry in mind, and Western musicians, who had been writing a ponderous kind of polyphony called *ars antiqua* for several generations, took flight with *ars nova* and began to write what they called "precisely measured songs." There was nothing quite like this half century again until the turn of the twentieth century, when the radio, radioactivity, Einstein, Picasso, and Schönberg swept Europe into a similar revolution.[29]

The quantificational signal appeared as Western Europe, circa 1300, reached its first peak in population and economic growth, and persisted as the West stumbled down into a century of horrors, of demographic collapse, chronic war, impromptu ravagings, a discredited church, periodic famines, and tidal waves of infection, the greatest of which was the Black Death. During that century Dante wrote his *Comedy;* William of Ockham wielded his incisive razor; Richard of Wallingford built his clock; Machaut composed his motets; and some Italian skipper ordered a helmsman to steer a compass course from Cape Finisterre across the Bay of Biscay to England, chosen not by consulting words, oral or written, but a maritime chart. Another Italian, possibly one who owned an interest in the vessel in question, made up something resembling a balance sheet. For the historian it is like watching a wounded hawk drift into an invisible thermal and soar and soar.

[29] Stephen Kern, *The Culture of Time and Space, 1880–1918* (London: Weidenfeld & Nicolson, 1983).

CHAPTER TWO

The Venerable Model

The mind's deepest desire, even in its most elaborate operations, parallels man's unconscious feeling in the face of his
universe: it is an insistence upon familiarity, an appetite for
clarity. Understanding the world for a man is reducing it to
the human, stamping it with his seal.

Albert Camus (1940)[1]

Pantometry is one of the neologisms that appeared in increasing numbers in the languages of Europe in the first half of
the second Christian millennium, words summoned into being by
new tendencies, institutions, and discoveries. *Milione* and *America*
are others. A general surge of *more* in the 1200s rendered the
awkward and seldom-used *a thousand thousand* obsolete and inspired a convenient replacement: *milione.* Columbus and Amerigo
Vespucci and the like created the need for *America* two centuries
or so later. These words were sparks thrown off by the wheels
of Western society veering and grating against the sides of old

---

[1] Albert Camus, *The Myth of Sisyphus,* trans. Justin O'Brien (New York:
Vintage Books, 1991), 17.

ruts. The veerings and gratings are the subject of this book, but first we must examine the ruts, that is to say, the view of reality that most medieval and Renaissance Western Europeans accepted as correct.

We can begin by putting aside the word *rut*. The old view of reality had to be discarded in time, but it served well for a millennium and a half, and for a great deal longer than that, if we consider that much of it had been standard for the classical world, too. It supplied a means by which tens of generations made sense of their surroundings, all the way from things immediately at hand out to the fixed stars. No, not a rut: *groove,* with its connotations of repetition, convenience, and ease, is better, though it is too generally applicable to be otherwise useful. I shall call the old view the Venerable Model, "venerable" because it is indeed old and deserving of respect.

The Venerable Model maintained a near monopoly in European common sense for so many generations because it had the cachet of classical civilization and, more important, because as a whole it squared with actual experience. Furthermore, it answered the need for a description of the universe that was clear, complete, and appropriately awesome without being stupefying. To illustrate: anyone could see that the heavens were vast, pure, and utterly different from the earth, but also that they revolved around the earth, which, though small, was the center of *everything*.

The Venerable Model provided structures and processes that a person could live with emotionally as well as comprehend intellectually – for instance, a time and a space of human dimensions.

Time was awesome, but not so as to exceed the capacity of the mind to encompass. Eusebius, circa A.D. 300, declared that God had created the universe and had wound time up and set it going 5,198 years before the Incarnation. The Venerable Bede, circa 700, was sure that Creation was even more recent: the figure according to his reckoning was 3,952 years before the Incarnation.[2] No medieval or Renaissance Westerner of repute suggested that the number of years since the beginning, from Creation to Incarnation to the present, was as high as 7,000. Two hundred and fifty to 300 or so human generations would surely suffice to include all time from the beginning to the present to the inevitable end. (Westerners of course believed in infinity – it was an attribute of God – but infinity was the antithesis of time, rather than its extension.)

Space was also vast, but not benumbingly so. Gossoin of Metz, writing about 1245, calculated that if Adam had set off straight up immediately after his creation at a rate of 25 miles a day (a good day's tramp, but not too much for a healthy young man), he would still have 713 years to go before he reached the fixed stars. A few decades later Roger Bacon calculated that a person walking 20 miles a day would take 14 years, 7 months, 29 days and a fraction to reach the moon. For some of the West's best-informed scholars the extent of the universe could still be described in terms of walking.[3]

Reality (a word I will use to mean everything material within time and space, plus those two dimensions per se) had humanly comprehensible dimensions and functioned in ways that people could understand or to which they could reconcile themselves, but that did not mean it was essentially uniform. They perceived reality as an uneven, heterogeneous sort of thing, perhaps a rare attitude today but a common one in the past shared, for instance,

---

[2] Ernst Breisach, *Historiography: Ancient, Medieval, and Modern* (Chicago: University of Chicago Press, 1983), 82, 92.

[3] Albert Van Helden, *Measuring the Universe: Cosmic Dimensions from Aristarchus to Halley* (Chicago: University of Chicago Press, 1985), 35–8; *The Opus Majus of Roger Bacon*, trans. Robert B. Burke (New York: Russell & Russell, 1962), 1: 251.

with the distant and unquestionably sophisticated Chinese.[4] Cats, so to speak, might always chase mice north of the equator and never vice versa, but who could say what might be the case in the antipodes? And what Christian could doubt that Methuselah lived 969 years in the first age after Creation, whatever might be the unlikeliness of such longevity in the present age.

Europeans dealt with reality's essential heterogeneity by acknowledging it in even the most immediate manifestations: fire rose and rocks fell not because they had different amounts of the same abstract thing, weight, but because they were different, *period*. Reality, however, was not absolutely chaotic – that would be very distressing, indeed – but its predictability derived not from itself per se, but from the one and only God. "The Creator has so ordered the laws of matter," wrote William of Canterbury, "that nothing can happen in his creation except in accordance with his just ordinance, whether good or bad."[5]

Did that make it quantifiable by mere humans? It well might, assuming that God deigned to be reasonable in human terms, though investigators' obsession with the immeasurable first cause, God, would for a long time divert attention away from immediately perceptible and possibly measurable secondary causes – velocity, temperature, and so on.

Believers in the Venerable Model doted on symbolism, which is more usefully sampled than abstractly described. Let us turn to examples, one from geography (space) and one from historiography (time). Christians agreed that the crucifixion of Jesus was the

---

[4] Derk Bodde, *Chinese Thought, Society, and Science: The Intellectual and Social Background of Science and Technology in Pre-Modern China* (Honolulu: University of Hawaii Press, 1991), 104.

[5] Benedicta Ward, *Miracles and the Medieval Mind: Theory, Record and Event, 1000–1215* (Philadelphia: University of Pennsylvania Press, 1987), 31.

pivot of all time – and therefore of the world. Jerusalem, the scene of His crucifixion, must be the center of the inhabited surface of the earth. Did not Ezekiel 5: 5 say, in anticipation of His agony, "This is Jerusalem: I have set it in the midst of the nations and countries that are round about her"?

Medieval Europeans commonly believed that that center had to be located on the Tropic of Cancer with the continents as then known gathered around, Asia to the east, Africa to the southwest, and Europe to the northwest. When Bishop Alculf visited Jerusalem in the seventh century he found a column raised up where contact with the Cross of the Lord had brought a dead man to life. This column supplied proof, he wrote, that the city was on the tropic: at noon on the summer solstice the column cast no shadow whatever. In the eleventh century Pope Urban II, in the sermon that launched the First Crusade, also described Jerusalem as at "the center of the earth" (and, in addition, as in the midst of a "land fruitful above all others, like another paradise of delights").[6] When Sir John Mandeville (probably a fictional character, but no matter) traveled in the Middle East three hundred years later, he repeated the common conviction that Jerusalem lay at the center of the portion of the globe occupied by humans.[7] Did anyone check a gnomon to see whether Jerusalem was on the tropic? No more than we would check the evidence of the gnomon by con-

---

[6] "The Pilgrimage of Alculfus," *The Library of Palestine Pilgrim's Text Society* (London: 1897), 3: 16; *Medieval History: A Source Book*, ed. Donald A. White (Homewood, Ill.: Dorsey Press, 1965), 352. Bernard the Wise observed the centrality of Jerusalem about 870; see John B. Friedman, *The Monstrous Races in Medieval Art and Thought* (Cambridge, Mass.: Harvard University Press, 1981), 219–20.

[7] *Mandeville's Travels*, ed. M. C. Seymour (London: Oxford University Press, 1968), 142. For further discussion, see Chapter 53 of Mark Twain's *Innocents Abroad*.

sulting the New Testament. The centrality of Jerusalem did not need confirmation; it was historically and theologically obvious.

All history, thought many, including historians, was embodied in the scheme of the Four Kingdoms derived from a passage in the Book of Daniel. Nebuchadnezzar dreams of a statue with a head of gold, chest and arms of silver, belly and thighs of bronze, legs of iron, and feet of iron intermixed with clay. (The clay feet live on in our aphorism about the inevitable weakness of even the powerful.) The head, the old Europeans believed, represented the Babylonian Empire, to be succeeded by empires of silver, then bronze, then iron for a total of four. The last, made of iron, would last a long time and was often identified as the Roman Empire, which would endure, in one form or another, until the events leading directly to the end of time. This obliged Christians to perform the trick of identifying the Carolingian and Ottonian empires as Roman. To do otherwise would have been to wreck an invaluable symbol that knit together a holy and distant past, a fleeting present, and a holy and impending future.[8]

Now, forewarned against thinking that "common sense" has been common through the ages, we can proceed to a brief assessment of three facets of the Venerable Model: time, space, and that which strikes us today as a very useful means of measuring and thinking about these dimensions, mathematics. We will troll through a millennium, from the decline of the Roman Empire through the Middle Ages and Renaissance, for materials for our assessment. Our criteria will not necessarily include intellectual respectability, but distribution and duration: how widely and for how long did Western Europeans hold a given attitude? Ours will be a "static approximation" (Carlo M. Cipolla's concept) emphasizing the consensus of a thousand years as if it were a unit.

[8] Daniel 2: 31–46; Breisach, *Historiography*, 83–4, 159.

This is a conceit, but a useful one. The "common sense" of a thousand years will serve as a backdrop against which innovations should show up clearly.[9]

We begin with time. Europeans did not think there was much of it, of time. St. Augustine warned against the effrontery of trying to calculate the totality of time, that is, the exact number of years from the Beginning to the appearance of the Antichrist, of Christ's second coming, of Armageddon, and of the end of time. A few tried anyway, but never agreed on a precise figure. They all, however, agreed that Judgment Day was much closer than the Beginning.[10]

In spite of that, medieval Europeans often paid little attention to the details of time. They could date events with painful precision — for instance, a certain Count Charles was murdered "in the year one thousand one hundred and twenty-seven, on the sixth day before the Nones of March, on the second day, that is, after the beginning of the same month, when two days of the second week of Lent had elapsed, and the fourth day was subsequently to dawn, on the fifth Concurrent, and the sixth Epact." But normally they dated events only vaguely. There is, to cite one example of many, an English document dated "after the king and Count Thierry of Flanders had talks together at Dover before the count went to set out for Jerusalem."[11] Peter Abelard, the West's philos-

---

[9] Carlo M. Cipolla, *Before the Industrial Revolution: European Society and Economy, 1000–1700* (New York: Norton, 1980), v, xiii.

[10] G. J. Whitrow, *Time in History: The Evolution of Our General Awareness of Time and Temporal Perspective* (Oxford: Oxford University Press, 1988), 80–1, 131; Patrick Boyde, *Dante Philomythes and Philosopher: Man in the Cosmos* (Cambridge University Press, 1981), 157.

[11] *Readings in Medieval History,* ed. Patrick J. Geary (Lewiston, N.Y.: Broadview Press, 1989), 420; M. T. Clancy, *From Memory to Written Record: English, 1066–1307* (Cambridge, Mass.: Harvard University Press, 1979), 237.

opher nonpareil in the early twelfth century, included few dates in his autobiography; such designations as "a few months later" and "one day" sufficed.[12] St. Thomas Aquinas, whose prominence during and fame after life might lead you to expect exactness in the recorded chronology of his life, was born in 1224, 1225, 1226, or 1227.[13]

Our chronic difficulty with medieval and Renaissance time is that, like an octopus, its shape was no more than approximate. Europeans of old had an enormous tolerence for anachronism. For example, in the sixth century Gregory of Tours knew people who had personally seen the chariot ruts in the bottom of the Red Sea made by the Israelites fleeing Pharoah's army, ruts miraculously renewed after every new accumulation of silt.[14] If true, then the exact year of the Exodus was not compellingly important, perhaps not even very interesting. Time, beyond the individual life span, was envisioned not as a straight line marked off in equal quanta, but as a stage for the enactment of the greatest of all dramas, Salvation versus Damnation.

Western Europeans had several ways of dividing that temporal stage. The divisions into two periods (from the Beginning to the Incarnation, and after) and into three periods (from Creation to the Ten Commandments, from the Commandments to the Incarnation, and from that event to the present and beyond to the

---

[12] Marc Bloch, *Feudal Society,* trans. L. A. Manyon (Chicago: University of Chicago Press, 1961), 1: 74; Alexander Murray, *Reason and Society in the Middle Ages* (Oxford: Oxford University Press, 1978), 175–7.

[13] James A. Weisheipl, *Friar Thomas D'Aquino: His Life, Thought, and Work* (Garden City, N.Y.: Doubleday, 1974), ix, 3.

[14] Gregory of Tours, *The History of the Franks,* trans. Lewis Thorpe (Harmondsworth: Penguin Books, 1974), 75–6; Jacques le Goff, *La civilisation de l'Occident médiéval* (Paris: B. Arthaud, 1964), 221–2; Murray, *Reason and Society,* 175–6, 177; William Langland, *Piers the Ploughman,* trans. J. F. Goodridge (Harmondsworth: Penguin Books, 1966), 82.

Second Coming) were familiar to all Christians.[15] A more abstruse but commonly cited system was that of the Four Kingdoms, derived from a passage in Daniel, which we have already considered. St. Augustine, the most important of the fathers of the Western Church, was the chief architect of a system of ages divided in accordance with the six days of Creation plus the Sabbath. The first six ages began, respectively, with Creation, the Flood, Abraham, David, the Captivity of Judah, and the Birth of Christ. The sixth age would end with the Second Coming. Then there would be a Sabbath and finally eternity.[16]

The ages, whatever their number, were qualitatively different. Salvation was impossible for all who had lived before Jesus, whatever their virtues, unless the Son of God rescued them in person. This explains why Dante came upon such good men as Homer, Horace, Ovid, Lucan, Socrates, Plato, and Ptolemy in Limbo, and not in Purgatory or Paradise.[17] The different qualities of the different ages could even cause quantitative differences. St. Augustine knew that the antediluvian people of the First Age had lived hundreds and hundreds of years each – the Bible said so – and also that they were much bigger than his contemporaries. Virgil and Pliny the Younger said so, and floods now and again turned up impressively large bones. Augustine wrote that he had seen a human tooth so big that, if divided into teeth of normal size, it would have made a hundred.[18]

Such beliefs were common because Europeans did not have a

---

[15] Breisach, *Historiography,* 83–5; "Historiography, Ecclesiastical," in *The New Catholic Encyclopedia* (Washington, D.C.: Catholic University of America, 1967), 7: 6.

[16] St. Augustine, *The City of God,* trans. Marcus Dods (New York: Modern Library, 1950), 867.

[17] Dante Alighieri, *The Divine Comedy: Inferno,* trans. and ed. Charles S. Singleton (Princeton, N.J.: Princeton University Press, 1970), 40–5.

[18] St. Augustine, *The City of God,* 489–90, 867.

vivid concept of causation through time, that is, of a lineage of factors, one leading to another, effecting significant change. The transitions from one age to another had been abrupt – for example, the Flood, the Incarnation – and, from the human point of view, arbitrary. Getting from giant predecessors who lived for centuries to us, small and of brief life span, in only a few thousand years is not hard if you have a notion of an omnipotent God where many of us have a notion of evolution.

Western Europeans had a reasonably accurate calendar, which they inherited from the Romans, from Julius Caesar, to be precise. By his time, Rome's civil or official year had drifted so far out of synchronization with the solar year that the spring equinox came in the winter. Caesar, never reluctant to exercise power, declared that the year which today we designate as 46 B.C. should have 445 days, bringing the civil year abreast of the solar year. (This was nicknamed "the year of confusion.") Thereafter the civil year would have 365 days, with a leap year of 366 days every fourth year.

This, the Julian calendar, was standard for Christendom for a millennium and a half, but many other temporal details remained unsettled. The date for the beginning of a given year – 1 January, the Roman choice; 25 March, the Annunciation and Christian choice; or what? – was such a detail. How to number the years was another. The Romans numbered theirs from the founding of their city and from the beginning of the reign of a given emperor or consul.[19] Westerners did their best to follow suit. The Synod of Hatfield (A.D. 680), for instance, was held "in the tenth year of the reign of our most devout lord Egfrid, King of the Northumbri-

---

[19] G. J. Whitrow, *Time in History: The Evolution of Our General Awareness of Time and Temporal Perspective* (Oxford: Oxford University Press, 1988), 66–7, 74, 119; D. E. Smith, *History of Mathematics* (New York: Dover, 1958), 2: 661.

ans; in the sixth year of King Ethelfrid of the Mercians; in the seventeenth year of King Aldwuolf of the East Angles";[20] and so on. Very awkward, that was, and far from universally informative in a decentralized Europe. After centuries of confusion the West adopted the system of Dionysius Exiguus, a sixth century monk who had pronounced the Christian Era to have begun with Christ's incarnation in the *anno Domini,* or A.D., number 1.[21]

Westerners were fortunate to have the Julian calendar, but it was not perfect. The actual solar year is a few minutes short of $365\frac{1}{4}$, and so the Julian calendar supplies a shade too many leap years. This mattered not at all to the peasants and nobles, but was a matter of great significance to meticulous churchmen struggling to adapt to a Middle Eastern religion with a vertiginously movable feast called Easter. Christians resorted to a bizarre combination of customary, lunar, and solar calendars to make sure that Easter would never fall on the same day as Passover. The Council of Nicaea declared in 325 Easter should fall on the first Sunday after the first full moon after the vernal equinox.[22] Easter darts about in the first weeks of spring like a reflection on moving water.

The difficulty of nailing down Easter's date nagged the astronomically and mathematically knowledgeable. New Year's Day might be this or that, as might the number of a given year, but Easter, upon which Christ's resurrection was commemorated and from which the dates of other movable feasts were measured, had to be on the right Sunday. That depended on the date of the vernal equinox, the Julian calendar's date for which, nudged along by the excess of leap years, was edging summerward. In the thirteenth

---

[20] Bede, *A History of the English Church and People,* trans. Leo Sherley-Price (Harmondsworth: Penguin Books, 1968), 234.

[21] Smith, *History of Mathematics,* 2: 661. Dionysius Exiguus started the current era not with zero, but with 1, which is why most of us do not know whether the next millennium will begin with the year 2000 or 2001.

[22] Whitrow, *Time in History,* 190–1.

century the divergence between the Julian and actual date was seven and then eight days. Roger Bacon wrote the pope suggesting that the calendar be reformed, but nothing came of his advice. Many of the greatest mathematicians and astronomers – Regiomontanus, Nicholas of Cusa, Copernicus – concerned themselves with this problem, but the political and church elites and the mass of the populace were so indifferent to calendrical detail that the Gregorian reform (see Chapter 4) came only at the end of our period.[23]

Hours, the ancient Middle Eastern units designating the divisions of day and night, were the smallest units with which people commonly concerned themselves. They of course knew there were shorter periods, but they could improvise ways to deal with them: fourteenth century cooking instructions directed novices to boil an egg "for the length of time wherein you can say a *Miserere*."[24] Hours, however, were too long and too important to guess at. Jesus Himself had said in John 9: 9, "Are there not twelve hours in the day?" (implying twelve for the night as well).

Europe did not straddle the equator, and so the durations of daytime and nighttime changed radically through the year. Even so, they had to have twelve hours each. Europeans had a system of unequal, accordian-pleated hours that puffed up and deflated so as to ensure a dozen hours each for daytime and nighttime, winter and summer.[25] To compound the confusion (ours, not

---

[23] Gordon Moyer, "The Gregorian Calendar," *Scientific American*, 246 (May 1982), 144–50; Smith, *History of Mathematics*, 2: 659–60; Whitrow, *Time in History*, 191.

[24] Don Lepan, *The Cognitive Revolution in Western Culture, 1: The Birth of Expectation* (London: Macmillan Press, 1989), 91.

[25] Yale College was still using this kind of hour in 1826 in order to take full advantage of sunlight. See Michael O'Malley, *Keeping Watch: A History of American Time* (Harmondsworth: Penguin Books, 1991), 4. Our daylight savings system is our inelegant way of doing the same.

theirs), these unequal hours, familiar to us at least to the extent of being duodecimal, were not the vernacular kind of hours. Most people, when they did not judge the time simply by glancing at the position of the sun in the sky, relied on a system of time proclaimed by church bells, the most effective information medium of the age. This was the system, still followed in monasteries today, of the seven canonical "hours" – matins, prime, tierce, sext, none, vespers, and compline – which indicated when certain prayers were to be said (Psalms 119: 64: "Seven times a day I praise Thee for thy righteous ordinances"). It served both the pious and the impudent. In the fifteenth canto of *Paradiso* Dante speaks of the bells of his Florence ringing tierce and none; and when Boccaccio notes specific times in his *Decameron,* he refers to a canonical hour.[26]

At the very beginning of the Middle Ages there were only three of these hours, then five, and finally seven, and they never were solidly moored to clock time. They were breadths, not points, of time. Choosing the moment within their durations to ring the church bell was problematic. We can get a sense of this by examining the saga of the heroic trek of *noon.* The word *noon* is derived from the canonical hour none, the name of which comes from the Latin for the ninth hour of the day, which, counting forward from sunrise, was originally rung at something like 3:00 or 15:00 in the *after*noon. During the Middle Ages the ringing of none migrated back through the day until it reached its final resting place, midday, as early as the twelfth century. The migration no doubt proceeded at different rates in different localities. In thirteenth century England, where Normans and Saxons had not yet fused

[26] Dante Alighieri, *The Divine Comedy: Paradiso,* canto 15, line 98; Giovanni Boccaccio, *The Decameron,* trans. G. H. McWilliam (Harmondsworth: Penguin Books, 1972); Giovanni Boccaccio, *Decameron* (Milano: Arnoldo Mondadori, 1985).

into Englishmen, the process seems to have been especially complicated: *none* may have meant midafternoon in French, but midday
in English.[27]

None's long march may have originated with monks who
could not eat until none during fasts, and therefore saw to it that
none was rung earlier and earlier. Indeed, St. Benedict, probably
the most important figure in the history of Western monasticism,
recommended in the sixth century that none "be said somewhat
before the time, about the middle of the eighth hour." His motive
was probably the famishing elongation of summer days.[28]

According to Dante, the ringing of none glided backward to
midday or sext because the latter meant six. The sixth hour was
"the most noble of the whole day, and the most virtuous," six
being the sum of its factors, 1, 2, and 3, and therefore – noble.
(We will get to poetically symbolic numbers in a few pages.) And
so the reading of the divine offices gravitated toward midday, the
earlier sliding forward and the later backward.[29] (How this would
work out in practice is not easy to understand.)

The migration of noon illustrates one sure characteristic of
most medieval Europeans. They were in their way as concerned
with time as we are, but their way was very different from ours. It

---

[27] W. Rothwell, "The Hours of the Day in Medieval France," *French Studies,*
13 (July 1959), 245.

[28] David S. Landes, *Revolution in Time: Clocks and the Making of the
Modern World* (Cambridge, Mass.: Harvard University Press, 1983),
404–5.

[29] *The Oxford English Dictionary,* s.v. "noon"; *The Oxford Dictionary of
English Etymology,* ed. C. T. Onions, (Oxford: Clarendon Press, 1966),
s.v. "noon"; Jacques le Goff, *Time, Work, and Culture in the Middle
Ages,* trans. Arthur Goldhammer (Chicago: University of Chicago Press,
1980), 44–5; *The Clockwork Universe, German Clocks and Automata,
1500–1650,* eds. Klaus Maurice and Otto Mayreds (New York: Neal
Watson, 1980), 146–7; *The Rule of St. Benedict,* trans. Cardinal Gasquet
(London: Chatto & Windus, 1925), 84–5; Dante Alighieri, *The Convivio
of Dante,* trans. Philip H. Wicksteed (London: J. M. Dent, 1912), 345–7.

had much to do with symbolic values and little to do with precision.

The concept of time that Europeans held was in at least one
way crucially similar to ours. The majority of humans – Greek
Platonists, Navajos, Hindus, Maya – believed that the patterns of
time in its larger dimensions were like the patterns right before
us – the round of seasons, the wheeling of the heavens, and so on.
They believed in cyclical time and did not worry about it unspool-
ing to the very end. Western Europeans also acknowledged the
cycles of life because the years are undeniably a repetitive round
of seasons, every sunset has been thus far matched with a dawn,
and so on. In addition, they believed that the Old Testament in
its details prefigured the New Testament. But because they were
Christians they could not embrace cyclicalism exclusively. God
had sacralized the concept of linear time by stepping into time in
order to provide humanity with the possibility of salvation. "Let
us therefore keep to the straight path, which is Christ," said St.
Augustine, "and with Him as our Guide and Saviour, let us turn
away in heart and mind from the unreal and futile cycles of
the godless."[30]
     Linear time had a beginning and will have an end. You can
count it from beginning to end – if you have a mind to.

The space of the Middle Ages and Renaissance was as assertively
finite as a goldfish bowl, spherical, and qualitative in structure.
Within its outermost sphere were a number of other spheres,
tightly nested, one inside the other. There was no emptiness between them: nature abhorred vacuums even more then than

---

[30] St. Augustine, *City of God*, 404. This and other matters pertaining to this
     subject are well summed up in Anne Higgins, "Medieval Notions of the
     Structure of Time," *Journal of Medieval and Renaissance Studies,* 19 (Fall
     1989), 227–50.

now.[31] The spheres, perfectly transparent, carried the heavenly bodies. The outermost sphere with visible freight carried the fixed stars, whose positions in relation to one another did not alter (at least not fast enough for anyone to notice in a lifetime or several lifetimes). These were what we would define exclusively as the stars. Within their sphere were the spheres carrying the planets, sun, and moon.

All the spheres and their visible freight moved in perfect circles because the heavens were perfect, and the circle was the most perfect and noble shape. Shapes had qualities, and the circle, like the number 6, was intrinsically noble. Motion in straight lines was antithetical to the nature of the heavens. The heavenly bodies and their spheres were all composed of the fifth and perfect element, which was changeless, stainless, noble, and entirely superior to the four elements with which humans were in contact. (We nod deferentially to this theory whenever we use the word *quintessence,* which refers to the fifth essence or element.)

Everything below the moon was changeable and ignoble, that is to say, composed of the four elements. Just below the moon was the sphere of fire, just below that the sphere of air, then that of water, and finally, at the center, earth, which was "the fundament of the universe." These elements were obviously not always neatly stacked in strata but were mixed, the dry land among the seas, for instance. The explanations were various and, some of them, quite audacious; one, for example, proposed that the waters withdrawn from the land were piled up somewhere.[32]

Here on earth, where wind blew grit in your eye and your

[31] E. J. Dijksterhuis, *The Mechanization of the World Picture,* trans. C. Dikshoorn (Oxford: Oxford University Press, 1960), 143.

[32] *On the Properties of Things: John Trevisa's Translation of Bartholomaeus Anglicus de Proprietatibus Rerum,* ed. M. C. Seymour (Oxford: Clarendon Press, 1975), 2: 690; Nicholas H. Steneck, *Science and Creation in the Middle Ages: Henry of Langenstein (d. 1397) on Genesis* (Notre

feet were often cold and wet, impermanence was the rule. In the thirteenth century Bartholomaeus Anglicus declared that the earth was the "most corpulent and hath leste of sutilte and of symplic-ite" of any of the bodies of the universe. Three hundred years later a Frenchman put it more plainly: the earth "is so depraved and broken in all kinds of vices and abominations that it seemeth to be a place that hath received all the filthiness and purgings of all the other worlds and ages."[33] In the sublunar zone natural motion was not perfect and circular, but straight and alterable only by violence. Left to its own devices, fire rose straight up toward its proper home in the sphere of fire, and stones, similarly motivated, fell straight down toward earth.

Our sublunary slum was heterogeneous, and not only in its climate, flora, and fauna, but in its plausibilities as well. Sir John Mandeville's *Travels,* one of the most popular books of the Re-naissance, soberly pronounces that in the Land of Prester John there was a waterless sea of gravel that "ebbeth and floweth in great waves as other seas do, and it is never still nor in peace." In Ethiopia people had only one foot, which "is so large that it shadoweth all the body against the sun when they will lie and rest them." (St. Augustine may have been Mandeville's source for this: the saint had heard that Ethiopians had two feet on one leg.)[34]

Geography was qualitative. The people of the Indies were slow

---

Dame, Ind.: University of Notre Dame Press, 1976), 78–80. There are many secondary sources on medieval astronomy; for accuracy and brev-ity, I recommend A. C. Crombie, *Medieval and Early Modern Science* (Garden City, N.Y.: Doubleday, 1959), 1: 19–20, 75–8.

[33] *On the Properties of Things,* 1: 442, 2: 690; E. M. Tillyard, *The Elizabe-than World Picture* (London: Chatto & Windus, 1958), 36. For a good secondary source on the medieval version of the earth, see "Dante's Geographical Knowledge," an appendix to George H. T. Kimble, *Geogra-phy in the Middle Ages* (London: Methuen, 1938), 241–4.

[34] *Mandeville's Travels,* 122, 210; St. Augustine, *City of God,* 530.

"because they be in the first climate, that of Saturn; and Saturn is slow and little moving," but Europeans, an active people, were of a land of the seventh climate, that of the moon, which "environeth the earth more hastily than any other planet."[35] Even the cardinal directions were qualitative. South signified warmth and was associated with charity and the Passion of Jesus. East, toward the location of the terrestrial paradise, Eden, was especially potent, and that is why churches were oriented east–west with the business end, the altar, at the east. World maps were drawn with east at the top. "True north" was due east, a principle to which we pay respect every time we "orient" ourselves.

Ignorance dictated that cartography be simple. For centuries T-O maps of the world, usually with Jerusalem at the center, were highly prized. T-O maps are called such because they were drawn like an O with a T inside – that is, a circle with one diametrical line and, at right angles to it, a line dividing one half into two parts. The longer line represented the Don River, the Black Sea, the Aegean, Jerusalem, and the Nile all together as a north–south divider, setting off Asia as one-half of the land mass of the globe. The other line represented the Mediterranean, dividing the other half of the pie into two wedges, Europe and Africa.[36]

Some Europeans believed that Europe, Africa, and Asia made up only a quarter of the land, which was separated from the three

[35] *Mandeville's Travels*, 126.
[36] Samuel Y. Edgerton, Jr., "The Art of Renaissance Picture-Making and the Great Western Age of Discovery," in *Essays Presented to Myron P. Gilmore*, eds. Sergio Bertelli and Gloria Ramukus (Florence: La Nuova Italia, 1978), 2: 148; C. Raymond Beazley, *The Dawn of Modern Geography* (London: Henry Frowde, n.d.), 2: 576–9; O. A. W. Dilke, *Greek and Roman Maps* (Ithaca, N.Y.: Cornell University Press, 1985), 173; David Woodward, "Medieval *Mappaemundi*," in *The History of Cartography*, 1: *Cartography in Prehistoric, Ancient, and Medieval Europe and the Mediterranean*, eds. J. B. Harley and David Woodward (Chicago: University of Chicago Press, 1987), 340–1.

other quarters by great seas, running north and south, east and west. It seemed unlikely that anybody lived in the three other quarters, and was possibly blasphemous to think so. How could anyone have traveled there from Mount Ararat, where Noah's ark, containing all the living descendants of Adam and Eve (that is to say, all humans) had grounded as the Flood receded? Not by land, obviously, and the distances by water were daunting. St. Augustine's opinion was that "it is too absurd to say that some men might have taken ship and traversed the whole wide ocean, and crossed from this side of the world to the other." Furthermore, they could have traveled to the two southern quarters from Mount Ararat only by passing through the uninhabitable, literally scorching tropics. Anyone who believed that people lived in the antipodes, said Dante, was a fool.[37]

The world, which God had created for His purposes and where Adam, Eve, Abraham, David, Solomon, Jesus and His saints, and Satan and his imps had performed, was adorned with localities of religious potency. Bethlehem, Jerusalem, and Judah could be visited and walked through, the Sea of Galilee drunk from and fished in, so why wouldn't one be able to find, for instance, Hell? The author of Mandeville's *Travels* wrote about an actual entry to Hell, a "Vale Perilous" with gold and silver to tempt mortals thither, where "anon they be strangled by devils." The author placed Eden in eastern Asia on top of a mountain so high it touched the orbit of the moon. In this terrestrial paradise there was a well "that casteth out the four floods that run by diverse lands," that is to say, the rivers Ganges, Tigris, Euphrates, and Nile. Men who attempted to ascend these rivers were deafened by the noise of the waters that "commeth down so outrageously

---

[37] St. Augustine, *The City of God*, 532; Kimble, *Geography in the Middle Ages*, 241; John Carey, "Ireland and the Antipodes: The Heterodoxy of Virgin of Salzburg," *Speculum*, 64 (Jan. 1989), 1–3.

from the high places above."[38] Columbus, on the coast of Venezu-ela in 1498, was sure that the Orinoco was one of these rivers and that he was near the terrestrial paradise.[39]

How did people who entertained such beliefs look at a map? How did Christians look at the Ebstorf map, the latest thing in world maps of the thirteenth century? We note its distortions, omissions, and outright mistakes and find them forgivable, consid-ering how little firsthand data or training in geometry the map-makers had. But we do not know what to make of the map as a whole. It is drawn on a background of Christ crucified, with His head in the Far East, pierced hands at the extreme north and south, and wounded feet off the shore of Portugal. What were the mapmakers trying to say? Certainly not that the Nile flows into the Mediterranean at precisely so many leagues south and west of Antioch. Their map was a nonquantificational, nongeometrical attempt to supply information about what was near and what was far – and what was important and what unimportant. It was more like an expressionist portrait than an identification photo. It was for sinners, not navigators.

In nothing we have touched on thus far is the way in which we think more different from that of medieval and Renaissance Westerners than in designations of quantity. They honored Ptol-emy and Archimedes, but had not inherited their taste for exact expression of quantity. Recipes for making glass, chalices, organs, and other things included very few numbers: "a bit more" and "a medium-sized piece" were precise enough. In the fourteenth cen-tury Paris had so many private dwellings that to count them would be like counting "stalks in a large field, or the leaves of a huge

[38] *Mandeville's Travels*, 234–6; see also *On the Properties of Things*, 1: 655–7.

[39] Samuel Eliot Morison, *Admiral of the Ocean Sea: A Life of Christopher Columbus* (Boston: Little, Brown, 1942), 556–8.

forest."[40] Medieval Europeans used numbers for effect, not for accuracy. The hero of the *Song of Roland* announces before the battle, "I will strike a thousand blows and follow them with seven hundred more, and you will see the steel of Durendal [his sword] running with blood." He dies in the battle and a hundred thousand Franks weep.[41]

In addition to a penchant for the general and impressionistic, Western Europeans, especially those who lived in what we call the Middle Ages, suffered from a lack of clear and simple means of mathematical expression. They had no signs for plus or minus or divide or equal or square root. Where they needed the clarity of algebraic equations, they, like the ancients, produced long, convoluted, almost Proustian sentences.[42] Their system of numerical expression, inherited from the Roman Empire, was adequate for the weekly market and for local tax collection, but not for anything grander. Roman numerals, with their repetitions of I, V, X, L, C, and M (with horizontal lines top and bottom to set numbers off from letters), were easy to learn, and understanding them in combination required little more than the simplest addition and subtraction (usually just addition because it was simpler to add more to the smaller number than to subtract from a bigger). But the Latin numerals were too clumsy for expressing large numbers. For instance, a number like 1,549 was usually written as Mccccccxxxxviiij. (The j on the end signified the end of the number, ensuring that no one could attach anything more.) Fortunately, the untheoretical Romans and medieval Europeans rarely had to use large numbers.[43]

Medieval Europeans wrote their numbers in Roman numerals,

[40] Murray, *Reason and Society,* 175, 176, 179.

[41] *Medieval Epics* (New York: Modern Library, n.d.), 126, 173.

[42] For examples of the mathematical prose of the Middle Ages, see *A Source Book in Medieval Science,* ed. Edward Grant (Cambridge, Mass.: Harvard University Press, 1974), 102–35.

[43] Smith, *History of Mathematics,* 2: 59–63.

but did not use that system for computation. They possessed in their hands and fingers a useful computer and, for more difficult operations, the abacus or counting board. The best description we have of the hands-and-fingers system is that of the Venerable Bede (673–735), who prefaced his treatise on chronology with a brief disquisition on "the necessary and ready skill of finger reckoning." Numbers up to 9 were designated by bending fingers: a bent little finger meant 1, a bent little finger and ring finger meant 2, and so on (6, being perfect, was indicated by bending the most noble finger, the ring finger, by itself). Ten and multiples of 10 were specified by various configurations of the fingers, by touching the thumb to certain joints of the fingers, for instance. Higher numbers involved complications, and Bede recruited hands, arms, elbows, and torso. Fifty thousand was signified by pointing the thumb of an extended hand to the naval. Complaints were made that the higher numbers required "the gesticulations of dancers."

Neither Bede nor any of his contemporaries in Western Europe knew about place value or zero, but finger reckoning enabled them to proceed as if they did. Finger joints supplied place value – one joint 10s, another 100s, and so on – and zero was indicated by the normal relaxed position of the fingers – by nothing, so to speak. The system was even capable of simple computation, 6×8, for instance, or even, with a little bit of multiplication in the head, 13 $\times$ 14.[44] (If you want to know how, I recommend Karl Menninger's fascinating *Number Words and Number Symbols*.)

But finger reckoning was inadequate for complicated operations. For that the Europeans turned to the abacus. Today the

[44] Karl Menninger, *Number Words and Number Symbols: A Cultural History of Numbers,* trans. Paul Broneer (Cambridge, Mass.: MIT Press, 1969), 202–18; Smith, *History of Mathematics,* 2: 196–202; Florence A. Yeldham, *The Story of Reckoning in the Middle Ages in English,* ed. Robert Steele (London: Early English Text Society, 1922), 66–9; Murray, *Reason and Society,* 156.

Figure 2. Calculators using Hindu-Arabic numerals and a counting board, 1503. Karl Menninger, *Number Words and Number Symbols* (Cambridge, Mass.: MIT Press, 1977), 350.

word *abacus*, though it is Greek and Latin in origin, refers to the East Asian device by which calculations are made by sliding beads along wires. For the Europeans of the Middle Ages and Renaissance the word meant a counting board on which lines served in place of wires and pebbles or counters were shifted about instead of beads (Figure 2).

The counting board was a device with which a skilled practitioner could swiftly and accurately make calculations of every kind, even those involving large numbers. It bestowed the advantages of both place value and zero without the disadvantage of having to think about them. If you wanted to express that difficult number 101, you placed one counter on the 100s line and another counter on the units line. You did not have to strain your brain about how to express *no* 10s or 5s or what have you in between, but simply left that line or those lines empty.

The abacus is still widely used over much of the world for the simple reason that it is one of humanity's cheapest and most felicitous inventions, and its absence from Western Europe between about A.D. 500 and 1000 is evidence of the nadir of civilization there. It is hard to believe that everyone forgot it, that for five centuries no one scratched lines in sand with a stick and pushed pebbles from one line to another with the toe of a sandal in order to confirm a guess as to how many cattle were in the seven herds that had come into market that morning. Whatever the truth about it may be, the fact is that the counting board did disappear from the written and archeological record for five hundred years.[45]

The revival of the counting board in the West is associated with the French monk Gerbert (later Pope Sylvester II), who in the second half of the tenth century studied in Spain, then sizzling with Islamic scholarship and science. He learned about Hindu-Arabic numerals and about the counting board, which he may have brought back home with him.[46] By the late eleventh and twelfth centuries treatises on elementary calculation were, by and large, treatises on the use of the counting board, and there was a new verb, *to abacus,* meaning to compute.[47] In the sixteenth century counting boards were so common that Martin Luther could offhandedly refer to them to illustrate the compatibility of spiritual egalitarianism and obedience to one's betters: "To the counting

[45] Menninger, *Number Words,* 322; Smith, *History of Mathematics,* 2: 186; Murray, *Reason and Society,* 163–4.

[46] Menninger, *Number Words,* 322–7; Murray, *Reason and Society,* 164.

[47] Gillian R. Evans, "From Abacus to Algorism: Theory and Practice in Medieval Arithmetic," *British Journal for the History of Science,* 10, pt. 2 (July 1977), 114; Smith, *History of Mathematics,* 2: 177.

master all counters are equal, and their worth depends on where he places them. Just so are men equal before God, but they are unequal according to the station in which God has placed them."[48]

Some time after Gerbert, perhaps in the thirteenth century, the lines of the Western European board made a quarter turn from vertical to horizontal. The reorientation strikes us as proper – the counters could now be read laterally, like words – but there is nothing about mathematics to dictate the change. Karl Menninger has suggested that the change may have been inspired by Guido of Arezzo's music staff, in which pitch was a matter of vertical position, but the notes were read and performed from left to right.[49] (We shall return to Guido in Chapter 8.)

Counting boards can handle big numbers and complicated calculations, so we cannot blame them for what we may call medieval Westerners' mathematical impotence. Their ignorance (G. R. Evans terms them, up to the mid-twelfth century, "sub-Euclidian")[50] explains a large part of their ineptness in reasoning about quantities, but there was more to it than just that. For us, except for a few superstitions such as triskaidekaphobia, numbers are utterly neutral, in and of themselves morally and emotionally free of all value, as purely tools as a shovel. Not so for the old Europeans: they thought of them as qualitative as well as quantitative.

"We must not despise the science of numbers," wrote St. Augustine, that fifth century font of Christian dogma. That science, he continued, is "of eminent service to the careful interpreter." God created the universe in six days because 6 was a

[48] Menninger, *Number Words*, 365–7; Yeldham, *Story of Reckoning*, 89.
[49] Menninger, *Number Words*, 340–1.
[50] Gillian R. Evans, "The Sub-Euclidian Geometry of the Earlier Middle Ages, up to Mid-Twelfth Century," *Archive for the History of Exact Sciences*, 16, no. 1 (1976), 105–18.

perfect number, as we have already learned from Dante. Seven was perfect, too. In the usage of his era 3 was the first odd number and 4 the first even number. Added together, they made the perfect 7. And had not God rested on the seventh day after completing the Creation? Ten, being the number of the Commandments, symbolized law, and so 11, which goes one beyond 10, signified transgression of the law – sin. Twelve, on the other hand, was the number of judgment because the two parts of the number 7, that is to say, 4 and 3, multiplied together, make 12. Forty, the number of the days of Lent and the number of days the Savior spent on earth after the Resurrection, represented to St. Augustine "life itself."[51]

Most of a millennium later St. Thomas Aquinas made 144,000, the sum of those whom Revelation promises will be saved at the end of time, into a cathedral of holy references. The *thousand* of 144,000 designated perfection (presumably because 1,000 is 10, the number of the Commandments, multiplied by itself 3 times over, 3 being the number of the Trinity and of the days between the Crucifixion and the Resurrection). The *one hundred and forty-four* of 144,000 is 12 times 12. Twelve signifies faith in the Trinity, that is to say, 3 multiplied by the 4 parts of the earth. One of the 12s to be multiplied can be taken to signify the number of the apostles and the other the number of the tribes of Israel.[52]

Today we utilize numbers when we want narrow focus on a given subject and maximum precision in our deliberations. The old Europeans preferred broad focus and settled for imprecision in the hope of including as much as possible of what might be important. Often they were reaching not for a handle on material

---

[51] Vincent F. Hopper, *Medieval Number Symbolism* (New York: Columbia University Press, 1938), 94–5.

[52] Ibid., 102.

reality, but for a clue as to what lay beyond the scrim of reality. They were as poetic about numbers as about words.

Much of the Venerable Model seems as peculiar to us as a Tungusic shaman's version of reality. We sniff and cluck at its mistakes – that the earth is the center of the universe, for instance – but our real problem with the Venerable Model is that it is dramatic, even melodramatic, and teleological: God and Purpose loom over all. We want (or think we want) explanations of reality leeched of emotion, as bloodless as distilled water. Our astrophysicists, looking for a title for the birth of time and space, have rejected *creation,* a word with references and reverberations that go on forever. They have chosen the nose-thumbing title *the big bang* in order to minimize the drama of the subject and the distortions and accelerations of rhapsodic thinking. Medieval and Renaissance Europeans, like the shaman, like all of us some of the time and some of us all of the time, wanted immediately conclusive and emotionally satisfying explanations. They longed for a universe that, in Camus's phrase, "can love and suffer."[53]

In such a universe the balance scale, the yardstick, and the hour glass were devices of little more than immediate practical convenience. The old Europeans' universe was one of qualities, not quantities.

[53] Camus, *Myth of Sisyphus,* 17.

CHAPTER THREE

Necessary but Insufficient Causes

In causal terms the presence of oxygen is a necessary but not a sufficient condition for fire. Oxygen plus combustibles plus the striking of a match would illustrate a sufficient condition for fire.

William L. Reese (1981)[1]

The raison d'être of this book is to describe an acceleration after 1250 or so in the West's shift from qualitative perception to, or at least toward, quantificational perception. Most particularly, we want to ferret out the source of that acceleration. The latter half of the assignment is daunting, and before we begin we must discuss just what we are looking for lest we convince ourselves we have found it before we get to it. For instance, the arrival of Hindu-Arabic numerals was extremely important, but no more than what logicians call a necessary but insufficient condition. We

---

[1] William L. Reese, *Dictionary of Philosophy and Religion: Eastern and Western Thought* (Atlantic Highlands, N.J.: Humanities Press, 1981), 381.

must not overlook such conditions (the oxygen and combustibles of the epigraph), but the final object of our search is the "striking of a match."

We will discuss in this chapter the oxygen and combustibles, that is, the rise of commerce and the state, the revival of learning, and other developments that are necessary but insufficient to explain the increase in quantificational thinking in the West during the Middle Ages and Renaissance.

In the following chapters, in order to ensure that we are not shadowboxing with mere reifications, we will examine actual evidence of the trend toward quantification, mechanical clocks, marine charts, and so on. Then, many chapters hence, we shall seek out the flaring match.

Western perceptions changed as Europeans' experience changed. The West's population doubled and may even have tripled between 1000 and 1340. Many people migrated to wetlands newly drained and forests newly cleared, and eastward to contend with the Slavs for fertile soils. Others became townsfolk, often to work in the new wool and linen industries, and new cities sprang up and old ones expanded. By the early fourteenth century Venice and London had perhaps ninety thousand inhabitants apiece, a fifth at the very most of Cairo's, but vast by the West's standards of previous centuries.[2] Then, with the eruption of the Black Death in the mid-1300s, Europe's population crashed by one-third and continued to fall well into the next century, with city populations probably shrinking faster than rural. Yet within a hundred years

---

[2] John H. Mundy, *Europe in the High Middle Ages* (London: Longman, 1973), 86–7; Ross E. Dunn, *The Adventures of Ibn Battuta: A Muslim Traveler of the 14th Century* (Berkeley: University of California Press, 1986), 45.

Westerners recovered and passed their earlier peak and the cities were growing again.[3]

Time and again, especially when population was expanding, Westerners marched and sailed away to invade Islamic and pagan lands for the sake of God, new fiefs, and commerce; and everywhere they went they saw things their experience did not equip them to understand. Fulcher of Chartres went on the First Crusade and wrote that the Levant had hippopotomuses, crocodiles, leopards, hyenas, dragons, griffins, and manticores, which had human faces, voices like flutes, and three rows of teeth each.[4]

Trade increased between the West's peasant millions and its cities' frenetic thousands. Long-range commerce increased between regions and even with the Abode of Islam and the barely imagined lands from which Marco Polo returned with implausible stories. The state began to coalesce, with its insatiable appetite for taxes. The Church, the font of mercy and salvation, taxed with such vigor that many Christians began to doubt whether the pope still possessed "that power granted from heaven to St. Peter, namely of binding and loosing, since he proved himself to be entirely dissimilar to St. Peter."[5]

New kinds of people sprouted up through the floors of medieval Europe's three-storied society (peasantry, nobility, clergy).

[3] J. C. Russell, "Population in Europe, 500–1500," in *The Fontana Economic History of Europe: The Middle Ages,* ed. Carlo M. Cipolla (Glasgow: William Collins, 1972), 36–41; Massimo Livi-Bacci, *A Concise History of World Population,* trans. Carl Ipsen (Oxford: Basil Blackwell, 1992), 44–5; Roger Mols, "Population in Europe, 1500–1700," in *The Fontana Economic History of Europe: The Sixteenth and Seventeenth Centuries,* ed. Carlo M. Cipolla (Glasgow: William Collins, 1974), 2: 38.

[4] Fulcher of Chartres, *A History of the Expedition to Jerusalem, 1095–1127,* trans. Frances R. Ryan (New York: Norton, 1969), 284–8.

[5] *Chronicles of Matthew Paris: Monastic Life in the Thirteenth Century,* trans. Richard Vaughan (Gloucester: Alan Sutton, 1984), 82, 275.

The new people were buyers, sellers, money changers, people who generated and who reveled in what Jacques le Goff has called "an atmosphere of calculation."[6] The new people were merchants, lawyers, scribes, masters of the stylus, quill, and counting board. They were the bourgeoisie, the citizens of the *bourg* or *burg,* or town, a meritocracy more literate and numerate than most European clergy and nobility. Philip the Fair of France, a monarch powerful enough to defy both the king of England and the pope, turned to a Genoese merchant to run his navy and a Florentine merchant to manage his finances. These two, Benedetto Zaccaria and Musciatto Guidi, respectively,[7] were men in the midrange of a social hierarchy that had theoretically no slot for anyone in the middle.

Many of these new people achieved their social positions through the wealth they had accumulated by using machines to exploit natural forces. Medieval Europe built tens of thousands of water mills for grinding grain, fulling cloth, and a score of other purposes. According to the Domesday Book, England had 5,624 at the time of the Norman Conquest, which would be approximately one for every fifty households. Westerners invented, apparently independently, the post mill, the kind of windmill with a horizontal axle and vanes extending out from it at right angles that most of us think of when we think of the Netherlands.[8] Post

---

[6] Jacques le Goff, "The Town as an Agent of Civilisation, 1200–1500," in *The Fontana Economic History of Europe: The Middle Ages,* 91; Jacques Bernard, "Trade and Finance in the Middle Ages, 900–1500," in ibid., 310.

[7] Robert S. Lopez, *The Commercial Revolution of the Middle Ages, 950–1350* (Cambridge University Press, 1976), 166.

[8] Jean Gimpel, *The Medieval Machine: The Industrial Revolution of the Middle Ages* (Harmondsworth: Penguin Books, 1976), 12, 16–17, 24, 167–8; Lynn White, Jr., *Medieval Technology and Social Change* (Oxford: Oxford University Press, 1964), 81–7.

mills were a common sight in the High Middle Ages, and in the early fourteenth century Dante could describe gigantic and winged Satan, confident that his readers would understand, as looking like "a mill which the wind turns."[9] By the fifteenth century and perhaps long before then, the West had a greater proportion of individuals who understood wheels, levers, and gears than any other region on earth, and Westerners north and south were becoming accustomed to the repetitive whirring and clunking of machines.

Change was not greater in the late medieval West than it would be in that society a half millennium later during the industrial revolution, but it may have seemed so. Europe in 1000 had no set way to think about change, certainly not social change, while Europe of 1750 was at least acquainted with the concept.

Yet the West, compared with contemporary Muslim, Indian, and Chinese civilizations, was uniquely prepared to survive and even to profit from such an avalanche of change. Western Europe had the characteristics that physicians seeking means to counter the disorders of senescence hope to find in fetal tissue, that is to say, not so much vigor per se, though that is surely valuable in itself, as a lack of differentiation. Fetal tissue is so young that it retains the potentiality for becoming whatever kind of tissue is required.

The West lacked firmness of political and religious and, speaking in the broadest generality, cultural authority. It was, among the great civilizations, unique in its stubborn resistance to political,

---

[9] Dante Alighieri, *The Divine Comedy: Inferno*, trans. Charles S. Singleton (Princeton, N.J.: Princeton University Press, 1970), 361. Those needing a corrective to Eurocentric interpretation of the history of technology might read Donald R. Hill, "Mechanical Engineering in the Medieval Near East," *Scientific American*, 264 (May 1991), 100–5.

religious, and intellectual centralization and standardization. It shared one thing with the universe as described by such mystics as Nicholas of Cusa and Giordano Bruno: it had no center and, therefore, had centers everywhere.

Western Europe was a warren of jurisdictions – kingdoms, dukedoms, baronies, bishoprics, communes, guilds, universities, and more – a compost of checks and balances. No authority, not even the vicar of Christ on earth, had effective political, religious, or intellectual jurisdiction. This became glaringly obvious with the Protestant revolt: for example, Joseph Justus Scaliger preserved both his religious faith and his skin by migrating from Catholic France to fervently Protestant Geneva and then to tolerant Leiden. The West's decentralization had saved dissenters before as well. When William of Ockham refused to accept John XXII's authority on evangelical poverty and other matters, the pope excommunicated him, that is to say, thrust him from the bosom of the Church into the absolute zero of a life without sacraments or the aid and comfort of any Christian – theoretically. The condemned man took refuge with the pope's enemy, the German emperor, Louis of Bavaria, continuing as before until silenced not by the pope but, probably, by the Black Death.[10] And, of course, those who disobeyed secular authority in obedience to Rome's could usually find refuge in the Church of Rome. Popes maintained for generations a stable of recusants and other such "traitors." In later and more secular ages kings, dictators, and premiers did likewise. Decentralized Europe has always had an attic room or at least a dry corner in the barn for émigrés.

The West's traditional elites, secular and sacred, were not united sufficiently to defend their own interests against their most

[10] Ernest A. Moody, "Ockham, William of," in *The Dictionary of Scientific Biography*, ed. Charles Coulston Gillispie (New York: Scribner's, 1970–80), 10: 172.

obvious and immediate rivals for power, which were not one another or the Tartars or Muslims, but the merchants with whom they, if city dwellers, rubbed elbows every day. The political and religious aristocracies of Asia and North Africa always ultimately united to keep the nouveau riche down. In the West, on the other hand, merchants and bankers even managed to establish their own family dynasties and to insinuate themselves into political prominence; most famous, of course, were the Medici, but there were also the Fuggers and a goodly number of lesser lineages of wealth and influence. Money changers were the yeast that the lump – peasant, priest, or noble – never could evict or sterilize, and that quickened and even recruited among the traditional classes.

The elites of palace and cathedral could not suppress the bourgeoisie because they lacked confidence that they could fulfill their own ambitions without access to the wealth and the skills of this cocky meritocracy. Before the upper classes could convert their scorn and nascent fear into effective policy, the merchants had created a civilization in which others could achieve their own satisfactions only by buying the services of and granting privileges to those who lived by counting.

The West was intellectually as well as socially unsolidified. It was unique among the great civilizations in its lack of a phylogenetic classical tradition. The classical syntheses of the others were deeply rooted in their pasts. Their precepts were a part of their ancient cultures, even those of the Muslims, the great majority of whom were not Bedouins but descendants of Persians, Egyptians, Greeks, and others. These sophisticates did not feel obliged to rethink their basic concepts of reality. They even lagged behind in inventing or adopting the scribal minutiae of arrangement and format – alphabetization (or some equivalent for Chinese characters), punctuation, indentation, capitalization, running heads, and so on – that proved, as we shall see presently, so helpful to the uninitiated in the West.[11] The anciently civilized had little sense of being uninitiated.

Westerners were, to put it simply, peripheral. For illustration we need only point to their most sacred shrines, which lay outside the West and, after the triumphs of Salah Al-Din Yussuf (Saladin), outside Christendom.[12] At least as troublesome as the alien origin of much of the Venerable Model were its internal contradictions. Its Greek and Hebrew elements, respectively rationalistic and mystical (grant me this oversimplification for the sake of brevity), were disharmonious. The West, unlike its rivals, had a chronic need for explainers, adjusters, and resynthesizers.

The theological and philosophical truth, the function of which was to *explain*, gained in ancient authority and contemporary refinement in the High Middle Ages and in consequence, paradoxically, became more a puzzle than a comfort. In the twelfth century Western scholars, Adelard of Bath, Robert of Chester, and others, studied with learned Jews and Muslims, usually in Spain, and returned home to bestow on Christendom Latin translations of works of some of the greatest minds of ancient Greek and current Islamic cultures: Plato, Ptolemy, Avicenna, and others. In the thirteenth century the translation of the entire corpus of Aristotle's writings arrived in the West like an amphora of wine rolling off a Greek bireme and into a North Sea cog.

For the first time Westerners had to cope with a complete body of detailed knowledge and highly sophisticated interpretation by a pagan. "The Philosopher," as they came to call him, explained just about *everything* – ethics, politics, physics, metaphysics, meteorology, biology. The Middle Age's standard textbook of theol-

[11] Toby E. Huff, *The Rise of Early Modern Science: Islam, China, and the West* (Cambridge University Press, 1993), 292.

[12] Samuel Y. Edgerton, Jr., "From Mental Matrix to *Mappamundi* to Christian Empire: The Heritage of Ptolemaic Cartography in the Renaissance," in *Art and Cartography: Six Historical Essays*, ed. David Woodward (Chicago: University of Chicago Press, 1987), 24–9.

ogy, Peter Lombard's *Summa sententiarum,* written in the mid-1100s, had, amid thousands of quotations from the church fathers, only three from secular philosophers; but St. Thomas Aquinas's *Summa theologica,* written between 1266 and 1274, had 3,500 quotes from Aristotle alone. Fifteen hundred of them were from works unknown in the West a hundred years before.[13]

The Venerable Model lost definition – not because Westerners decided it was wrong, but because sometimes the past's various explanations were not precisely coterminous or were not precisely adequate for present requirements. For example, the four elements according to the ancient Greeks and Romans were earth, air, fire, and water, but the story of Creation as set forth in Genesis omits mention of air. St. Thomas Aquinas explained that Moses "makes no express mention" of this invisible element by name, "to avoid setting before ignorant persons something beyond their knowledge."[14] Another example: in 1459 Fra Mauro made a world map in which Asia was so large that it pushed Jerusalem out of the most honorable position, the center. He explained that

> Jerusalem is indeed the centre of the inhabited world latitudinally, though longitudinally it is somewhat to the west, but since the western portion is more thickly populated by reason of Europe, therefore Jerusalem is also the center longitudinally if we regard not empty space but density of population.[15]

The Venerable Model lost definition in the glare of clarification.

---

[13] R. W. Southern, *Medieval Humanism* (New York: Harper & Row, 1970), 46.

[14] *A Source Book in Medieval Science,* ed. Edward Grant (Cambridge, Mass.: Harvard University Press, 1974), 26; Thomas S. Kuhn, *The Copernican Revolution: Planetary Astronomy in the Development of Western Thought* (Cambridge, Mass.: Harvard University Press, 1957), 110.

[15] G. R. Crone, *Maps and Their Makers: An Introduction to the History of Cartography* (Folkestone, Kent: William Dawson, 1978), 28–9.

According to some of the wisest modern historians of the later Middle Ages – Johan Huizinga, Lynn White, Jr., William J. Bouwsma – the West was floundering in a slough of cultural despond, a condition of perceptual confusion, during the late thirteenth to the sixteenth century.[16] Its traditional ways of perceiving and explaining were failing in their primary function, which was, in Bouwsma's words, "to impose a meaning on . . . experience that can give to life a measure of reliability and thus reduce, even if it cannot altogether abolish, life's ultimate and terrifying uncertainties."[17]

Westerners began, very slowly, tentatively, and often unconsciously, to improvise a new version of reality out of inherited elements and out of current, often commercial, experience. The emerging New Model, as we shall call it, was distinctive in its growing emphasis on precision, quantification of physical phenomena, and mathematics.

The individuals chiefly responsible for the New Model were townspeople, the yeastiest citizens in Western as in most societies. In the way that the cells of a fetus *are* growth, these people *were* change, even when members of ancient elites: for instance, the bishop in his new, vast, and exorbitantly expensive urban cathedral. Some of the townsfolk were members of nascent elites, of the cultural avant-garde, and to them we owe special attention. They spent their working hours in one of two centers, the university and the marketplace.

---

[16] J. Huizinga, *The Waning of the Middle Ages* (New York: Doubleday, 1954); Lynn White, Jr., "Death and the Devil," in *The Darker Vision of the Renaissance: Beyond the Fields of Reason,* ed. Robert S. Kinsman (Berkeley: University of California Press, 1974), 25–46; William J. Bouwsma, "Anxiety and the Formation of Early Modern Culture," in *After the Reformation: Essays in Honor of J. H. Hexter,* ed. Barbara C. Malament (Philadelphia: University of Pennsylvania Press, 1980), 215–46; Donald R. Howard, "Renaissance World-Alienation," in ibid., 47–76.

[17] Bouwsma, "Anxiety and the Formation of Early Modern Culture," 228.

The latter was older than writing or the wheel, but Westerners had to invent the former for themselves. Expanding population, burgeoning church and state, proliferating knowledge, and the threat of various heresies together produced a demand for more teachers, scholars, bureaucrats, and preachers, overwhelming the old cathedral schools and giving rise to the universities.

The first half of the twelfth century was the heroic period of Western higher education, a time in which students spontaneously gathered around masters like the radically rationalistic Peter Abelard, even following them from town to town if necessary. The masters dispensed knowledge and wisdom, sometimes with a fillip of skepticism, but could not grant degrees or effectively claim legal prerogatives for themselves or defend their students in town-versus-gown struggles. Students could not obtain formal certification of acquired erudition nor assurance that the masters would not show up drunk to lecture or move away or even quit, nor could the students defend themselves against local prejudice and exploitation. The masters and the students, in other words, were not institutions.[18]

In the twelfth century the two groups coalesced into institutions. The University of Paris, which specialized in teaching the popular liberal arts in a city capable of providing enough food, housing, entertainment, and panache for legions of scholars, was the most influential. By the middle decades of the next century the University was sufficiently large and prestigious to ensure that it and universities in general would be a permanent and vital element in Western civilization.[19]

The Parisian masters, sometime between 1150 and 1200, fol-

---

[18] R. W. Southern, "The Schools of Paris and the School of Chartres," in *Renaissance and Renewal in the Twelfth Century,* eds. Robert L. Benson, Giles Constable, and Carol D. Lanham (Toronto: University of Toronto Press, 1991), 114–18.

[19] Nathan Schachner, *The Mediaeval Universities* (New York: Barnes, 1962), 59–73.

lowing the example of physicians, merchants, and craftsmen, set themselves up as a guild or *universitas*. The chancellor of the city cathedral fought a long battle with the masters for control of the new institution, which the masters, backed by a papacy seeking to weaken episcopal authority, won. The city government and populace opposed the masters' claims of special privileges and the students' rowdy ways, and even busted a few heads to make that point clear; but again the University won, in this case also with the backing of Capetian kings who wanted to cultivate the prosperity and prestige of their capital city. In 1231 Pope Gregory IX issued a bull recognizing the University of Paris as a corporation under papal protection, buttressing the institution's claim of exemption from local authority.

The West had invented an enduring institution whose function was to provide employment for professional thinkers and learners. In the twelfth century celebrants of the status quo had hounded Abelard out of Paris and out of teaching, but in the thirteenth century Albert the Great, Thomas Aquinas, Bonaventure, and even, for a while, the quasi-heretical Siger of Brabant enjoyed, as masters at the University of Paris, considerable job security as well as a degree of freedom of thought and speech.[20]

As a reward for indulging the universities, the Church and state received generations of literate, bright, intellectually rigorous bishops, administrators, and assorted bureaucrats who had attended and often taught at universities.[21] For instance, Nicole Oresme and Philippe de Vitry, products of the University of Paris

---

[20] Hastings Rashdall, *The Universities of Europe in the Middle Ages* (London: Oxford University Press, 1936), 1: 269–583.

[21] Willis Rudy, *The Universities of Europe, 1100–1914* (London: Associated University Presses, 1984) 20–6; Southern, "The Schools of Paris and the School of Chartres," 119, 129; John W. Baldwin, "Masters at Paris from 1179 to 1215: A Social Perspective," in *Renaissance and Renewal in the Twelfth Century,* 141–3, 151–8.

of whom we will hear more, were advisers to kings of France and became, respectively, the bishops of Lisieux and Meaux.

The teachers of philosophy and theology in the universities, the Schoolmen, were the most influential intellectuals of the medieval West. They were among the grandparents, if not parents, of the New Model, though they were not intentional innovators. They did not believe they had to invent or discover wisdom, but only to rediscover it. St. Bonaventure called them "compilers and weavers of approved opinions."[22] They can be better understood as heirs than as prophets, so let us begin with their past.

Their intellectual ancestors of the early Middle Ages were devoted to salvage scholarship. They constructed summaries and encyclopedias of the ancient heritage, adapting and simplifying in accordance with Christian beliefs the little they had and often, like archaeologists cataloging potsherds, becoming engrossed in minutiae. The seventh century's St. Isidore of Seville, for instance, produced an encyclopedia of all human knowledge, *Etymologiae*, the most popular in Western Europe for centuries, in which he explained quite nearly everything of importance, often by mean of incorrect analyses of the origins of words.[23]

Concentration on compilation, arrangement, and language per se was characteristic of the later Middle Ages, too. The difference between the scholarly effort of the two periods was that the first was an attempt to save as much as possible from a shrinking body of knowledge – a grasping at straws, as it were – and the second

---

[22] Jorge J. E. Gracia, "Scholasticism and the Scholastic Method," in *The Dictionary of the Middle Ages,* ed. Joseph R. Strayer (New York: Scribners', 1982–9), 11: 55.

[23] Frederick B. Artz, *The Mind of the Middle Ages, A.D. 200–1500* (Chicago: University of Chicago Press, 1980), 193; Ernest Brehaut, *An Encyclopedist of the Dark Ages* (New York: Columbia University Press, 1912), 215–21.

was an attempt to make sense of an expanding body of knowledge as a whole hay mow spilled onto the barn floor.

The Schoolmen had to solve the daunting problem of how to organize the massive bequest from the pagan, Islamic, and Christian past before they could effectively confront the even tougher problem of reconciling the contradictions of Christian and non-Christian thinkers – and even of saint and saint. The comfortably ignorant or the confidently cynical would have solved both difficulties by throwing away what seemed excessive or did not fit. But the Schoolmen were intensely, if narrowly, learned and terribly earnest.

The texts, sacred and profane, as first received from the ancients, were undifferentiated lumps, unsegmented and without handles, as awkward to manage as beached whales. The Schoolmen invented chapter titles and running headlines (often coded by size of initials and by color), cross-references, and even citations of quoted authors. Around 1200 Stephen Langton (soon to become the archbishop of Canterbury who counseled the barons and King John in the crisis that produced the Magna Carta) and colleagues devised the chapter and verse system for the books of the Bible, until then trackless forests.[24] In the next century Hugh of St. Cher, a Dominican at the University of Paris, led a team of scholars in writing, among other masterpieces of reference aids, the massive *Correctoria*, a list of the variant readings of the Vulgate. These and like scholars produced concordances for the Scriptures, key-word and subject indexes to the church fathers, and then to Aristotle and other ancients.[25] When they used numbers in their scholarly scaffolding, they substituted for Roman numerals

---

[24] Beryl Smalley, *The Study of the Bible in the Middle Ages* (Oxford: Basil Blackwell, 1952), 222–4.

[25] Ibid., 222–4, 333–4; "Hugh of St. Cher," in *Dictionary of the Middle Ages,* 6: 320–1; Lloyd William Daly, *Contributions to a History of Alphabetization in Antiquity and the Middle Ages* (Brussels: Latomus Revue d'Études Latines, 1967), 74; Richard H. Rouse and Mary A. Rouse,

the bright new Hindu-Arabic numerals, before most merchants and bankers made the same transition.[26]

For generations the Schoolmen were at a loss for a principle by which to arrange masses of information for easy retrieval. They believed that the principle should pertain chiefly to the relative importance of bits of information. In library catalogs, for instance, the Bible should come first, then the church fathers, and so on, with books on the liberal arts last. But ordering by prestige alone did not always work well, especially at the level of minutiae, and so the Schoolmen supplemented it with a system occasionally used in the ancient world and now and again since, but never often or consistently: alphabetization. As abstract as a progression of numerals, it required no judgment about the relative significance of what it arranged and, paradoxically, was therefore universally useful. One could use it to organize dictionaries of words, concordances of the pronouncements of God or of the statements of ancient Greeks, catalogs of books, collections of government documents. The Schoolmen supplied alphabetized handbooks and dictionaries of sermon materials for the preachers who at the end of the twelfth century were competing with heretics for the souls of the inhabitants of the burgeoning cities. And we have been alphabetizing ever since.[27]

Perhaps the most innovative and useful of all the Schoolmen's

---

Preachers, Florilegia and Sermons: Studies on the Manipulus florum *of Thomas of Ireland* (Toronto: Pontifical Institute of Mediaeval Studies, 1979), 4.

[26] Brian Stock, *The Implications of Literacy: Written Language and Models of Interpretation in the Eleventh and Twelfth Centuries* (Princeton, N.J.: Princeton University Press, 1983), 63; Rouse and Rouse, *Preachers, Florilegia and Sermons,* 32–3.

[27] Daly, *Contributions to a History of Alphabetization,* 74, 96; Smalley, *Study of the Bible,* 333–4; Rouse and Rouse, *Preachers, Florilegia and Sermons,* 4, 7–15; Mary A. Rouse and Richard H. Rouse, "Alphabetization, History of," in *Dictionary of the Middle Ages,* 1: 204–7; Stock, *The Implications of Literacy,* 62.

discrete inventions was the system of the analytical table of contents. Greece and Rome had never arranged their texts so that a novice could proceed confidently from the general to the topic to the subtopic to the specific point, and then back again. The Schoolmen did. Their system is an aid not only to finding a given item in a book, but to following lines of argument and, like mathematical technique, to thinking clearly. It is a sieve of several levels, graded from coarse to fine, into which we dump our confused ideas. First to be sifted out are general subjects, designated in our adaptation of this Scholastic invention as I, II, and so on. Next selected are the topics, A, B, and so on; then the subtopics, 1, 2, and so on; and these, if necessary, are further divided into a, b, and on and on. Alexander of Hales, the Franciscan master, may have been the first to introduce the system. He divided the whole into *partes* and then into *membra* and *articuli*. St. Thomas Aquinas, who never lost track of where he was in an argument, divided the whole into *partes,* and these into *quaestiones* or *distinctiones,* and these into *articuli.*[28]

The Schoolmen's organizing skills combined with their dead seriousness to deprive them of the refuge of both obscurantism and cynicism. They had full command of their texts, knew them to be correct, knew them often to be seemingly contradictory, and tried hard to think their way through the maze they insisted on constructing for themselves. They did not succeed in doing so, of course, but in the process they reinvented rigor in logic and lucidity in formal expression for the West. They meticulously analyzed their texts, carefully climbed ladders of syllogisms from premise to conclusion, and perfected in their prose a suitable instrument for the expression of their careful thoughts.

[28] Erwin Panofsky, *Gothic Architecture and Scholasticism* (Latrobe, Pa.: Archabbey Press, 1951), 32–5, 95–6; see also Otto Bird, "How to Read an Article of the *Summa,*" *New Scholasticism,* 27 (Apr. 1953), 129–59.

No Schoolman performed more skillfully or with greater economy of means than St. Thomas Aquinas. The armature of his logic is right there to be seen and tested, and his prose is a bony minimum stripped of alliteration, figures of speech, or even metaphor, except where tradition demanded otherwise. (He could not very well reject the poetry of the Psalms, but he did criticize Plato for extravagance in language.)[29] His reasoning and language are almost mathematical: our translators sometimes use algebraic letter symbols as the best means to express in twentieth century English what he wrote in thirteenth century Latin, although such symbols did not appear even in mathematics until the latter part of the Renaissance. For an example of his logic and his prose, let us examine a few sentences from the first of his proofs for the existence of God:

> Now the same thing cannot at the same time be both actually x [*sit simul* in the Latin original] and potentially x, though it can be actually x and potentially y [*secundum diversa*]: the actually hot cannot at the same time be potentially hot, though it can be potentially cold. Consequently, a thing in process of change cannot itself cause the same change: it cannot change itself. Of necessity therefore anything in process of change is being changed by something else.[30]

(This ultimate agent, of course, turns out to be God a few sentences later.)

In our time the word *medieval* is often used as a synonym for muddle-headedness, but it can be more accurately used to indicate precise definition and meticulous reasoning, that is to say, *clarity*.

[29] M.-D. Chenu, *Toward Understanding Saint Thomas,* trans. A.-M. Landry and D. Hughes (Chicago: Henry Regnery, 1964), 59–60, 117–19.
[30] St. Thomas Aquinas, *Summa theologiae* (London: Blackfriars, n.d.), 2: 12–13.

Thomas Aquinas, a saint, was a favorite of René Descartes,[31] a crown prince of rationalist philosophy and virtual inventor of coordinate or analytic geometry.

Careful organization, logic, and precision in language, if followed to their extremes, lead to mathematics. That next step beyond St. Thomas was not as long as we might consider it today because most of mathematics beyond counting and simple arithmetic was still expressed verbally. Yet it was a long stride conceptually, so great that the Schoolmen never completed it. They were not able or very rarely were able to get beyond what twentieth century scholars have called "logicomathematical philosophy." The Schoolmen did not have the advantage of the signs for plus, minus, square root, and other operations. They did not have the advantage of many of the most basic kinds of decisions about what and how to measure, decisions they began to make for us. For instance, in matters of temperature were coldness and hotness two different entities or different aspects of one? Most important, the Schoolmen, the heirs more to qualitative sages like Plato and Aristotle than to the quantitative Ptolemy, were still not adept at or comfortable thinking in terms of measured quantities.

Oxford's Richard Swineshead, for example, was ingenious not in dealing with exact measurement, but in avoiding the subject. He did not measure weight, but found ways to think about it without measuring it. He pondered over what we could call thought experiments about weight. If a rod fell vertically to and through the center of the universe (the earth), the part that first passed through would then be "falling" up, which would affect the rest of the rod, still falling down. Would the midpoint of the

---

[31] Albert G. A. Balz, *Descartes and the Modern Mind* (New Haven, Conn.: Yale University Press, 1952), 26; René Descartes, *Correspondance*, eds. C. Adam and G. Milhaud (Paris: Presses Universitaires de France, 1941), 3: 301; Adrien Baillet, *La vie de Monsieur Des-Cartes* (Paris: Daniel Honthemels, 1891), part 1, 286.

rod ever coincide with the center of the universe? This was a problem to challenge the sharpest logician, a problem that has inspired Swineshead's interpreters to produce streams of algebra, but one that smells more, much more, of the scholar's lamp than the bench scientist's Bunsen burner.[32]

Even so, in the fourteenth century certain Schoolmen – Swineshead and his fellow monks at Merton College, Oxford, and, most productively, Nicole Oresme of Paris – made great progress in mathematics-without-measurement. Englishmen were more successful than any Westerners yet in utilizing algebra in the consideration of what Aristotle termed qualities: velocity, temperature, and so on. Oresme pushed further on, geometrizing qualities, even speed in its most perplexing manifestation, acceleration. He produced what amounted to graphs (rather like music staffs; see Chapter 8) in which the progression of time was expressed with a horizontal line and the variable intensity of a quality with vertical lines of various heights. The end result was an elegant and pure abstraction, a geometrical depiction of a physical phenomenon varying through time[33] (Figure 3).

Impressive as the work of these people might be, one is amazed over and over by the absence of actual measurement. They did not have translations of, or studiously ignored, the mensural sections of Ptolemy and Euclid and other classical quantifiers. As with Aristotle, the Schoolmen considered things as more and less than each other, but not in terms of multiples of a definite quantity such as inches, degrees of arc, degrees of heat, and kilometers per hour. The Schoolmen, paradoxically, were mathematicians without being quantifiers.[34]

---

[32] John Murdoch and Edith Sylla, "Swineshead, Richard," in *Dictionary of Scientific Biography*, 3: 185, 189, 198–9, 204–5.

[33] David C. Lindberg, *The Beginnings of Western Science* (Chicago: University of Chicago Press, 1992), 294–301.

[34] Anneliese Maier, *On the Threshold of Exact Science*, trans. Steven D. Sargent (Philadelphia: University of Pennsylvania Press, 1982), 169–70.

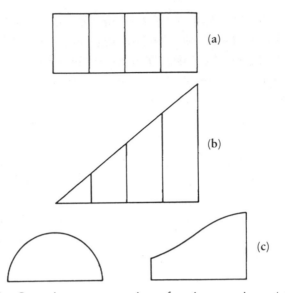

Figure 3. An Oresmian representation of various motions: (a) uniform velocity, (b) uniformly accelerated motion, (c) nonuniform velocities. David C. Lindberg, *The Beginnings of Western Science* (Chicago: University of Chicago Press, 1992), 299.

There were exceptions, Roger Bacon being the most famous of them. At the end of the thirteenth century he called mathematics "the gate and key" to knowledge, which saints had discovered at the beginning of the world. Mathematics was, he said, our unfailing guide in astronomy, weather, geography, and other things of this world, and in philosophy and beyond, even theology.[35] He sometimes actually measured things, for instance, the 42-degree angle between the arc of a rainbow and the line of sun's rays striking the measurer's back. The influence (or lack thereof) of this venture into practical metrology, however, was what you and I must consider odd. Other medieval researchers in the field of

[35] *The Opus Majus of Roger Bacon,* trans. Robert B. Burke (Philadelphia: University of Pennsylvania Press, 1928), 1: 116, 117, 120, 123, 128, 200, 203–4.

optics paid little heed to Bacon's measurement, and the most successful of them, Theodoric of Freiberg, seems to have reduced it by half in his treatise on rainbows. Was this his mistake or some copyist's? What is more important is that the mistake seems to have troubled no one for hundreds of years.[36]

Another source for the quantifying tendency, one more important than the Schoolmen's struggle to get beyond verbalism, brings us back to what may or may not be the root of all evil but which is surely the taproot of modern civilization. Many of the Schoolmen concerned with quantifying qualities – Roger Bacon, Albert of Saxony, Walter Burley, Henry of Hesse, Gregory of Rimini, and Jean Buridan – also wrote about *money*.[37] Nicole Oresme composed an entire treatise on the subject, focusing on the mystery of inflation, by which more mysteriously became less. Yes, he said, debasement of coins made more money, but money of less value, impoverishing society. He tried, in vain, to dissuade the French kings from the practice.[38]

Money was second only to God in its power and ubiquity. St. Thomas Aquinas acknowledged its power:

> It is true that money is subordinated to something else as its end; still to the extent that it is useful in the quest for all material goods by its power it somehow contains them all. . . . This is how it has some likeness to beatitude.[39]

---

[36] A. C. Crombie, "Quantification in Medieval Physics," in *Change in Medieval Society: Europe North of the Alps, 1050–1500*, ed. Sylvia L. Thrupp (New York: Appleton-Century-Crofts, 1964), 195.

[37] Joel Kaye, "The Impact of Money on the Development of Fourteenth-Century Scientific Thought," *Journal of Medieval History*, 14 (Sept. 1988), 260.

[38] Ibid., 254, 257–8, 260.

[39] St. Thomas Aquinas, *Summa theologiae* (London: Blackfriars, 1964–6), 41: 261.

The Roman Empire had functioned on cash, but initially the West did not. There was little trade, and much of that was barter. Coins had little abstract value beyond the value of their metal. Powerful men with specie gave it to followers to cultivate their loyalty or strewed it among the poor; a nobleman in the Limousin even sowed a field with pieces of silver for the sake of prestige. It was not unusual to melt money, and recast and horde it as plate, crowns, crucifixes, and chalices, or to bury it with the dead.[40] Currency ceased to circulate for the lack of commerce, commerce curdled for lack of currency, and money taught few the advantages of quantification.

But in time Muslim and Viking raiders either stayed home or settled down, feudal lords established law and order of a sort, and agricultural productivity edged upward. New techniques and devices appeared – a kind of harness to enable horses to pull with their shoulders, not their necks; heavy plows to ease through the clayey soils of Atlantic Europe; and a score of other individually minor but collectively major improvements.[41]

Supply grew, commerce and towns revived, avarice blinked and rubbed its eyes at the sight of money. Specie rose up out of hidden caches and seeped in from abroad. England, which had only ten mints in 900, had seventy in 1000. Cities and then nations began to issue coins, and Western replaced non-Western coinage as the commonest kind of money.[42]

Westerners found themselves sliding into a cash economy, each item in their lives reduced to a single standard in the process. "Every saleable item is at the same time a measured item,"[43] said

---

[40] Marc Bloch, *Feudal Society,* trans. L. A. Manyon (Chicago: University of Chicago Press, 1961), 1: 66, 2: 311; Alexander Murray, *Reason and Society in the Middle Ages* (Oxford: Clarendon Press, 1985), 34–5.

[41] Lopez, *The Commercial Revolution,* 30–57.

[42] Murray, *Reason and Society,* 50–8.

[43] Kaye, "The Impact of Money," 260.

Walter Burley of Merton College in the fourteenth century. Wheat, barley, oats, rye, apples, spices, woolens, silks, carvings, and paintings developed prices; and that was relatively easy to understand because they could be eaten, worn, touched, and observed. It was harder to understand when money substituted for obligations of service and labor set long ago by custom. When time proved to have a price – that is to say, interest on a debt calculated in accordance with the passage of months and years – that strained the mind and the moral sense as well because time was God's exclusive property.[44] If time had a price, if time were a thing that could have a numerical value, then what about other unsegmented imponderables, like heat or velocity or love?

Price quantified *everything*. The seller set a price on what he or she had to sell because everything the seller needed or wanted had to be paid for in turn. In 1308 Pope Clement V proclaimed the price of pardoning a year's worth of sins to be the contribution of one pence, Tours currency, to the good cause of crusading against the Muslims.[45] "O most excellent gold!" exulted Christopher Columbus two centuries after. "Who has gold has a treasure with which he gets what he wants, imposes his will on the world, and even helps souls to paradise."[46]

Northern Italian cities minted the first Western gold coins to circulate widely in a very long time, Genoa the genois and Florence the florin, both in 1252, and Venice the ducat in 1284.[47] These

---

[44] Jacques le Goff, *Your Money or Your Life: Economy and Religion in the Middle Ages,* trans. Patricia Ranum (New York: Zone Books, 1988).

[45] William E. Lunt, *Papal Revenues in the Middle Ages* (New York: Octagon Books, 1965), 2: 458; Elisabeth Vodola, "Indulgences," in *Dictionary of the Middle Ages,* 6: 446–50.

[46] *Journals and Other Documents on the Life and Voyages of Christopher Columbus,* trans. Samuel Eliot Morison (New York: Heritage Press, 1963), 383.

[47] Le Goff, "The Town as an Agent of Civilization," 81.

coins were supposed to be worth not only what their metal would bring in the marketplace, but what the governments that issued them declared they were worth. Some of them retained that value in the market for considerable periods: a new and abstract measurement of worth appeared in Western Europe. When even the value of the genois and florin and ducat wavered, or when a transaction could not be closed because the number of coins offered in one currency was worth a fraction too much or too little of a whole number of the coins in the currency in which the price was expressed, or when currencies flew up and down in value so fast no one was confident of knowing their relative values – when all was in flux and yet bills had to be proffered and paid, Westerners took another giant step into abstraction. They extended as never before the useful fiction of "money of account," an idealized scale consisting of what after a while was the arbitrarily fixed ratios of the values of prestigious coins. The system was so abstract that it continued to function even after some of these coins fell out of circulation.[48]

The abstraction of Western merchants' scale of value puts one in mind of some of Plato's airier speculations, but this one was the product of the shrewd practices of those men whose livelihoods depended on the balance of expenditure and profit. Money of

---

[48] Kaye, "The Impact of Money," 259; P. Spufford, "Coinage and Currency," in *Economic Organization and Policies in the Middle Ages,* eds. M. M. Poston, E. E. Rich, and Edward Miller, Cambridge Economic History of Europe, 3 (Cambridge University Press, 1963), 593–5; F. P. Braudel, "Prices in Europe from 1450 to 1750," in *The Economy of Expanding Europe in the Sixteenth and Seventeenth Centuries,* eds. E. E. Rich and C. H. Wilson, Cambridge Economic History of Europe, 4 (Cambridge University Press, 1967), 379; Elgin Groseclose, *Money and Man: A Survey of Monetary Experience* (Norman: University of Oklahoma Press, 1976), 66–7; Carlo M. Cipolla, *Money, Prices, and Civilization in the Mediterranean World, Fifth to Seventeenth Century* (New York: Gordian Press, 1967), 38–52.

account was as useful and as strange as a system of measurement of time that musicians just down the city street invented: *tempora* (tempi), which were homogeneous, each equal to every other, though composed of sound or of silence. In the dizzy vortex of a cash economy the West learned the habits of quantification.

Western Europe's economy was not the first to be monetized, not by thousands of years: why, then, did that alteration have such distinctive, even unique, effects in the West? Its chronic shortage of specie surely contributed. Western Europe did not have great deposits of easily mined gold and silver and, therefore, when it took the hook of a cash economy, did not have enough precious metal of its own for its economy to function efficiently. The West suffered from a chronic balance-of-payments problem until some time in the sixteenth century. Specie flowed from Northern Europe to the Mediterranean ports and thence to trading partners in the East. In the 1420s Venice exported something like fifty thousand ducats a year to Syria alone. The flow of gold eastward was so steady and lasted for so long that the Spanish had a special name for it: *evacuación de oro*.

Europe took what specie it could out of its own mines, imported gold from as far away as tropical Africa, and, after its manufacturing revived, sold its goods for specie whenever possible, but always the precious metals swept away to the East. Rates of interest, therefore, were as high as 15 percent on long-term loans to respectable merchants and institutions such as the commune of Florence, 30 percent and higher on loans to kings and princes. Governments decreed maximum interest rates – 15 percent in Genoa throughout the 1200s, 20 percent in France in 1311 – which suggests that actual rates tended to be even higher.[49]

---

[49] Cipolla, *Money, Prices, and Civilization*, 63–5; Geoffrey Parker, "The Emergence of Modern Finance in Europe, 1500–1730," in *The Fontana Economic History of Europe: The Sixteenth and Seventeenth Centuries*,

Westerners were obsessed with what they could not hold on to, money. Marco Polo waxed eloquent about the abundance of gold in parts of the East. Columbus fixated on finding it in his new world. Cortés and his Spaniards hungered for it, said the Aztecs, "like pigs."[50] There were no people on earth more concerned with coins than Westerners, no people who worried more about their weight and purity, who played more tricks with bills of exchange and other pieces of paper that represented money – no people on earth more obsessed with counting and counting and counting.

527–9; Harry A. Miskimin, *The Economy of Early Renaissance Europe, 1300–1460* (Englewood Cliffs, N.J.: Prentice-Hall, 1969), 155; Harry A. Miskimin, *The Economy of Later Renaissance Europe, 1460–1600* (Cambridge University Press, 1977), 22–3, 28, 35–43.

[50] *The Broken Spears: The Aztec Account of the Conquest of Mexico*, ed. Miguel Leon-Portilla (Boston: Beacon Press, 1962), 50–1.

CHAPTER FOUR

Time

The Horologium – not only does it show and register the hour to our eyes, but also its bell announces it to the ears of those who are far away or staying at home. Hence in a way it seems to be alive, since it moves of its own accord, and does its work on behalf of man, night and day, and nothing could be more useful or more pleasant than that.

Giovanni Tortelli (1471)[1]

Time puzzled St. Augustine: "I know well enough what it is, provided that nobody asks me; but if I am asked what it is, and try to explain, I am baffled."[2] Measurements are usually *of* something distinctively itself – a hundred meters of road, of meadow, of lake – but a hundred hours, happy or sad, is a hundred hours of . . . time.

Time's insubstantiality defied St. Augustine's understanding

---

[1] Alex Keller, "A Renaissance Humanist Looks at 'New' Inventions: The Article 'Horologium' in Giovanni Tortelli's *De Orthographia,*" *Technology and Culture*, 11 (July 1970), 351–2, 354–5, 362, 363.

[2] St. Augustine, *Confessions,* trans. R. S. Pine-Coffin (Harmondsworth: Penguin Books, 1961), 264.

and defies ours, but allows humans to press upon it their own conceptions of its parts. It is not odd that medieval Western Europeans took in measuring time their first giant step forward in practical metrology. Nor is it odd that they did so in measuring hours, rather than in calendar reform. Hours were not bounded by natural event, but were arbitrary durations and susceptible to arbitrary definition. Days, in contrast, had such boundaries in darkness and light, and, furthermore, calendars were artifacts of millennia of civilization, stiff with encrustations of custom and sanctity.

To illustrate: when, in 1519, Jerónimo de Aguilar met Christians after years of being stranded among the Maya of Yucatán, his first question was as to the day of the week. When his rescuers said that it was, as he thought, Wednesday, confirming that he had been able to keep track of the days of the week despite his isolation, he burst into tears. What so moved him was not that his calendar was correct according to the stars, but that he had been able to maintain his schedule of prayer while among the infidel.[3] This keeper of calendars, typical of his era and people, was not interested in accuracy per se but vis-à-vis tradition and the possibility of salvation.

For peasants schedules were approximate: weather, dawn, and sunset dictated their tempi. But hours were of central significance to city dwellers, whom buying and selling had already initiated into the vogue of quantification. Their time was already what Benjamin Franklin, a man they prefigured, would call it: money.

In 1314 the city of Caen installed a clock on a bridge and inscribed it thus: "I give the hours voice / To make the common

[3] Francisco López de Gómara, *Cortés: The Life of the Conqueror by His Secretary*, trans. Lesley Byrd Simpson (Berkeley: University of California Press, 1964), 31.

folk rejoice."[4] (Remember that the common people then included everyone except members of the aristocracy and the Church.) A fifteenth century petition for a city clock for Lyons proclaimed, "If such a clock were to be made, more merchants would come to the fairs, the citizens would be very consoled, cheerful and happy and would live a more orderly life, and the town would gain in decoration."[5]

The English word *clock* is related to the French *cloche* and the German *Glocke,* words for bell. In the Middle Ages and Renaissance, life in the cities was paced by bells – "a city without bells," said even the antipunctual Rabelais, "is like a blind man without a stick."[6] But the hours they rang at the start of the second millennium were canonical and imprecise, and there were too few per day to provide a suitable tempo for urban schedules.

The burghers understood the practical value of clocks, were comfortable with quantification and adept with machinery, but that does not necessarily mean they invented the mechanical clock. If history were logical, then an astrologer or a monk would have to have done the deed because they were members of the two groups in medieval European society dedicated to keeping a schedule at night, cloudy or bright, when judging the time was difficult. Astrologers, for example, had to fix the positions of moving planets in relation to each other when kings, popes, and wealthy patrons were getting born, dying, initiating battles, and so on. Monks had to arise in the dark to recite the proper prayers at the proper times. Getting the day under way at matins was tricky: St. Benedict's Rule decreed, "If anyone shall come to matins after the

[4] David S. Landes, *Revolution in Time: Clocks and the Making of the Modern World* (Cambridge, Mass.: Harvard University Press, 1983), 81.
[5] Carlo M. Cipolla, *Clocks and Culture, 1300–1700* (London: Collins, 1967), 42.
[6] François Rabelais, *The Histories of Gargantua and Pantagruel,* trans. J. M. Cohen (Harmondsworth: Penguin Books, 1955), 78.

Gloria of the 94th Psalm, which on this account we wish to be said slowly and leisurely, he shall not take his place in the choir, but go last of all, or to some place apart which the abbot may appoint for those who so fail in his sight."[7]

The early mechanical clocks were so huge and expensive that I doubt an individual astrologer or astronomer built the very first of them, though such a wizard might have if sponsored by a duke or a bishop. My guess is that a monk, a member of a large and probably wealthy organization, did the deed. If history were logical, he would have been a monk of the technologically advanced Cistercian order, whose abbots were certain that grace somehow correlated with efficiency and, therefore, with water mills and windmills, cogs and wheels.[8]

Logic would further suggest that the inventing was done in the north. There, the seasonal variation in day length and the inequality of the unequal hours was greater than in Mediterranean Europe and the water in water clocks more apt to freeze. Northern France, the motherland of Gothic architecture and polyphony, where innovation was bounding ahead in the thirteenth century, seems a sensible choice.

So much for logic, which history often ignores. We do not know who built the European prototype of our mechanical clocks or where, and probably never will. As for when, that was in the last decades of the thirteenth century just before or soon after the invention of spectacles (which was more than a coincidence: the West was beginning its long frenzy of devising technological aides for human senses).[9] We cannot pin down the year, but the decade was probably the 1270s. At its beginning Robertus Anglicus re-

[7] *Rule of St. Benedict,* trans. Charles Gasquet (London: Chatto & Winders, 1925), 36, 78; Landes, *Revolution in Time,* 68.

[8] Jean Gimpel, *The Medieval Machine: The Industrial Revolution of the Middle Ages* (Harmondsworth: Penguin Books, 1976), 67–8.

[9] Edward Rosen, "The Invention of Eyeglasses," *Journal of the History of Medicine and Allied Sciences,* 11 (Jan. 1956), 28–9.

marked on attempts to construct a wheel that would make one complete revolution every twenty-four hours. In the same decade someone at the court of Alfonso El Sabio in Spain sketched a weight-driven clock regulated by the flow of mercury from one compartment of a hollow wheel to another.[10] About then or soon afterward the poet Jean de Meun, co-author of *The Romance of the Rose,* included in this, the era's "best-seller," a Pygmalion who was quite a mechanic. He invented several kinds of musical instruments – a tiny organ, for instance, which he pumped and played while "he sang motet or triplum or tenor voice" – and clocks that chimed "by means of intricately contrived wheels that ran forever."[11] If the poet had not seen clocks, he had heard about them.

After 1300 there is no doubt that the mechanical clock was a reality, because there was a great increase in the number of references to time-measuring machines.[12] Dante, in the twenty-fourth canto of *Paradiso,* written about 1320, utilized reduction gearing as a metaphor for souls in bliss, spinning in ecstasy:

> As the wheels within a clockwork synchronize
> So that the innermost, when looked at closely
> Seems to be standing, while the outermost flies.[13]

---

[10] Pierre Mesnage, "The Building of Clocks," in *A History of Technology and Invention through the Ages,* ed. Maurice Daumas, trans. Eileen B. Hennessy (New York: Crown, 1969), 2: 284; H. Alan Lloyd, *Some Outstanding Clocks over Seven Hundred Years, 1250–1950* (n.c.: Leonard Hill, 1958), 4–6.

[11] Guillaume de Lorris and Jean de Meun, *The Romance of the Rose,* trans. Charles Dahlberg (Hanover, N.H.: University Press of New England, 1986), 343.

[12] J. D. North, "Monasticism and the First Mechanical Clocks," in *The Study of Time: Proceedings of the Second Congress of the International Society for the Study of Time,* eds. J. T. Fraser and N. Lawrence (New York: Springer, 1975), 2: 384–5.

[13] Dante Alighieri, *The Divine Comedy,* trans. John Ciardi (New York: Norton, 1961), 541; Ernest L. Edwardes, *Weight-Driven Chamber Clocks*

In 1335 Galvano della Fiamma described a "wonderful clock" in Milan in the Chapel of the Blessed Virgin (now the San Gottarde) with a hammer that struck twenty-four hours in the day and night:

> At the first hour of the night it gives one sound, at the second, two strokes, at the third, three, and so on at the fourth, four; and thus it distinguishes hour from hour, which is in the highest degree necessary for all conditions of men.[14]

Clocks had only bells — no faces or hands yet — but already Western Europe had entered the age of quantified time, perhaps already too deeply to turn around.

Most inventions are improvements or adaptations of previous devices, but the mechanical clock was, in its key mechanism, truly original. Time had seemed to most people an unsegmented flow. Therefore, experimenters and tinkerers wasted centuries attempting to measure time by imitating its flowing passage, that is, the flow of water, sand, mercury, ground porcelain, and so on — or the slow and steady burning of a candle out of the wind. But no one has ever devised a practical way of measuring long periods by such means. The substance in motion grows gelid, freezes, evaporates, clots, or the candle perversely burns too fast or too slow or gutters out — something goes wrong.

Solving the problem becomes possible when one stops thinking of time as a smooth continuum and starts thinking of it as a succession of quanta. St. Augustine suggested that one could, for instance, measure a long syllable as twice a short one: "But when two syllables sound one after the other — the first short, the second long — how shall I keep hold of the short one?"[15] The answer

---

of the Middle Ages and Renaissance (Altrincham: John Sherratt, 1965), 19–21. See canto 10 of Dante's Paradiso for another clock-related image.

[14] Edwardes, Weight-Driven Chamber Clocks, 46–7.

[15] The Human Experience of Time: The Development of Its Philosophical Meaning, ed. Charles M. Sherover (New York: New York University Press, 1975), 92, 93–4.

technologically (not philosophically) was the escapement. With it, the short syllable became the duration between *tick* and *tock*.

Western Europe was full of mills, levers, pulleys, and toothed gears when Robertus Anglicus described a time measurer driven by a weight hanging from a line wound around a cylinder, and the idea of using some of this technology to measure time must have occurred to a number of protomachinists. The problem was how to prevent the weight in Robertus's proposed machine from dropping in a rush or lagging and sticking ungraciously. The descent of the weight could be slowed easily enough, but how could it be done so as to ensure a steady turning of the cylinder? How could one ensure that the first hour so measured would be of the same duration as the last?

The answer was what we call the escapement. This "simple" oscillating device regularly interrupts, in thousands upon thousands of repetitions a day, the descent of the clock's weight, ensuring that its energy is expended evenly.[16] The escapement did nothing to solve the mysteries of time, but it did domesticate it.

Westerners were not the first to have mechanical clocks. The Chinese had several giant ones as early as the tenth century. Indeed, it is conceivable that news of these spurred the invention of the West's first clocks.[17] Whatever may be the truth of that, it is unquestionable that the West was unique in its enthusiasm for clocks (we will get back to that soon) and in its headlong shift from unequal to equal hours. As far as we know, from the beginning the West's mechanical clocks measured time in terms of equal

---

[16] Landes, *Revolution in Time*, 6–11.

[17] Joseph Needham, Wang Ling, and Derek J. de Solla Price, *Heavenly Clockwork: The Great Astronomical Clocks of Medieval China* (Cambridge University Press, 1960), 55–6; Landes, *Revolution in Time*, 17–24. These Chinese devices might be more accurately called astronomical machines rather than clocks, as some would say about the first European clocks, too.

hours, winter or summer. This was not because the problem of creating a clock for seasonally variable hours was insoluble: the Japanese did so after the mechanical clock arrived from Europe.[18] That was centuries later, and medieval technology was probably not up to such a task. Even so, it is interesting that the record includes no mention of any attempt to do so. Perhaps early capitalists wanted equal hours so they could grind a full hour's worth of labor out of workers in the gloomiest and briefest days of winter. Perhaps Westerners were already beginning to think of time as homogeneous, as thirteenth century polyphony hints.

Be all that as it may, equal hours began to displace unequal hours in general usage as early as 1330 in Germany and about 1370 in England. In the latter year Charles V of France decreed that all the clocks of Paris should count the hours in agreement with the clock he was installing in his palace on the Ile de la Cité. (The quai de l'Horloge, with a clock, is still there.) Jean Froissart, the historian of the Hundred Years' War, shifted from canonical hours to the new clock hours halfway through writing his *Chronicles* – the 1380s seems a good guess.[19]

"It was in the European city," says A. J. Gurevich, "that time began, for the first time in history, to be 'isolated' as a pure form, exterior to life."[20] Time, though invisible and without substance, was fettered.

The clock's effects were manifold and tremendous. The clock was a complicated machine that demanded in its building and encouraged in its maintenance the skills of a good machinist and of a practical mathematician. For evidence, let me refer you to

---

[18] Landes, *Revolution in Time,* 77.

[19] Edwardes, *Weight-Driven Chamber Clocks,* 3; W. Rothwell, "The Hours of the Day in Medieval French," *French Studies,* 13 (July 1959), 249.

[20] A. J. Gurevich, "Time as a Problem of Cultural History," in *Cultures and Time,* ed. L. Gardet et al. (Paris: UNESCO Press, 1976), 241.

Richard of Wallingford, abbot of St. Albans from 1326 to 1336, who built a tower clock for his abbey and wrote a treatise on clock making. More like a mechanic than a monk, he must have cut and filed and adjusted and tightened and tested scores of bits of metal, and, of necessity, he spoke in numbers:

> The wheel of the weight for the day movement is divided into 72 teeth. The centre of the wheel is separated from the base by a distance of 13 teeth of the same wheel, and is a chord of 6 teeth from the centre line of the entire device, the length of its arbor being a chord of 15 teeth beyond the tenon.[21]

The quantitative abbot was a ghost of the Hellenistic past or, more likely, of the future.

The clock provided Westerners with a new way of imagining – of meta-imagining. Lucretius, the Roman poet, had created the image of the *machina mundi,* "the world machine," back in the first century A.D. and others had now and again used it since, but the firmly specific "clockwork universe," which many would say has been the dominant metaphor of Western civilization, did not appear until the fourteenth century. Nicole Oresme, in his theories and techniques, anticipated the great sixteenth and seventeenth century astronomers, especially in his reference to God having created the heavens so they functioned "so tempered, and so har-monized that . . . the situation is much like that of a man making a clock and letting it run and continue its own motion by itself."[22]

---

[21] *Richard of Wallingford: An Edition of His Writings,* ed. and trans. J. D. North (Oxford: Clarendon Press, 1976), 1: 465, 471, 473–4.

[22] Nicole Oresme, *Le livre du ciel et du monde,* trans. Albert D. Menut, eds. Albert D. Menut and Alexander J. Denomy (Madison: University of Wisconsin Press, 1968), 289. See also Nicholas H. Steneck, *Science and Creation in the Middle Ages: Henry of Langenstein (d. 1297) on Genesis* (Notre Dame, Ind.: University of Notre Dame Press, 1976), 149; Otto Mayr, *Authority, Liberty and Automatic Machinery in Early Modern Europe* (Baltimore: Johns Hopkins Press, 1986), 39.

When Johannes Kepler, three centuries after Oresme, tried to explain the idea that guided his awesome speculations, he wrote:

> My aim is to show that the heavenly machine is not a kind of divine, live being, but a kind of clockwork (and he who believes that a clock has a soul, attributes the maker's glory to the work), insofar as nearly all the manifold motions are caused by a most simple, magnetic, and material force, just as all motions of the clock are caused by a simple weight.[23]

Oresme's metaphor guided the thoughts of the men who gave us classical physics and, one could argue, was equally important for the creators of classical economics and Marxism.

So much for the geniuses; what about the rest of the people, whose ultimate decision on quantified time, as on everything, would be decisive? We know next to nothing about what peasants, the great majority, thought of the clock, but we can be sure that urbanites held the time machine in high esteem. Every big city and many smaller ones taxed themselves severely in order to have at least one clock, which in their first century or so were huge, usually sat in towers, and were very expensive. It may be that no complicated machine in the entire history of technology before the seventeenth century spread so rapidly as the clock.

Jean Froissart, who, with his prolific quill and average tastes, is more valuable to the social historian of medieval Europe than any genius, was infatuated with the new machine. His poem "L'Horloge amoureuse" features the clock as an image for a lover's heart. The beauty of the poem's beloved lady motivates her lover just as the weight drives the clock. His desire would be uncontrollable if it were not checked by fear, like the escapement regulating the fall of the weight. Froissart found images for all the allegorical dwellers in the realm of love – Loyalty, Patience,

---

[23] Arthur Koestler, *The Sleepwalkers: A History of Man's Changing Vision of the Universe* (Harmondsworth: Penguin Books, 1964), 345.

Honor, Courtesy, Valor, Humility, Youth – in the mechanisms of the new time machine.[24] The poem is itself a sort of love song to the clock because the machine tells the hours even when there is no sun:

> Hence do we hold him for valiant and wise
> Who first invented this device
> And with his knowledge undertook and made
> A thing so noble and of great price.[25]

Some of the most spectacular clocks ever made were constructed within the first few generations after the invention of the escapement. The famous Strasbourg clock, begun in 1352 and finished two years later, told the hours and included an automated astrolabe, a perpetual calendar, a carillon that played hymns, statues of the Virgin with Christ child and three worshiping Magi, a mechanical rooster that crowed and flapped its wings, and a tablet showing the correlation between the zodiac and the parts of the body, indicating the proper times for bloodletting.[26] To say that the city's clock told time and to say no more would be like saying that its cathedral's stained-glass windows admitted light and saying no more.

For generations the town clock was the one complicated machine that hundreds of thousands saw every day, heard over and over again every day and night. It taught them that invisible, inaudible, seamless time was composed of quanta. It, like money, taught them quantification.

The modern style of disciplined industrial time appeared as far

---

[24] Jean Froissart, *Chronicles*, trans. Geoffrey Brereton (Harmondsworth: Penguin Books, 1978), 9–10; F. W. Shears, *Froissart, Chronicler and Poet* (London: Routledge, 1930), 202–3.

[25] Landes, *Revolution in Time*, 82.

[26] F. C. Harber, "The Cathedral Clock and the Cosmological Clock Metaphor," in *The Study of Time*, 2: 399.

back as the first half of the fourteenth century. For instance, on 24 April 1335 Philip VI granted power to the mayor and aldermen of Amiens to ordain and control by a bell the time when the workers of the city should go to work in the morning, when they should eat and return to work after eating, and when they should quit work.[27] When two hundred years later Rabelais's Pantagruel proclaimed "that no clock keeps better time than the stomach,"[28] his was a voice crying in a quantified urban wilderness.

"The calendar," writes Eviatar Zerubavel in a particularly felicitous sentence, "is the warp of the fabric of society, running lengthwise through time, and carrying and preserving the woof, which is the structure of relations among men, and the things we call institutions."[29] That being true, the fact that Western Europeans were slower to reform their calendar than to build and obey clocks is not surprising. In fact, that they did it at all is more surprising than that they procrastinated about it.

Philip Melanchthon, the Lutheran reformer, tells of a "doctor" (holder of a university degree) who said that there was no need for precision in the divisions of the year, because "his peasants knew perfectly well when it was day, when it was night, when it was winter, when it was summer." Many people would have agreed, but the learned and pious Melanchthon proclaimed that someone should "shit a turd" into the aforesaid doctor's hat "and put it back on his head." The Protestant theologian declared (and on this the Catholic Jerónimo de Aguilar would have agreed), "It is

---

[27] Jacques le Goff, *Time, Work and Culture in the Middle Ages,* trans. Arthur Goldhammer (Chicago: University of Chicago Press, 1980), 45–6.

[28] Rabelais, *Gargantua and Pantagruel,* 588.

[29] Eviatar Zerubavel, "Easter and Passover: On Calendars and Group Identity," *American Sociological Review,* 47 (Apr. 1982), 289.

one of God's great gifts . . . that everyone can have the weekday letters on his wall."[30]

The entry of God into time with the incarnation of Christ had sacralized certain dates, especially Easter. The Council of Nicaea had declared that the date of Easter should be the first Sunday following the first full moon after the vernal equinox.[31] A tricky calculation, but not all that hard to make – if you know the date of the vernal equinox. But the makers of the Julian calendar, as noted in Chapter 2, had misjudged the length of the solar year, a mistake that produced a few too many leap years and a calendar date for the vernal equinox that was sliding away from the actual astronomical event and toward summer. That meant that Easter might be celebrated on the wrong Sunday, an intolerable situation for the meticulously pious. Christian astronomers and mathematicians – Roger Bacon, Nicholas of Cusa, Regiomontanus, Johannes Schöner, Paul of Middelburg, and Nicholas Copernicus – pointed to the parlous condition of the calendar whenever asked. The discrepancy between the Julian calendar and solar reality amounted to eleven days by 1582.

In that year Pope Gregory XIII assembled a conference of experts – Roman Catholic experts – to reform the calendar. They debated, brooded, and offered to the pope a revised version of the Julian calendar known ever since as the Gregorian calendar. On their recommendation, he proclaimed that Thursday, 4 October 1582, would be immediately followed by Friday, 15 October 1582. As for the difference between the abstract calendar year of

---

[30] Anthony Grafton, *Defenders of the Text: The Traditions of Scholarship in an Age of Science, 1450–1800* (Cambridge, Mass.: Harvard University Press, 1991), 104; see also Michel de Montaigne, *The Complete Essays,* trans. M. A. Screech (Harmondsworth: Penguin Books, 1991), 1160.
[31] Zerubavel, "Easter and Passover," 284–9.

whole days and the actual solar year of 365 and a fraction, the Gregorian reform retained the Julian system of an extra day every four years, with a slight but important correction: centurial years are leap years *only* if divisible by 400 (like 1600 and 2000).[32]

Many were upset with the reform. The Catholic Michel de Montaigne complained, "I grit my teeth, but my mind is always ten days ahead or ten days behind: it keeps muttering in my ears: 'That adjustment concerns those not yet born.' "[33] Orthodox and Protestant Christians clung to the Julian calendar as if to a piece of the True Cross, and in many cases continued to do so for centuries. "The English mob," wrote Voltaire, "preferred their calendar to disagree with the Sun than to agree with the Pope."[34] The experts, the real ones and the self-proclaimed ones, heaped up a reef of treatises around the Gregorian calendar. Joseph Justus Scaliger, a Calvinist, judged the new calendar a poor excuse for a good calendar and called its chief defender, the Jesuit Christoph Clavius, a "German fat-belly." Clavius smothered this and other criticisms with his 800-page *Romani calendarii a Gregorio XIII P. M. restituti explicatio*.

The battle went on long after Scaliger and Clavius were in their graves, and the Gregorian reform won. It won not because it was perfect, but because of its practicality: it would not lose a whole day of the solar year for well over 2,000 years. Johannes

---

[32] Gordon Moyer, "The Gregorian Calendar," *Scientific American,* 246 (May 1982), 144–52.

[33] Montaigne, *Complete Essays,* 1143. One should always be reluctant to correct Montaigne, but technically he was eleven days, not ten, out of step. The confusion arises from the fact that when the pope inserted eleven days into the month of October 1582, i.e., when 4 October was followed by 15 October, what would have been the 5th became the 15th, a difference of ten.

[34] George Sarton, *Six Wings: Men of Science in the Renaissance* (Bloomington: Indiana University Press, 1957), 69–72.

Kepler, mathematician, astronomer, and Protestant, found the reform's imperfect definition of the lunar month, basic to setting up the Church calendar, acceptable: "Easter is a feast, not a planet."[35]

As I said before, it is more surprising that the Gregorian reform was accomplished at all than that it came late and was often ill-received. If the Julian calendar had never been adjusted and repaired, we would today be only about two weeks out of synchronization with the solar year, not enough to make a difference in the lives of farmers and fishermen and such. The Muslims, then as now, managed quite nicely with a lunar calendar that designated religious holidays on days of the solar year with what would seem wild abandon to anyone but an attentive astronomer. Ramadan, the holy month of fasting, reels from one end of the solar calendar to the other every thirty-two and a half years. Calendrical chaos does not seem to disconcert the practical worshipers of Allah. There are lay calendars for those who, for one reason or another, need solar dates.[36]

But four hundred years ago a slight unrigorousness in the dating of Easter triggered a major reform in the West, where the entry of God into time had unnerved Christian chronologists forever and where the descendants of the barbarian heirs of Rome were still uncomfortable in the presence of the shibboleths of their Middle Eastern religion.

The Gregorian recalibration was an enormous improvement calendrically, but not enough so to satisfy the truly doctrinaire quantifiers, of whom the West had more who were both fanatical and devoted to the application of mathematics to actual chronol-

---

[35] Moyer, "Gregorian Calendar," 144–52.
[36] Louis Gardet, "Moslem Views of Time and History (with an Appendix by Abdelmajid Meziane on the Empirical Apperception of Time among the Peoples of the Maghreb)," in *Cultures and Time,* 201.

ogy than any other society. Another sixteenth century example of
calendrical reform, the Julian period, was more nearly perfect,
albeit stunningly impractical for common use.

Joseph Justus Scaliger, mentioned earlier as a critic of the new
Catholic calendar, was a monumental scholar in an age of great
scholars: contemporaries called him a "sea of sciences" and a
"bottomless pit of erudition."[37] His industriousness and powers
of concentration verged on the superhuman. He was in Paris on
St. Bartholomew's Day in 1572 but, by his own account, was so
intent on studying his Hebrew that he almost missed the massacre
of his fellow religionists, not noticing for some time "the clash of
arms ... the groans of children ... the wailing women, [or] the
shouting men."[38]

As a young man he learned his trade from his father, one of the
most prominent scholars of the mid-sixteenth century, absorbed
languages – a dozen or so eventually – and honed his skills by
editing the works of Catullus, Tibullus, and Procopius. When he
had made himself into arguably the greatest philologist and student of classical literature of his era, he turned his laserlike attention to *chronologia* (like *America,* a term coined in answer to new
demands).[39] He scorned preceding and contemporary chronologists, "who seem all to have sworn never to tell the truth," and
offered an antidote to their mistakes in his massive tome, *De
emendatione temporum* (1583), which changed chronology from
a pseudoscience to a true science.[40]

Scaliger gathered together the oldest and best editions of the

---

[37] Moyer, "Gregorian Calendar," 144.
[38] *The Autobiography of Joseph Scaliger,* trans. George W. Robinson (Cambridge, Mass.: Harvard University Press, 1927), 76, 77.
[39] Arno Borst, *The Ordering of Time from the Ancient Computus to the
Modern Computer,* trans. Andrew Winnard (Chicago: University of Chicago Press, 1993), 104.
[40] Anthony T. Grafton, "Joseph Scaliger and Historical Chronology: The
Rise and Fall of a Discipline," *History and Theory,* 14, no. 2 (1975), 158.

classics of chronology and all the calendars available, more than fifty, whatever their origins, Christian, Islamic, or what have you. Though a devout Christian, he granted no special credence to the Bible, declaring that truth is sacred even if heard from profane lips. He sought not to discover a divine order in history, but to achieve calendrical accuracy and the correlation of every prominent dating system with every other.[41]

He created what he called the Julian period (named after Caesar) as a basis for a new system of time. He derived the period by multiplying three familiar chronological cycles, an 18-year solar cycle, a 19-year lunar cycle, and the 15-year cycle devised by the old Romans for tax purposes. The product of the multiplication was 7,980 years, the Julian period. All three cycles began together at the start of this purely abstract invention; they would not be so synchronized again until the end of the period. It would be possible to obtain a Julian period date for any event dated in any of the three cycles and to translate that into a date in the other two cycles. Hebrew, Christian, Roman, Greek, Arabic, and other chronologies could be correlated.[42]

Scaliger decided, after research and further calculation, that Christ had been born in the period's 4,713th year. As we would put it, the period had begun at 4,713 B.C. It had some 1,700 years to go. Of course, the period started before even the earliest Judeo-Christian dates for Creation, which made literalists queasy, but Scaliger was seeking a mathematical convenience, not the date upon which God of Genesis had moved over the face of the waters. He wanted a period long enough to include all recorded events in a system in which the three cycles could be precisely correlated.[43]

De emendatione temporum was a masterpiece of chronology, perhaps the greatest of all, but it was never read widely. It was hard going for the reader, and the Julian period system far too cumbersome and alien for nonmathematicians. Then, when Egyp-

---

[41] Ibid., 159–61, 167.   [42] Ibid., 162.   [43] Ibid., 162–3.

tian dates showed up that allegedly fell before 4713 B.C., Scaliger had to add a period that preceded his Julian period, robbing his system of its inclusive neatness, one of its greatest recommendations. Not until after the seventeenth century Jesuit Domenicus Petavius put the finishing touches on our current A.D./B.C. (C.E./ B.C.E.) system, cutting the Gordian knot of choosing a beginning date by having none, was a satisfactory way of annual dating popularized.[44]

But Scaliger's system did not fall into the dustbin. Astronomers, driven to distraction by the complications of common calendars, with their weeks of seven days all out of coordination with everything else and their twelve months of variable lengths, adopted it. Imagine the difficulties in trying to state the exact number of days between Halley's comet's swing past the sun on 16 November 1835 and the next repetition of that event on 20 April 1910. Astronomers, utilizing the one and only quantum of the Julian period, the mean solar day (Julian day), can say there were exactly 27,183 Julian days between Halley's comet's two nineteenth century visitations to the sun.[45]

The fee that obsession with temporal precision exacted for its services was anxiety. Intelligence, a character in the fourteenth century's *Piers the Ploughman,* proclaims that "of all things on earth, God knows, nothing is more hated by those in Heaven than waste of time."[46] Leon Batista Alberti, an early Renaissance man

---

[44] Ibid., 171–3; Gordon Moyer, "The Origin of the Julian Day System," *Sky and Telescope,* 16 (Apr. 1981), 311–12; Donald J. Wilcox, *The Measure of Times Past: Pre-Newtonian Chronologies and the Rhetoric of Relative Time* (Chicago: University of Chicago Press, 1987), 203–8.

[45] Moyer, "Origin of the Julian Day System," 311–12; "Julian Period," in *The World Almanac and Book of Facts for 1995* (Mahwah, N.J.: Funk & Wagnalls, 1994), 289.

[46] William Langland, *Piers the Ploughman,* trans. J. F. Goodridge (Harmondsworth: Penguin Books, 1959), 108.

(whom we shall meet again in Chapter 9), declaimed, "I flee from sleep and idleness, and I am always busy about something." When he rose in the morning he made a list of what had to be done that day and assigned to each a time[47] (thus anticipating Benjamin Franklin by three hundred years).

Petrarch paid strict attention to time in a most untraditional fashion. We know, therefore, that he was born at the break of dawn on Monday, 20 July 1304. We know that he fell in love with Laura on 6 April 1327, that she died on 6 April 1348, and that he died on 19 July 1374.[48] We know that time never slipped through his fingers; "rather it was torn from me. Even when I was involved in some business or in the delights of pleasure it would still dawn on me 'Alas, this day is irretrievably gone.' "[49]

He admonished his reader to discard the traditional concept of his or her life as "a ship moving this way and that according to the various winds and waves." No, he insisted, the truth is that

> one unalterable speed is the course of life. There is no going back or taking pause. We move forward through all tempest and whatever wind. Whether the course be easy or difficult, short or long, through all there is one constant velocity.[50]

Three centuries later this kind of time, bleached even of despair, became the time of classical physics. In 1687 Sir Isaac Newton would define it thus: "Absolute, true, and mathematical time, of itself, and from its own nature, flows equably without relation to anything external."[51] I am writing this line at 22:38 Greenwich Mean Time on the 2,449,828th Julian day.

---

[47] Ricardo J. Quinones, *The Renaissance Discovery of Time* (Cambridge, Mass.: Harvard University Press, 1972), 191.

[48] Ibid., 109, 110, 113.   [49] Ibid., 135.   [50] Ibid., 108.

[51] Isaac Newton, *Mathematical Principles of Natural Philosophy and His System of the World*, trans. Andrew Motte and Florian Cajori (Berkeley: University of California Press, 1934), 6.

CHAPTER FIVE

Space

Henceforth I spread confident wings to space:
I fear no barrier of crystal or of glass:
I cleave the heavens and soar to the infinite.

Giordano Bruno (1591)[1]

The shift in Westerners' perception of space was not as dra-matic as the change in their perception of time. There was no jackrabbit start like the invention of the mechanical clock. Gio-vanni Tortelli, writing circa 1450 about all the new things that were transforming his world — the clock, compass, pipe organ, sugar, tallow candle — mentioned only one pertaining to the mea-surement of extension, a new kind of maritime chart, the *porto-lano,* and allowed that he was not as impressed with it as the others because "it is the work of long labors and careful diligence rather than of a divine challenge."[2] The transformation in Western

---

[1] Dorothea Waley Singer, *Giordano Bruno, His Life and Thought* (New York: Greenwood Press, 1968), 249.

[2] Alex Keller, "A Renaissance Humanist Looks at 'New' Inventions: The Article 'Horologium' in Giovanni Tortelli's *De Orthographia,*" *Technology and Culture,* 11 (July 1972), 352.

perception of space, which culminated in changes as radical as those that shook physics at the beginning of the twentieth century, started like a tortoise.

The compass, acquired from Asia early in the second millennium, persuaded sailors to risk the long run from Cape Finisterre to England or across the Mediterranean in winter when clouds covered the pole star. They needed, of course, to be sure of the correct compass course, and for that it would be convenient to have charts, that is, accurate drawings of bodies of water and of the surrounding coasts in relation to each other, with indications of the shortest compass courses between the most prominent features, visually and commercially, of those coasts.[3]

The first useful maps in Western Europe for laying compass courses were called *portolani*. The earliest dated example that has survived was drawn in 1296, in those same wondrous few decades in which the first clock was built.[4] The *portolani*, short on references in comment or sketch to God, gods, or monsters, were utilitarian drawings of coastlines with the waters, adjacent and between, scored with rhumbs (compass courses) traced with straightedge. A navigator consulting a *portolano* often found rhumbs already drawn from major port to major port, often the course he wanted. If not, he could often find a rhumb parallel to the one he needed, and could then take his heading from that.

The *portolani* were devised for enclosed or nearly enclosed waters, like the Mediterranean, the Bay of Biscay, and the North and Baltic seas. For these they served their purpose well because they were reasonably accurate and the distances between landfalls were short. Distortions, inevitable because no one knew about

[3] Frederic C. Lane, "The Economic Meaning of the Compass," *American Historical Review*, 47 (Apr. 1963), 613–14.
[4] Ibid.

compass deviation and unavoidable because the *portolani* were geometrically naive flat pictures of the curved surface of the earth, were insignificant. But these charts were dangerously illusory over long distances. Oceanic sailors needed maps that would enable them to set courses across the surface of the planet as depicted on geometrically rigorous charts.[5] The next stride in cartography would be toward taking the measure of area and shape, in addition to direction and distance.

The concept of drawing maps in accordance with a gridwork of lines already existed in Western Europe and elsewhere in the first half of the fourteenth century.[6] Some of the surviving *portolani* were so drawn, but their cartographers probably resorted to gridworks only as an aid to reproducing mariners' sketches. In order to flourish, the technique needed the mathematics and theory of ancient science. Enter (or re-enter) Claudius Ptolemy, the ancient Hellene without whom Western Europeans would have taken much longer than they did to become themselves.

About 1400 a copy of Ptolemy's *Geographia* arrived in Florence from Constantinople. If there was anything equivalent in the shift in spatial perception to the appearance of the escapement in temporal perception, this was it. News of the *Geographia* flowed

---

[5] Jonathan T. Lanman, *On the Origin of Portolan Charts* (Chicago: The Newberry Library, 1987), 49–54; Lee Bagrow, *History of Cartography,* 2d ed. (Chicago: Precedent, 1985), 62–6; A. C. Crombie, *Medieval and Early Modern Science* (Garden City, N.Y.: Doubleday, 1959), 1: 207–8; C. Raymond Beazley, *The Dawn of Modern Geography* (London: Henry Frowde, n.d.), 3: 512–14; John N. Wilford, *The Mapmakers: The Story of the Great Pioneers in Cartography from Antiquity to the Space Age* (New York: Vintage Books, 1981), 51; Tony Campbell, "Portolan Charts from the Late Thirteenth Century to 1500," in *The History of Cartography,* 1: *Cartography in Prehistoric, Ancient, and Medieval Europe and the Mediterranean,* eds. J. B. Harley and David Woodward (Chicago: University of Chicago Press, 1987), 372.

[6] Lanman, *On the Origin of Portolan Charts,* 54.

westward with Italian commerce and capital to Iberia, whose sailors, noodling down the coast of Africa and probing out into the Atlantic, needed charts for voyages long beyond known landmarks or even any sight of land.[7]

Ptolemy's contribution to cartography was, put simply, to treat the earth's surface as neutral space by slapping a gridwork on it, a crosshatch of coordinates calculated in accordance with the positions of heavenly bodies. He provided fifteenth century Europe with three different methods, mathematically consistent, by which the curved surface of the earth could be represented on flat maps with the unavoidable distortions managed in ways for which the informed could make allowances.[8] By the next century Ptolemy's techniques were part of the common currency of Western European mapmakers. Their earth was now a sphere caught in a network of latitudes and longitudes, its theoretical surface as uniform as that of a billiard ball.[9] When the Americas and the Pacific burst into Western perception, the means to depict them accurately already existed.

The history of Western cartography is a story of catch-as-catch-can practice bounding out ahead of theory and of theory trying to catch up. The parallel history of astronomy (often, then, astrology) is one of theory, in this case more verbal than mathematical,

[7] Crombie, *Medieval and Early Modern Science*, 1: 209; Marie Boas, *The Scientific Renaissance, 1450–1630* (New York: Harper & Row, 1962), 23–4; Samuel Y. Edgerton, Jr., *The Renaissance Rediscovery of Linear Perspective* (New York: Basic Books, 1975), 97–9.

[8] Samuel Y. Edgerton, Jr., *The Heritage of Giotto's Geometry: Art and Science on the Eve of the Scientific Revolution* (Ithaca, N.Y.: Cornell University Press, 1991), 99–110.

[9] In reality the earth is not that simple, as mapmakers in time learned. It is squashed at the poles, a bit obese at the equator, and subject to compass variations.

drifting like smoke and of practice, in this case exact observation and calculation, trying to catch up.

The Venerable Model's version of space was too restrictive and ignoble for some of the freer spirits among the Schoolmen. Why would God have placed the earth at the center of the universe, a position that most kings reserved for themselves? And if stability was more noble than motion (a self-evident truth, you must realize), why were the heavens in motion and the earth the one body at rest? Could it be possible that the earth turned and the sphere of the fixed stars was stable? After all, it was hard to decide at sea, looking from one ship to another, which was moving, so how could it be any easier looking from earth to the heavens? Nicole Oresme (c. 1325–82), friend of Petrarch, took the discussion a step toward Copernicanism, pointing out, as had a few others, that reason did not provide the means to decide whether the heavens or the earth was turning.[10]

Oresme teetered on the brink of relativism and heresy, and drew back. After all, the Bible said that at the Battle of Jericho God had halted the sun, not the earth. Oresme passed off his speculation as a "diversion or intellectual exercise."[11] Indeed, it may have been exactly that: some Schoolmen delighted in intellectual high jinks.

In the next, the fifteenth, century, philosophers and protoscientists tended to play for keeps. The West's avant-garde (Italy's, usually) veered from Aristotelianism toward Platonism. (I should say Neoplatonism because much had been added since the Athen-

[10] *A Source Book in Medieval Science,* ed. Edward Grant (Cambridge, Mass.: Harvard University Press, 1974), 46–8, 500–10; Richard C. Dales, *The Scientific Achievement of the Middle Ages* (Philadelphia: University of Pennsylvania Press, 1973), 127–30; Ernest A. Moody, "Buridan, Jean," in *The Dictionary of Scientific Biography,* ed. Charles C. Gillispie (New York: Scribner's, 1970–80), 2: 603, 607.
[11] *Source Book in Medieval Science,* 510.

ian's day from Christian and pagan sources.) Cosimo de' Medici
sponsored a Platonic Academy at Florence, where Marsilio Ficino
translated Plato and Plotinus into Latin and urged the imitation of
Socrates as next best to the imitation of Christ.[12] Thinkers like
Ficino reveled in the mystical elements of the classical heritage,
leaning toward a kind of Christian sun worship and a more pagan
than Christian faith in mathematics. God's message would un-
doubtedly be symbolic and mysterious, but He might well express
it in quantifiable dimensions.

Johannes Regiomontanus (1436–76), a German who spent his
many productive years in Italy, translated and published the works
of ancient mathematicians and, as well, published the works of
contemporary mathematicians, including his own. He made careful observations of astronomical phenomena and produced tables
and books on the behavior of the heavens. His Ephemerides
(1490) listed the positions of heavenly bodies for every day from
1475 to 1506. Columbus took a copy with him on his fourth
voyage and was able to predict a lunar eclipse on 29 February
1504, confounding and disarming the hostile Indians of Jamaica.[13]

Nicholas of Cusa (c. 1401–64), born in the Rhineland the son
of a commercial shipper, may well have grown up in "the atmosphere of calculation." Then, as cardinal, calendar reformer, Vati-
can statesman, philosopher, and mystic, he ascended to circles in
which familiarity with the hermetic writings of Dionysius and
Meister Eckhart, the pellucid treatises of Ptolemy and Euclid, and
faith that God was a geometrician were de rigueur.[14] Nicholas
declared that God was beyond all possibility of human under-

---

[12] James Hankins, Plato in the Italian Renaissance (Leiden: Brill, 1990),
1: 344.
[13] Edward Rosen, "Regiomontanus, Johannes" in Dictionary of Scientific
Biography, 11: 348–51.
[14] Edgerton, The Heritage of Giotto's Geometry, 288.

standing, the center and the circumference of all things, the ground in which opposites were reconciled in the way that a segment of the circumference of a circle would be a straight line if the circle were infinitely large. Nicholas is also credited (and there is no paradox here, not in the fifteenth century) with being the author of two of the earliest scale maps of land areas, longitude and latitude and all, in Europe.[15]

Nicholas saw the universe as containing everything except God, Who contained it. Such a universe had no limit, no edge. The earth could not be the center of it because the universe had no center. There was no edge, center, up or down, or any other absolute dimension. Space was homogeneous. The earth was not necessarily different from other heavenly bodies, which might also have life.[16]

Nicholas of Cusa, in a society in which rigorous qualitative analysis, the intellectual tool of choice of Aristotle and the School-men, seemed to be losing its edge, searched for new tools. He found them in quantification. "Think of precision," he wrote, "for God is absolute precision itself,"[17] and "Mind is a living measure which achieves its own capacity by measuring other things."[18]

In *Idiota,* one of Nicholas's most famous dialogues, the guru is not an ancient philosopher or a Schoolman or an intellectual of any kind, but a layman. (In the Latin of the period *idiota* did not

[15] Alexandre Koyré, *From the Closed World to the Infinite Universe* (Baltimore: Johns Hopkins Press, 1957), 12; P. D. A. Harvey, *The History of Topographical Maps: Symbols, Pictures, and Surveys* (London: Thames & Hudson, 1980), 146; P. D. A. Harvey, "Local and Regional Cartography in Medieval Europe," in *The History of Cartography,* 1: 497.

[16] J. E. Hofmann, "Cusa, Nicholas," in *Dictionary of Scientific Biography,* 3: 512–16; Koyré, *From the Closed World,* 6–23.

[17] Nicholas de Cusa, *The Layman on Wisdom and the Mind,* trans. M. L. Führer (Ottawa: Dovehouse, 1989), 41.

[18] Nicholas de Cusa, *Idiota de Mente. The Layman: About Mind,* trans. Clyde L. Miller (New York: Abaris Books, 1979), 43.

mean an idiot, but a common man who could not read Latin.) Idiota proclaims that God's wisdom "cries out in the streets." And what and how does it speak? asks his listener, who from where he is sitting in a barbershop opening onto the marketplace sees only the changing of money, the weighing of wares, and the measuring out of oil. These, answers Idiota, are exactly what I mean. "Brutes cannot number, weigh, and measure."[19]

Nicholas's *De staticis experimentis,* written in 1450, is a treatise on how we can learn about nature by means of what was his century's most accurate measuring device, one easily found in the marketplace: the balance scale. For instance, weigh the water that runs through an hour glass, and thereby measure the changing day length throughout the year or the duration of an eclipse. To measure the difference between the strengths of the sun in different climates, measure the difference between the weights of plants produced by the sowing of a thousand similar seeds in the different climates.[20]

Nicholas simplified very complicated problems and was as reluctant as any Schoolman to try experiments for himself. And he was more concerned with the deity behind the material scrim than with the scrim itself. He was more like St. Augustine than Galileo, but his thoughts are evidence that the West had begun to shift from thinking of the world in terms of qualities to thinking of the world in terms of quantities.[21]

Ironically, the closer these armchair thinkers got to discarding the concept of a finite and hierarchical universe, the less was their immediate influence. Oresme influenced other Schoolmen and that

---

[19] Nicholas de Cusa, *Layman on Wisdom,* 21, 22.

[20] *Unity and Reform: Selected Writings of Nicholas de Cusa,* ed. John P. Dolan (Notre Dame, Ind.: University of Notre Dame Press, 1962), 239–60 passim.

[21] Nicholas de Cusa, *Layman on Wisdom,* 22.

is all, and may or may not have been read carefully or read at all by the likes of Copernicus and Galileo two centuries later. The pope thought well enough of Regiomontanus to call him to advise on calendar reform, but as we know, to no effect.[22] This astronomer is important chiefly for having left accurate observations behind for later and more daring astronomers to use. Nicholas of Cusa's contemporaries largely ignored him, except insofar as he was a statesman of the Church. As of the opening of the sixteenth century, the Venerable Model's version of space seemed solid.

Nicholas Copernicus (1473–1543), a Pole who spent several years around 1500 studying and teaching in Italy, was a Neoplatonist insofar as he sought elegance in nature and was intrigued by the majesty of the sun. He revived an idea so old, lost for a thousand years in the shadow of Aristotle and Ptolemy, that we might credit it as having been nearly original with him. He turned their universe inside-out, snatching the earth from the center and replacing it with the sun. He justified his extravagant act with arguments similar to those of Oresme and Nicholas of Cusa. Yes, the sun appeared to course through the sky from east to west every day, but the appearances would be the same if the earth rotated from west to east and the sun stood still. How could anything as huge as the heavens circle the earth in a day? Would it not be easier to imagine the earth, a mere point in comparison, doing so? He even resorted to a justification that smacked of pagan sun worship: "For in this most beautiful temple [the universe], who would place this lamp in another or better position than that from which it can light up the whole thing at the same time?"[23]

If he had left off with these pleasantly persuasive arguments,

---

[22] Rosen, "Regiomontanus," 351.
[23] *Nicholas Copernicus on the Revolutions,* trans. Edward Rosen (Baltimore: Johns Hopkins Press, 1978), 13, 16, 22.

he would probably have had no great influence, and the sun would have languished another generation or two in earthly orbit. Even as it was, he failed to persuade Michel de Montaigne, the humanist, who shrugged his shoulders over the divergence of the traditionalists and Copernicus: "For all we know, in a thousand years' time another opinion will overthrow them both."[24] But Copernicus, unlike Montaigne or even Nicholas of Cusa, was a mathematician to the marrow of his bones. His great book, *De revolutionibus orbium coelestium,* includes page after page of calculations. He was the first astronomical theorist in a millennium to express himself chiefly in mathematics, the native tongue of science and more persuasive than words for the minority who would remake astronomy and physics in the seventeenth century.[25]

The influence of the Copernican revolution was immense not only in its demotion of the earth (about which much has been written), but also in its implications for the quantity and quality of space itself. In the Aristotelian-Ptolemaic system, in order to leave room for the other heavenly bodies and their spheres, the fixed stars had to be a great distance from earth, but not an inconceivable distance. In the Copernican system the distance had to be immense, quite nearly inconceivable, because the stars' positions did not change in relation to nearer bodies as the observer swung from one extreme of the earth's orbit around the sun to the other. (This is a matter of *parallax.*) The volume of a Copernican universe had to be *at least* 400,000 times as great as that of the traditional universe.[26]

Medieval and all but a very few Renaissance Europeans

[24] Michel de Montaigne, *The Complete Essays,* trans. M. A. Screech (Harmondsworth: Penguin Books, 1987), 642.

[25] Thomas S. Kuhn, *The Copernican Revolution: Planetary Astronomy in the Development of Western Thought* (Cambridge: Mass.: Harvard University Press, 1957), 139.

[26] Ibid., 160.

thought of space as hierarchical, a view that Ptolemaic theory enforced. If the earth were the center to which everything heavy fell, then it obviously was intrinsically different from the rest of creation. But if the sun were the center, and the earth wheeled around it just like other planets, then where was the earth's uniqueness?

The first individual, at least the first of renown, to proclaim unrestrainedly the implications of Copernican theory for the nature of space was Giordano Bruno (1548–1600), who began as a Dominican but ended at the stake in Rome. He proposed a space without center or edge, top or bottom, that offended Aristotelians, Catholics, Calvinists, and every person who could not live comfortably cheek and jowl with infinity. His version of space was homogeneous, infinite, populated with infinite worlds – outrageous:

> There is a single general space, a single vast immensity which we may freely call Void: in it are innumerable globes like this one on which we live and grow; this space we declare to be infinite, since neither reason, convenience, sense-perception nor nature assign to it a limit.[27]

Bruno was executed for heresy in 1600 – to no avail. The cat, already out of the bag, was having kittens.

If space were homogeneous and measurable, and therefore susceptible to mathematical analysis, then human intellect could reach around the world and out into the interstellar void. I offer two examples.

In the 1490s Spain and Portugal were squabbling over which

---

[27] Koyré, *From the Closed World*, 40, 41; Max Jammer, *Concepts of Space: The History of Theories of Space in Physics* (Cambridge, Mass.: Harvard University Press, 1954), 83–4. See also Paul H. Michel, *The Cosmology of Giordano Bruno*, trans. R. E. W. Maddison (Paris: Hermann, 1973).

had rights to the entire non-Christian world. How could they draw borders in alien realms where no Spaniard or Portuguese had ever been, borders that for the most part would run through the high seas? They drew said boundary, first with the pope's help in 1493, and again, after some modification, in the Treaty of Tordesillas in 1494, from north to south, from pole to pole, "three hundred and seventy leagues west of the Cape Verde Islands, *being calculated by degrees.*"[28] The italics (mine) emphasize the obvious fact that distances measured and lines drawn on water can, as a practical fact, be calculated only in degrees.

In another generation the Iberians needed an equivalent boundary in the western Pacific. In the Treaty of Zaragoza (1529) they extended the Tordesillas line over the poles and the rest of the way around the world, creating a border 297½ leagues or *19 degrees* east of the Moluccas.[29]

The line drawn at Tordesillas and Zaragoza proved to have, in point of fact, little importance. The Portuguese violated it in Brazil and the Spanish in the East Indies, and no one could calculate longitude accurately yet, anyway. That line, however, does serve as evidence of Renaissance Europeans' confidence in the homogeneity of the world's surface even in lands and seas that neither they nor, as far as they knew, any other human had ever seen. They saw themselves not only as powerful enough to split the world like an apple, but as being able to do so in a way that was precise in theory and before long could be precise in fact.

In November 1572 people all over the world saw a new star, a nova, as we would call it, so bright that it was visible in daylight. Theodore Beza, Calvin's successor as the leader of scorchingly

---

[28] *Documents of American History*, ed. Henry Steele Commager (New York: Appleton-Centuy-Crofts, 1958), 2–4.

[29] F. Soldevila, *Historia de España*, 2d ed. (Barcelona: Ariel, 1962), 3: 347–8.

Protestant Geneva, saw it and supposed it the second star of Bethlehem and a portent of the Second Coming of Christ. Tycho Brahe, an observational astronomer, the West's first real one since ancient times and perhaps the best ever before the telescope, also saw it, measured the angular distance between the new star and the nine known stars of Cassiopeia, and made notes on its magnitude and color. He continued to do so for the seventeen months that the star remained visible.[30]

Authority proclaimed that the heavens were perfect, that change could take place only in the sublunar sphere, beneath the moon.[31] Therefore, this *new* star must be close to the earth, a more likely subject for meteorology than astronomy. Yet according to Tycho's meticulous measurements, it never changed its position in relation to the fixed stars, the most distant of all objects in the sky, as it surely would have had it been within the sphere of the moon. Brahe's observations indicated that the new star, for all its mutability, must be in the sphere of the stars.[32]

In 1577 a large comet swept across the heavens, the first of a number of "fiery meteors" in the next half century. If there was validity to the traditional and hierarchical universe model, then comets, the most spectacularly unstable of all objects aloft, had to be within perturbations of the upper air. Brahe observed the new comet, made his usual meticulous measurements, and deduced from them that it was not within the moon's sphere but far beyond, something like six times farther away than the moon. Moreover, the comet seemed to be moving not in a perfect circle but in an oval, a gimcracky orbit that perforce cut through the planetary

---

[30] Boas, *Scientific Renaissance,* 109–12.

[31] Kuhn, *Copernican Revolution,* 92.

[32] John A. Gade, *The Life and Times of Tycho Brahe* (Princeton, N.J.: Princeton University Press, 1947), 41–2; Antonie Pannekoek, *A History of Astronomy* (New York: Interscience, 1961), 207–8; C. Doris Hellman, "Brahe, Tycho," in *Dictionary of Scientific Biography,* 2: 402–3.

spheres. The crystal spheres, which had served European astronomical speculation for millennia, could not exist.[33]

By the end of the sixteenth century the Venerable Model's version of space was shattered. Conservatives camped in its ruins for generations to come, but moving to the alternative was inevitable. The alternative was what Isaac Newton defined as "absolute space," which "in its own nature, without relation to anything external, remains always similar and immovable,"[34] that is to say, uniformly measurable: the space of classical physics. This is the amoral void that Blaise Pascal, another mathematician and, as well, a mystic, called terrifying.[35]

---

[33] Hellman, "Brahe," 407–8; Pannekoek, *History of Astronomy*, 215–16. See also C. Doris Hellman, *The Comet of 1577: Its Place in the History of Astronomy* (New York: Columbia University Press, 1944).

[34] Isaac Newton, *Mathematical Principles of Natural Philosophy and His System of the World*, trans. Andrew Motte and Florian Cajori (Berkeley: University of California Press, 1934), 6.

[35] Blaise Pascal, *Pensées* (New York: Dutton, 1958), 61.

CHAPTER SIX

Mathematics

Wherefore in all great works are Clerks so much desired?
Wherefore are Auditors so well fed? What causeth Geometri-
cians so highly to be enhaunsed? Why are Astronomers so
greatly advanced? Because that by number such things they
finde, which else would farre excell mans minde.

Robert Recorde (1540)[1]

Certain Western Europeans of the late Middle Ages and Renaissance began tentatively to consider the possibilities of
absolute time and space. The advantages were that absolute properties, by definition, were permanent and universal, which meant
that it was worth the effort to measure them and to analyze and
manipulate the measurements in various ways. Measurement is
numbers, and the manipulation of numbers is mathematics.
Thomas Bradwardine, Schoolman and archbishop of Canterbury
in the fourteenth century, said, "Whoever then has the effrontery
to study physics while neglecting mathematics, should know from

---

[1] Franz J. Swetz, *Capitalism and Arithmetic: The New Math of the 15th
Century* (La Salle, Ill.: Open Court, 1987), epigraph.

the start that he will never make his entry through the portals of wisdom."[2]

Roger Bacon, John Buridan, Theodoric of Freiberg, Nicole Oresme, and others of a like mind prefigured Kepler and Galileo with their glorification of geometry and, particularly in the case of Oresme, with a conviction that numbers could be imposed where they had previously been thought inappropriate. Oresme (who spent much of his life in Paris and must have heard Charles V's authoritarian clock many times) wrote in a treatise entitled *The Geometry of Qualities and Motion* that for the measurement of things of "continuous quantity" – for instance, motion or heat – "it is necessary that points, lines, and surfaces, or their properties be imagined. . . . Although indivisible points, or lines, are non-existent, still it is necessary to feign them."[3] Why? Because then you could count them (see Figure 3).

The stage was ready or nearly ready for swift progress in mathematics and in its application to material reality. In the thirteenth century Leonardo Fibonacci of Pisa, the West's greatest mathematician yet, had stepped onto that stage, making free use of Hindu-Arabic numerals and other borrowings from Islamic lands, experimenting with number theory, and devising what we still call the Fibonacci series. He was a fresh advance in mathematics all by himself – but left few or no disciples.[4]

Mathematics was not ready for swift advance. Its symbols and

[2] James A. Weisheipl, "The Evolution of Scientific Method," in *The Logic of Science*, ed. Vincent E. Smith (New York: St. Johns University Press, 1964), 82.

[3] *Nicole Oresme and the Medieval Geometry of Qualities and Motions*, trans. and ed. Marshall Claget (Madison: University of Wisconsin Press, 1968), 165.

[4] Paul L. Rose, *The Italian Renaissance of Mathematics: Studies on Humanists and Mathematicians from Petrarch to Galileo* (Geneva: Librairie Droz, 1975), 82.

techniques were inadequate. The moment had arrived for a trumpet solo, and the only instrument available was a hunting horn. Furthermore, mathematics was not, in a manner of speaking, homogeneously equal to homogeneous time and space. Numbers and concepts were still resonating with nonmathematical significance. Yes, 3 was 1 plus 1 plus 1 or the square root of 9, and so on, but it was also at unpredictable moments a direct reference to the Trinity.

But let us deal first with getting from the hunting horn to the trumpet. Let us look at counting, arithmetic, and simple algebra. As discussed in Chapter 2, counting, especially if the numbers got high, was very difficult in Roman numerals. St. Augustine described the limitlessness of eternity by saying that it was infinitely greater than even a sum so large that "it could no longer be expressed in numbers,"[5] a statement that confuses rather than enlightens today. Complicated computation with Roman numerals was impractical, if not impossible, and the mixing and confusion of numbers and letters were hard to avoid because, of course, Roman numerals were Roman letters.

The counting board helped enormously with these difficulties, but this Western version of the abacus had its own disadvantages. It could not handle very large numbers and very small numbers at the same time and was a device for computing, not recording. Its users of necessity erased their steps as they calculated, making it impossible to locate mistakes in the process except by going back to the beginning and repeating the entire sequence. As for permanently writing down the answers, that was done in Roman numerals, which brings us right back to the problem of writing long numbers.

If medieval Europeans had had the kind of abacus common in

[5] St. Augustine, *The City of God*, trans. Marcus Dods (New York: Modern Library, 1950), 392.

the Far East and elsewhere today, the kind with beads on wires that experts flick back and forth almost with the speed of thought, Westerners might never have accepted Hindu-Arabic numerals. But counters had to be picked up and moved or shoved from place to place on the counting board, and a bump with a knee or a careless brush with a sleeve could knock them to the floor, eliminating all the results of a long calculation. Fortunately, Europeans never saw the oriental abacus. (This is not the last time I shall point to the advantages of philistinism.) In 1530 John Palegrave declared that he could calculate six times faster with Hindu-Arabic numerals than "you can caste it ones by counters."[6]

Little is clear about the origin of what we usually call Arabic numerals except that the Arabs did not invent them. They got them from the Hindus, who may be their inventors, but it is just possible that the Indians got them from the Chinese.[7] We will call them Hindu-Arabic numerals. Whatever the truth about their origin, the Arabs, who knew a good thing when they saw it, adopted and adapted them to their own ends. The Muslim whose name is most closely associated with the new system is the scholar and author Abu Jafar Muhammed ibn Musa al-Khwarizmi, who lived in the ninth century. His book on the new numbers traveled west to Spain, and the new system soon percolated into Europe. In the twelfth century an Englishman, Robert of Chester, translated al-Khwarizmi's book into Latin, and after that the influence of the new numerals in the West was continuous.[8]

European tongues turned *al-Khwarizmi* into various ancestors

---

[6] Alexander Murray, *Reason and Society in the Middle Ages* (Oxford: Oxford University Press, 1978), 166, 454; Keith Thomas, "Numeracy in Early Modern England," *Transactions of the Royal Society,* 5th series, 37 (1987), 106–7.

[7] Swetz, *Capitalism and Arithmetic,* 327, n. 17.   [8] Ibid., 27–8.

of our twentieth century words *algorithm* and *algorism*. These have special meanings today, but during the Middle Ages and Renaissance and for long thereafter they simply referred to Hindu-Arabic numerals and the kind of computation that went along with them.[9]

The superiority of Hindu-Arabic over Roman numerals and counting board strikes us as obvious now, and we are correct if the competing systems are viewed by someone who has had no previous experience with either. There were only ten symbols, "as here bene writen for ensampul, 0987654321." With them any number could be written, however huge. The process of "pen reckoning," as calculation with Hindu-Arabic numerals was sometimes called,[10] did not efface itself as it occurred, and thus could be easily checked; and calculating and recording could be done with the same symbols.

But Hindu-Arabic numerals did not seem necessarily advantageous to the old Europeans. The existing system was comfortably familiar, and it was 1514 before the final arithmetic book in Roman numerals was published. Yes, the mathematician cued to this latest fashion could write *any* number he wanted, and all would understand, but only if he and they understood place value and the mysterious and bizarre zero. Place value was difficult to grasp. On the counting board you could see the counters and could follow positionally what was being done with them. But with algorism there were only chicken tracks on the slate (or parchment or paper, if you could afford them). And the terrible zero, a sign for what was *not*, was as conceptually discomforting as the idea of a vacuum. The zero presented a real problem, as we

---

[9] Ibid., 28–9.

[10] Lambert L. Jackson, *The Educational Significance of Sixteenth Century Arithmetic* (New York: Columbia University Teachers College, 1906), 27.

can infer from contemporary explanations. In the thirteenth century John Sacrobosco wrote in *The Crafte of Nombrynge,* Europe's most popular guide to algorism:

> A cifre tokens nought, bot he makes the figure to betoken that comes after hym more than he schuld & he were away, as thus 10. here the figure of one betokens ten, & yf the cifre were away, & no figure by-fore hym he schuld token bot one, for then he schuld stonde in the first place.[11]

Translation: 1 is only 1, but putting a zero to the right of it promotes it tenfold. Ignore "by-fore hym." It may be an echo of the Arabic practice of writing from right to left.

Centuries passed before Europeans would grant that zero was a real number. One fifteenth century Frenchman wrote, "Just as the rag doll wanted to be an eagle, the donkey a lion, and the monkey a queen, the *cifra* put on airs and pretended to be a digit." Astrologers, however, were relatively quick to adopt algorism numerals, including the zero, possibly because it raised their status, like secret writing.[12] Incidentally, it is likely that the "cipher" in *encipher* and *decipher* traces back at least in part to the once-mystical reputation of zero.[13]

---

[11] *The Earliest Arithmetics in English,* ed. Robert Steele (London: The Early English Text Society, 1922), 5.

[12] Karl Menninger, *Number Words and Number Symbols: A Cultural History of Numbers,* trans. Paul Broneer (Cambridge, Mass.: MIT Press, 1969), 286, 422–3; *Earliest Arithmetics in English,* 4.

[13] But by the beginning of the seventeenth century familiarity with the zero was widespread enough for Shakespeare to use it as a metaphor for deep gratitude in *Winter's Tale* (act 1, scene 2, line 6), without bewildering the groundlings:

> Like a cypher (yet standing in rich place),
> I multiply with one, "We thank you,"
> Many thousands more, that go before it.

It was perhaps inevitable that algorism would triumph in the West, with its burgeoning economy and technology, but the change was slow and accomplished without grace. For generations Western Europeans put off the day of surrender to algorism by jumbling the various systems together. To avoid the trouble of recording a large number with Roman numerals, they would sometimes write said number as dots arranged in the pattern of counters expressing the number on a counting board. In a preface to a calendar of 1430 the maker of the calendar defined a year as consisting of "ccc and sixty days and 5 and sex odde howres." Two generations later another author expressed the then-current year as MCCCC94, that is, two years after Columbus's discovery of America. Sometimes Europeans would adopt Hindu-Arabic numeral place value and the zero, but express them with Roman capitals, a particularly confusing compromise. IVOII is (and how would you ever know unless told?) 1502: that is, I in the thousands slot, V in the hundreds slot, none in the tens slot, and II in the digits slot. The painter Dirk Bouts placed on his altar at Louvain the number MCCCC4XVII, which designates – what? My guess would be 1447. What is yours?

In the earliest account books of the Imperial Free City of Augsburg all the numbers were written in Latin words. Then the accountants used Hindu-Arabic numerals to designate the year (not much possibility that some unscrupulous accountant would add a fifth numeral to the year). When the accountants finally started using the new numerals to express other amounts, they recorded the numbers in Roman numerals as well. That was in 1470; more than a half century passed before Hindu-Arabic numerals completely deposed Roman numerals from Augsburg's records.

The triumph of the Hindu-Arabic system over the Roman was so gradual that it cannot be cited as having happened in any single decade or even the longest of lifetimes. It certainly had not happened by 1500, though perhaps it was inevitable by that year: by then the Medici bank accountants were using the new system exclusively, and even the illiterate were beginning to adopt the new numerals. It surely had happened by 1600, though conservatives continued to cling to the old numerals. Roman numerals did not completely disappear from the British Exchequer's books until the mid-seventeenth century; and we still use them for such pompous matters as inscribing dates on cornerstones and designating American football superbowls.[14] Be that as it may, the change, however slow, was one of enormous consequences. As Western Europeans turned away from one supernational, superregional language, Latin, in favor of their several vernacular tongues, they accepted and embraced another and truly universal language, algorism.

Tagging along behind the revolutionary adoption of the new numerals came a change in operational notation, a change essential for most of the advances made in mathematics, science, and technology since. The simplest of operational signs, + and −, came late to European arithmetic, much later than Hindu-Arabic numerals. Leonardo Fibonacci used the new numerals with great skill in the thirteenth century, but had to express their relationships and operations rhetorically, with words.[15] Words were ambiguous. "And," as in "2 and 2 equal 4," seems clear enough, but sometimes could be used to indicate simply that there were several, as in "a 2 and a 2 and a 2," with no intention of addition. In the last half of the fifteenth century Italians were using signs, or at

[14] Florence Yeldham, *The Story of Reckoning in the Middle Ages* (London: George G. Harrap, 1926), 86; Murray, *Reason and Society*, 169, 170; J. M. Pullan, *History of the Abacus* (New York: Praeger, 1968), 43, 45–7; Menninger, *Number Words*, 287–8.

[15] Florian Cajori, *A History of Mathematical Notations* (La Salle, Ill.: Open Court, 1928), 1: 89.

least abbreviations, for plus and minus: p̄ for plus and m̄ for minus. They, too, could promote confusion, especially if you wanted to use them in algebraic notation, that is, a p̄ b m̄ c = x. The familiar plus and minus signs, + and −, appeared in print in Germany in 1489. Their origins are obscure: perhaps they sprang from the simple marks that warehousemen chalked on bales and boxes to indicate that they were over or under the expected size or weight. The German marks fought for acceptance against the Italian p̄ and m̄ all through the sixteenth century, and did not win until French algebraists adopted them. Robert Recorde made the decision for the English about 1542, announcing that "thys fygure +, whiche betokeneth to muche, as this lyne, − plaine without a crosse lyne, betokeneth to lyttle." He was referring to their use in algebra, and in England as elsewhere they were used by algebraists long before they were accepted by simple folk doing arithmetic.[16]

The equals sign, =, appears to be an English invention. In the mid-sixteenth century Recorde, to avoid the tedious repetition of "is equal to," used a pair of horizontal parallel lines "because noe 2 thynges can be moare equalle." The history of the Anglo-American signs for multiplication and division, × and ÷, is more complicated, longer, and not at all as happy, as was prefigured by their origins. An "x" appeared in medieval manuscripts and, later, in printed books as a mathematical sign with eleven or more different functions. If used in algebraic expressions along with letter symbols, it was bound to create confusion. Algebraists omit multiplication signs or use a dot, and arithmeticians did not settle on the × for multiplication for centuries. The Anglo-American

[16] Ibid., 107, 128, 230–1, 235; D. E. Smith, *History of Mathematics* (New York: Dover, 1958), 2: 398–9, 402.

sign for division, ÷, has a dangerously close resemblance to the sign for subtraction. The process of making operational symbols universal, which began in the Middle Ages, is still incomplete.[17]

Luca Pacioli, the most famous bookkeeper of the Renaissance, stated that "many merchants disregard fractions in computing and give any money left over to the house," but customers would not put up with that forever. Businessmen took part in complicated transactions involving participants varying over time, involving simple and compound interests, and two, three, and more currencies rising and falling like a choppy sea. In the fifteenth century they often used fractions like 197/280, and sometimes found themselves sinking into the quicksand of fractions like 3345312/ 4320864. They were pulled out by the decimal system, which may have existed in embryo as early as the early thirteenth century, but lacked a useful notation system for another three hundred years.

Simon Stevin's *De thiende* (*The Tenth*), which came out in both Flemish, his native language, and French in 1585, was the most influential work on the subject. In it Stevin indicated the place of a given digit to the left and right of the decimal point (as we would put it) by writing in little circles over the digits a 0 for a whole number and 1, 2, 3, 4, and so on for the fractions: for instance, he would have written pi or π

⓪	①	②	③	④
3	1	4	1	6

His contribution lay not in that particular notation per se, but in providing a careful explanation and at least one kind of clear notation for the system of decimal fractions. Our way of expressing decimal fractions did not arrive until the next century, and to

---

[17] Cajori, *History of Mathematical Notations,* 1: 239, 250–68, 272; Smith, *History of Mathematics,* 2: 404–6, 411.

this day there is no universal system. Some societies use a point and some a comma between whole numbers and their decimal fractions. But we have had the inestimable benefit of one kind or another of a workable system of decimal fractions ever since the heyday of Simon Stevin.[18]

Hindu-Arabic numerals, enhanced by even the most primitive operational signs, equipped Europeans for the efficient manipulation of numbers, opening the door for other advances. "This relief from a struggle with arithmetical details," according to Alfred North Whitehead, "gave room for a development which had already been faintly anticipated in later Greek mathematics. Algebra now came upon the scene, and algebra is the generalisation of arithmetic."[19] The Hindu and Arab algebraists did not use simple symbols (x or y or what have you) but words or, at best, abbreviations of words. In the early thirteenth century Leonardo Fibonacci in one instance used a letter in place of a number in his algebra, but let the innovation drop there. His contemporary, Jordanus Nemorarius, used letters as symbols for knowns and unknowns more frequently, but had no signs of operation, for plus, minus, multiplication, and so on. He invented his own system, using letters so freely, said one historian of mathematics, "that the letters became as much an impediment to rapid progress on a train of reasoning as the legs of a centipede are in a marathon race."[20]

Algebraic notation remained a mishmash of words, their abbreviations, and numbers until French algebraists, particularly Francis Vieta late in the sixteenth century, took the step of system-

---

[18] Swertz, *Capitalism and Arithmetic*, 287, 338 n. 64; Smith, *History of Mathematics*, 2: 221, 235–46; Cajori, *History of Mathematical Notations*, 1: 154–8; Carl B. Boyer, *A History of Mathematics* (Princeton, N.J.: Princeton University Press, 1985), 347–8.

[19] Alfred North Whitehead, *Science and the Modern World* (New York: Macmillan, 1925), 43.

[20] Smith, *History of Mathematics*, 2: 427.

atically using single letters to denote quantities. Vieta used vowels for unknowns and consonants for knowns. (In the next century Descartes tidied up Vieta's system, using the first letters of the alphabet for knowns and the final letters for unknowns. *A* and *B* and their neighbors are knowns, *X* and *Y* and their neighbors are the mysteries to be solved.)[21]

As algebra became more and more abstract and generalized, it became clearer and clearer. Because the algebraist could concentrate on the symbols and put aside for the moment what they represented, he or she could perform unprecedented intellectual feats. Nonmathematicians sometimes find algebraic notation confusing and repellent, and jeer along with Thomas Hobbes, who condemned a treatise on conic sections as "so covered over with the scab of symbols, that I had not the patience to examine whether it be well or ill demonstrated."[22] But what he condemned as scabs are really little magnifying glasses for wondrously focusing the attention. As Alfred Hooper has put it, "By means of algebraic symbolism a kind of 'pattern' or mathematical 'machine tool' is provided, which guides the mind as swiftly and unerringly to an objective as a jig guides a cutting tool on a machine."[23] Galileo, Fermat, Pascal, Newton, and Leibnitz inherited a refined algebraic jig from Vieta and used it to earn for the seventeenth century the title of the century of genius.[24]

Parallel with the advances in mathematical symbology was a

[21] Cajori, *History of Mathematical Notations,* 1: 379–81, 2: 2–5; E. T. Bell, *The Development of Mathematics* (New York: McGraw-Hill, 1945), 97, 107, 115–16, 123; Smith, *History of Mathematics,* 2: 427.

[22] "Mathematics, the History of," in *The New Encyclopaedia Britannica,* 15th ed. (Chicago: Encyclopaedia Britannica, 1987), 23: 612.

[23] Alfred Hooper, *Makers of Mathematics* (New York: Random House, 1948), 66–7.

[24] Raymond L. Wilder, *Mathematics as a Cultural System* (Oxford: Pergamon Press, 1981), 130.

change at least as important in the perception of the *meaning* of mathematics. Numbers are, on their faces, symbols of quantities devoid of qualities, and that is why they are so useful. They mean what they say, and that is all they mean. For instance, the relationship between the circumference, radius, and area of a circle is a matter of π, which is $3\frac{1}{7}$ or 3.14 or 3.1416. We can refine it further, adding more decimal places, but that process only emphasizes that π is what it is. No politician, priest, general, saint, genius, movie star, or maniac can make it as little as 3 or as much as 4, or make it end in a whole number. π is π everywhere and forever, in hell and in heaven, today and doomsday.

But our minds, which are at least as metaphorical and analogical as logical, are intolerant of short, straight paths that stop short at their destinations. We like twisting paths through bosky dells, and therefore have often adapted mathematics for nonmathematical motives. Thus most of our tall buildings lack a thirteenth floor because 13 is more than 10 plus 3: it is *unlucky.* Western mathematics seethed with messages like that in the Middle Ages and Renaissance. Even in the hands of an expert – or, *especially,* in the hands of an expert – it was a source of extraquantitative news.

Roger Bacon, for instance, tried very hard to predict the downfall of Islam numerically. He searched through the writings of Abu Ma'shar, the greatest of the astrologers who wrote in Arabic, and found that Abu Ma'shar had discovered a cycle in history of 693 years. That cycle had raised up Islam and would carry it down 693 years later, which should be in the near future, Bacon thought. The cycle was validated in the Bible in the Revelation of St. John the Divine 13: 18, which Bacon thought disclosed that "the number" of the Beast or Antichrist was 663, a number certain to be linked to other radical changes.

Bacon's analysis had two defects. First, the number of the Beast of Revelation is 666, not 663: Bacon probably had a defective copy of Revelation. The other defect is more interesting. Abu

Ma'shar's 693 and the Bible's 663 (or 666, if you want) are not the same number. If you believe that arithmetic is always numbers and never messages, at this point you check for mistakes or discard your hypothesis. But Bacon believed that the message is more important than its vehicle, numbers. So he fudged the numbers, justifying himself by saying, "Scripture in many places takes something from a complete number, for this is the custom of Scripture" and "Perhaps God willed that this matter should not be explained fully, but should be somewhat veiled, like other matters which are written in the Apocalypse."[25]

Mathematics is glorious because in its specificity it makes obvious such manipulations as Bacon's. Mathematics is also glorious because in its generality it is powerful enough to tempt us to tackle the biggest mysteries – for instance, the nature of the universe, physical and metaphysical – with its aid. What could be more general than 2, which can represent two galaxies or two pickles, or one galaxy plus one pickle (the mind doth boggle), or just 2 gently bobbing – where? It, like God, is an *I am* and many have thought that it must be a precipitate of ultimate reality.

In the fifteenth century Nicholas of Cusa, echoing Plato two thousand years before, wrote, "The number in our mind is the image of the number in God's mind." Five hundred years later Eugene P. Wigner, Nobel laureate, looked at the mystery of the relation of numbers and physical reality from a much higher plateau of knowledge and skill than Cusa or any deceased Neoplatonist, but his conclusion was similar to theirs: "It is difficult to avoid the impression that a miracle confronts us here."[26] Our

[25] *The Opus Majus of Roger Bacon,* trans. Robert B. Burke (Philadelphia: University of Pennsylvania Press, 1928), 1: 287, 2: 644–5.
[26] Nicholas de Cusa, *Idiota de Mente. The Layman: About Mind,* trans. Clyde L. Miller (New York: Abaris Books, 1979), 61; Wilder, *Mathematics as a Cultural System,* 45.

obsessions with the numbers 13 and 666 are silly, but there is nothing silly about mystical mathematicians per se. Mysticism is one of our ways of facing up to mystery, and mathematics is mysterious.

Physics, chemistry, astronomy — the hard sciences — have empirically justified our intuitive faith that reality is mathematical (or perhaps that we can comprehend only what is mathematical, but that is another concern). That faith is a prerequisite of science — indeed, of most of the kind of civilization we have — but it does not necessarily lead to Newtonian physics, to give but one example. Such a faith, in addition to being intellectually challenging, is aesthetically satisfying, even addictively so. It can make a mathematician a computational virtuoso completely unmoored from materiality, like Plato contemplating the "perfect number," probably the anciently numinous 60 to the fourth power, 12,960,000, or Buddhist monks who claim that the young Gautama was so incomprehensibly great that he could divide a *yoyana* (a mile) into bits to the number of 384,000 to the tenth power.[27]

Christian number-smiths started down the path to mathematics as an expression of awe. In the second century Bishop Papias, one of the apostolic fathers, wrote that the days will come when vines shall grow, each with 10,000 branches, and each branch with 10,000 twigs, and each twig with 10,000 shoots, and each shoot with 10,000 bunches, and each bunch shall have 10,000 grapes, and each grape shall yield twenty-five "metres" of wine; "And when one of the saints takes hold of a cluster, another shall

[27] *The Collected Dialogues of Plato,* ed. Edith Hamilton and Huntington Cairns (Princeton, N.J.: Princeton University Press, 1961), 775; Smith, *History of Mathematics,* 1: 89; Sal Restivo, *The Social Relation of Physics, Mysticism, and Mathematics* (Dordrecht: Reidel, 1983), 218; Menninger, *Number Words,* 136–8.

cry out, 'I am a better cluster, take me.' "[28] Roger Bacon and Piero della Francesca a thousand years later wanted to baptize geometry not for the purpose of laying the groundwork for modern optics or to spur the invention of eyeglasses or telescopes per se. Their intentions had less in common with Galileo's than with Queen Elizabeth's magus and mathematician, John Dee, who soared out of sight on a thermal of mathematical mysticism:

> Arise, clime, ascend, and mount up (with Speculative winges) in spirit, to behold in the Glas of Creation, the *Forme* of *Formes,* the *Exemplar Number* of all *thinges Numerable:* both visible and invisible, mortall and immortall, Corporall and Sprituall.[29]

India, the home of Buddha, has produced and continues to produce a disproportionate number of brilliant pure mathematicians. The West, in spite of John Dee, has produced most of the good applied physicists, engineers, and accountants. (This may or may not be true of late, but I am speaking historically.) One of history's most interesting problems is the question of why.

A simple but false answer would be that in the West number mysticism retreated as practical mathematics advanced. The truth is that the Renaissance and Reformation seem to have stimulated rather than discouraged wizards to read the past, present, and future in accordance with numbers and computations. Astrology was more popular during the Renaissance than during the Middle Ages, employing hundreds of number-smiths and astronomers in the production of horoscopes of increasing mathematical sophistication. In the Reformation, when sectarianism thrived, Petrus Bun-

[28] Edward H. Hall, *Papias and His Contemporaries* (Boston: Houghton, Mifflin, 1899), 121–2.

[29] Christopher Butler, *Number Symbolism* (New York: Barnes & Noble, 1970), 47.

gus calculated that the name of his century's most outrageous rebel, if spelled in a then-current Latin system – LVTHERNVC – and added up in accordance with the numerological value of its letters, produced – well, of course – 666. Lutherans leapt to reply, and found that the words emblazoned on the papal tiara – VICARIUS FILII DEI (Vicar of the Son of God) – added up to 666, too, after you dropped the *a, r, s, f,* and *e* because they had no numerological value.[30]

While some used mystical mathematics like handfuls of mud, the young Neoplatonic Copernican Johannes Kepler misled himself into a sort of mania about the five Platonic solids, which are the tetrahedron, cube, octahedron, dodecahedron, and icosahedron. They are "perfect" because the faces of each are identical (that is, the four square faces of the cube are the same, and the twenty equilateral triangles of the icosahedron are the same) and because these five solids can be inserted within a sphere with all their vertices (corners) touching its surface or imposed around a sphere with all the centers of their faces touching its surface. In 1595 Kepler decided that they explained the universe. These five, he was sure, could be fitted inside the orbits (spheres) of the six known planets, the vertices holding the outer spheres out and the faces holding the inner spheres in – a divine example of God's taste for Platonic order. "I saw," Kepler wrote, "one symmetrical solid after the other fit in so precisely between the appropriate orbits, that if a peasant were to ask you on what kind of hook the heavens are fastened so that they don't fall down, it will be easy for thee to answer him."[31]

[30] George Ifrah, *From One to Zero: A Universal History of Numbers,* trans. Lowell Blair (Harmondsworth: Penguin Books, 1987), 307.
[31] Arthur Koestler, *The Sleepwalkers: A History of Man's Changing Vision of the Universe* (Harmondsworth: Penguin Books, 1964), 251–5, 270, 279.

Tragically, observations expressed in exact numbers (Tycho Brahe's usually) proved him wrong. Kepler next tried a model of the solar system based on the harmonies of the Pythagorean scale. That failed, too, and still he persisted. He checked every theory in all its variations against the numbers, year after year, and after Herculean calculation divined his three laws of planetary motion, the foundation upon which Newton built.

Kepler's faith was that the merciful Deity had created and placed humans in the only kind of universe they could possibly understand, a mathematical universe. In 1599 he asked:

> What else can the human mind hold besides numbers and magnitudes? These alone we apprehend correctly, and if piety permits to say so, our comprehension is in this case of the same kind as God's, at least insofar as we are able to understand it in this mortal life.[32]

It was a faith for which evidence had accumulated more swiftly in the sixteenth than in any previous century.

[32] Ibid., 535, 611.

PART TWO

Striking the Match: Visualization

Science and technology have advanced in more than direct ratio to the ability of men to contrive methods by which phenomena which otherwise could be known only through the senses of touch, hearing, taste, and smell have been brought within the range of visual recognition and measurement and thus become subjects to that logical symbolization without which rational thought and analysis are impossible.

William N. Ivins, Jr., *On the Rationalization of Sight* (1938)

CHAPTER SEVEN

Visualization: An Introduction

The eye is the master of astronomy. It makes cosmography.
It advises and corrects all human arts. . . . The eye carries
men to different parts of the world. It is the prince of mathematics. . . . It has created architecture, and perspective, and
divine painting. . . . It has discovered navigation.

Leonardo da Vinci (1452–1519)[1]

In the sixteenth century a new culture burgeoned in Western
Europe, especially in its cities, as Bruegel celebrated in his print
Temperance, discussed in Chapter 1. Hours were equal, mapmakers envisioned the earth's surface in degrees of arc, and ambitious
men like Shakespeare's Cassio and Shylock, though their fingers
might still flutter in reckoning insignificant transactions, calculated
and recorded their major transactions and increasingly thought in
Hindu-Arabic numerals.

---

[1] Samuel Y. Edgerton, Jr., "From Mental Matrix to *Mappamundi* to Christian Empire: The Heritage of Ptolemaic Cartography in the Renaissance,"
in *Art and Cartography: Six Historical Essays,* ed. David Woodward (Chicago: University of Chicago Press, 1987), 15.

It all seems quite normal to us, but only because we are Cassio's and Shylock's direct heirs. We are blinded by our "common sense" to the magnitude of the revolution in *mentalité* that produced our quantitative approaches to reality. A half millennium before Bruegel the quantitative trait in the Western European personality (if we may speak of such an entity) was recessive and, in the modern view, bizarre. Dozens of factors could override requirements for numerical clarity and exactness in measurement. As brilliant a thinker and mathematician as Roger Bacon was so passionately engaged in the pursuit of the numinous that he could accept 693 as close enough to the number of the Beast of Revelation to be just that. Quanta differed in magnitude not only from region to region, as you might expect in a decentralized society, but even from transaction to transaction in the same locality. A bushel of oats was no more or less than as many oats as a bushel basket contained, but a bushel presented to a lord might well be a *heaped* bushel and one received by a peasant no more than level with the rim.[2] The variation (broad enough to evoke squeaks of protest from a modern economist) was not cheating, like our proverbial butcher's thumb on the scale, but right and proper, like elongation of a summer and shriveling of a winter daytime hour.

The advantages that came with the advance of quantificatory appreciation of reality strike us as obvious, but were not necessarily so in its early stages. The town clocks were wildly expensive, as well as egregiously inaccurate, losing or gaining many minutes an hour and often stopping dead.[3] The first maritime charts, freehand sketches of coastlines barely worth a practical sailor's effort

[2] Witold Kula, *Measure and Men,* trans. R. Szreler (Princeton, N.J.: Princeton University Press, 1986), 104.

[3] David S. Landes, *Revolution in Time: Clocks and the Making of the Modern World* (Cambridge, Mass.: Harvard University Press, 1983), 78–9, 83.

to draw or consult, were not then or for long after more than supplements to the traditional verbal or written sailing directions (pilot books; "rutters" in English), which included information not only about compass bearings and distances, but about anchorages, depths, tides, muddy or sandy or gravelly bottoms, when and where pirates might be expected, and so on.[4] The shift toward quantitative measurement and procedure was, in its initial stages, not as immaculately rational as we, who view it through the medium of succeeding centuries of habitual quantification, may think. The shift was part of something subliminal, a sea change of *mentalité*.

Johan Huizinga, who may well have been more familiar with the art, music, literature, and manners of late medieval Western Europe than any other scholar of the first half of our century, and who was certainly one of the keenest historians of any generation, perceived the change in its larger dimension:

> One of the fundamental traits of the mind of the declining middle ages is the predominance of the sense of sight, a predominance which is closely connected with the atrophy of thought. Thought takes the form of visual images. Really to impress the mind a concept has first to take visible shape.[5]

Huizinga, a student of so-called high culture, looked upon the transmutation of the civilization that had produced Dante and St. Thomas Aquinas, and then for generations failed to produce poets and philosophers of like stature, as ipso facto in decline. Huizinga found in the literature of the fourteenth and fifteenth centuries an increasing obsession with details of superficial appearance and a

---

[4] E. G. R. Taylor, *The Haven-Finding Art: The History of Navigation from Odysseus to Captain Cook* (New York: Abelard-Schuman, 1957), 104–9, 131.

[5] J. Huizinga, *The Waning of the Middle Ages* (New York: Doubleday, 1954), 284.

growing preference for prose rather than poetry because it is a more effective medium for exact physical description. He dismissed Froissart, the nonpareil chronicler of the Hundred Years' War, as having had the "soul of a photographic plate."[6]

Jump a century and a half forward from Froissart and look again at Bruegel's *Temperance* (Figure 1). Notice that everything the humans depicted are actually *doing* (with the exception of the debaters at center right and the actors in the upper left corner) — measuring, reading, calculating, painting, singing — is visual. Even the singers are reading, reading in order to know what sounds they must make for the delectation of the ear.

The shift to the visual is the "striking of a match" that we did not locate among the "necessary but insufficient causes" of the late medieval and Renaissance surge of quantification cited in Chapter 3. There is evidence for it at the loftiest peaks of high culture. For example, Marsilio Ficino, the quattrocentrist aesthete, wrote, "Nothing reveals the nature of the Good more fully than the light," and called it, in one of the most striking metaphors of the Renaissance, "the shadow of God."[7]

The shift in religious and aesthetic thought that inspired Ficino's remarks was but one sign of a movement down in the magma of common attitude that supports and lifts the peaks of high culture. There the change was manifest as a new way not so much of thinking about the infinite and ineffable as of seeing and manipulating matters of finite and daily actuality.

It occurred in many fields of human exertion, as we shall see

---

[6] Ibid., 292, 296, 297, 302.

[7] Thomas S. Kuhn, *The Copernican Revolution: Planetary Astronomy in the Development of Western Thought* (Cambridge, Mass.: Harvard University Press, 1957), 130; *The Letters of Marsilio Ficino,* trans. Members of the Language Department of the School of Economic Sciences, London (London: Shepheard-Walwyn, 1975), 1: 38.

in the next three chapters. Let us begin with literacy, not because it was *the* cause – many peoples have advanced in literacy without altering their basic appreciation of physical reality, and I cannot see that the first advances in literacy in medieval Europe appeared any earlier than those in other fields – but because literacy was at least as much an effect as a cause. Furthermore, it is patently visual and universally acknowledged as important, and is therefore illustrative. It did not necessarily point the way for Western Christendom, but it can do so for us.

The practice of communicating and preserving information by means of stylus, quill, and ink surged in the thirteenth century. Pope Innocent III (1198–1216) dispatched at most a few thousand letters a year; Boniface VIII (1294–1303) as many as fifty thousand. England's Royal Chancery used on average 3.63 pounds of wax per week for sealing its documents in the late 1220s and 31.9 pounds in the late 1260s.[8] A society in which the chief conduit of authority was the ear, tilted to the recitation of Scripture and the church fathers, to the somniferous repetition of myths and epics, began to become a society in which the recipient of light ruled: the eye. The word *audit* (from the same root as *audible* and *auditory*), which meant to examine by listening to testimony, was off on its queer trek to meaning, almost without exception, to examine by reading in dead silence.[9]

For centuries heirs of the Roman alphabet have taken for granted their ability to write and read swiftly, comfortably, and silently. It was not always so. Writing and reading in late antiquity and the early Middle Ages were tough. The practice of easeful cursive writing had several starts, but scribes for the most part

---

[8] M. T. Clanchy, *From Memory to Written Record: England, 1066–1307* (Cambridge, Mass.: Harvard University Press, 1979), 45, 258.

[9] Ibid., 215.

formed letters separately and, you might almost say, painfully. A scribe working with a stylus and wax tablet could take dictation quickly, but transcribing that onto more permanent materials was laborious.

Reading was also laborious: there were few or no divisions between words, and when scribes did leave spaces, they did so not necessarily after every word but wherever was comfortable for them, whether convenient for the reader or not. There were perforce no divisions between sentences or paragraphs; nor was there much, if anything, in the way of punctuation.[10]

Writing was no more than speech on a page, and so it is not surprising that the literate of antiquity and the early medieval centuries did most of their writing and reading aloud. That is why St. Augustine thought it necessary to explain to us how it was that when his mentor, St. Ambrose, "read, his eyes scanned the page, and his heart, explored the meaning, but his voice was silent and his tongue was still." Augustine offers explanations, the likeliest being, he guesses, that the older saint was saving his voice, which was subject to hoarseness. Whatever the reason for Ambrose's odd behavior, Augustine was "sure it was a good one."[11]

There was, of course, some silent reading – Julius Caesar could manage that trick with a love letter, and St. Augustine with Paul's Epistles – but most of the time writers mumbled and readers declaimed, and scriptoria and libraries were unquiet, even noisy. Writing and reading aloud were slow but, we should note, may have helped the reader because the ear could be a better guide to where a word or sentence started and stopped than the eye. How-

---

[10] Paul J. Achtemeier, "*Omne verbum sonat:* The New Testament and the Oral Environment of Late Western Antiquity," *Journal of Biblical Literature,* 109 (Spring 1990), 10, 17; Paul Saenger, "Silent Reading: Its Impact on Late Medieval Script and Society," *Viator,* 13 (1982), 371, 378.

[11] St. Augustine, *Confessions,* trans. R. S. Pine-Coffin (Harmondsworth: Penguin Books, 1961), 114.

ever, it remains true that reading was closer to walking, however adeptly, on stilts than sweeping down a snowy slope on skis.[12]

The literate of Western Europe were driven by their provincialism and general lack of sophistication to alter and improve late Roman script and the general procedures associated with writing and reading. Romans might know Latin so well that they had no need for word separation, certainly not as an aid to pronunciation, but not Saxon and Celtic priests in the far and misty marches of Christendom. Roman and early medieval writers and readers might not have such a load of work to do as to persuade them to plump for cursive scripts, plus improvise a way to read faster, but the literate of the West's High Middle Ages – intimidated and inspired by the sheer volume of the classics of the ancient world, the Bible, canon law, the works of the church fathers, the interminable glosses thereon of the Schoolmen, the documents pouring out of church and royal bureaucracies – did.

They had devised by the early fourteenth century new and cursive scripts, with word separation and punctuation, enabling scribes to write faster and readers to read faster. Poor Charlemagne had never learned to write, though he had kept writing tablets under the pillows of his bed to try to form letters in free moments. Charles V (he who established *the* clock and *the* correct time for his capital, Paris) corrected drafts of his letters in his own handwriting and signed them.[13]

The cursive Gothic or black letter (or, in more recent form, fraktur) script spread across Western Europe, often displacing provincial ways of writing. Roman script eventually superseded it

---

[12] Plutarch, *The Lives of the Noble Grecians and Romans,* trans. John Dryden (New York: The Modern Library, n.d.), 1189; St. Augustine, *Confessions,* 178; Saenger, "Silent Reading," 368.

[13] Saenger, "Silent Reading," 406; Einhard and Notker the Stammerer, *Two Lives of Charlemagne,* trans. Lewis Thorpe (Harmondsworth: Penguin Books, 1969), 79.

(tardily in German-language areas), but – rightfully, one might say – it was Gothic script that provided Gutenberg with the model for his type faces.[14]

A new way of reading arose and disseminated by which the habit of visualization, with its special inclusions and exclusions, took a firmer hold on the mind of the West. By the thirteenth century silent reading – swift and psychologically interior – was accepted as perfectly normal in the abbeys and cathedral schools and was spreading to courts and countinghouses. Miniatures have come down to us from the fourteenth century of Charles V seated in his, the first true royal, library, not listening to someone else read, but alone and reading for himself, his lips firmly sealed. Before his century pictures showed God and His angels and saints always communicating with humans by speech. Shortly after 1300 an Anglo-French prayerbook showed the Virgin Mary pointing to words in a book. An equivalent today would be a picture of Holy Mary pointing to a computer screen.

In the next century universities – the Sorbonne by custom, Oxford and Angers by regulation in 1412 and 1431 – established that libraries, which had once been small and as noisy as refectories, were to be not only larger but also quiet: that is to say, that silence and an appreciation of what was in books went together.[15] Reading was now silent and swift: much more could be perused and, possibly, learned. Reading was now a more individual – and potentially heretical – act.

People for whom the written word had swerved free of speech were also engaged in other ventures into the domain of visualiza-

[14] Albert Kapr, *The Art of Lettering: The History, Anatomy, and Aesthetics of the Roman Letter Forms* (New York: Saur Müchen, 1983), 57–63.

[15] Saenger, "Silent Reading," 384, 397, 402–3, 407. By the fifteenth century the practice was so common that Oxford's 1412 regulations declared the library to be a place of silence and in 1431 the University of Angers forbade conversation and even murmuring in its library.

tion. The first were made by very smart individuals who were a notch and more lower than poets and philosophers in the hierarchy of the professions and crafts as ranked by celebrants of literary culture like Huizinga. We have already cited some of these innovators: clock and *portolani* makers, for example. Few of these, being mere artisans or sailors, wrote about what they were doing or attracted the approval of the kind of people whose writings have been preserved. (Richard of Wallingford was not really an exception: he was an abbot, as well as a clock maker.) We know as much about the first clock and maritime chart makers as we ever will, barring miraculous discoveries in ancient archives and attics.

Fortunately, there were others of similar perception of whom we know more. The prestige of their patrons guaranteed their places in history, as did the praise or at least plagiarism of university professors and writers like Oresme, Petrarch, and Luca Pacioli. In addition, these others were men whose works generations since have admired and preserved.

I speak of composers, painters, and bookkeepers. They were devotees of a visual and quantitative perception of the stuff of their crafts; and, even if befuddled with Neoplatonic balderdash, they had to do more than speculate. They had to actually *do* things, to sing, make pictures, and balance their books. Doing these involved counting – that is, comprehending reality as composed of quanta, which could and should be counted – and that is why these ancient workers are still a presence in our lives.

CHAPTER EIGHT

Music

It is no longer a surprise that man, the ape of his Creator, should finally have discovered the art of singing polyphonically, which was unknown to the ancients, namely in order that he might play the everlastingness of all created time in some short part of an hour by means of an artistic concord of many voices and that he might to some extent taste the satisfaction of God the Workman.

Johannes Kepler (1618)[1]

The specific conditions of musical development in the Occident involve, first of all, the invention of modern notation. A notation of our kind is of more fundamental importance for the existence of such music as we possess than is orthography for our linguistic art formations.

Max Weber (c. 1911)[2]

I have been encouraged in writing this chapter by Géza Szamosi's "Law and Order in the Flow of Time: Polyphonic Music and the Scientific Revolution," in his book *The Twin Dimensions: Inventing Time and Space* (New York: McGraw-Hill, 1986).

[1] Johannes Kepler, *The Harmonies of the World,* in *Great Books of the Western World,* ed. Robert Hutchins (Chicago: Encyclopaedia Britannica, 1952), 16: 1048.

[2] Max Weber, *The Rational and Social Foundations of Music,* trans. Don Martindale, Johannes Riedel, and Gertrude Neuwirth (Carbondale: Southern Illinois University Press, 1958), 83.

M usic is a physically measurable phenomenon moving through time. It is universal to humanity: the tendency to make music is right there in our nervous systems with our propensity for speech, so it provides material for the assessment of all societies and ages.[3]

If we want to investigate medieval and Renaissance Europeans' sense of time as a part of their perception of reality, we can hardly do better than to examine their music. They, like the ancient Greeks, believed that it was an emanation of the basic structure of reality, even part of that structure. "Without music," wrote St. Isidore of Seville, the Middle Ages' favorite encyclopedist, "there can be no perfect knowledge, for there is nothing without it. For even the universe is said to have been put together with a certain harmony of sounds, and the very heavens revolve under the guidance of harmony."[4] A thousand years later Johannes Kepler asked, "Which Planet Sings Soprano, Which Alto, Which Tenor and Which Bass?"[5]

We begin with the earliest written music of Western Europe, the plainsong of the Church, specifically Gregorian chant. According to hallowed tradition, Gregory the Great, pope from 590 to 604, is supposed to have composed the body of liturgical chant named for him (or, as depicted long after, to have written it down at the

---

[3] G. Rochberg, "The Structure of Time in Music: Traditional and Contemporary Ramifications and Consequences," in *The Study of Time: Proceedings of the Second Conference of the International Society for the Study of Time,* eds. J. T. Fraser and N. Lawrence (New York: Springer, 1975), 2: 147.

[4] Ernest Brehaut, *An Encyclopedist of the Dark Ages: Isidore of Seville* (New York: Burt Franklin, 1964), 137.

[5] Eric Werner, "The Last Pythagorean Musician: Johannes Kepler," in *Aspects of Medieval and Renaissance Music,* eds. Martin Bernstein, Hans Lenneberg, and Victor Yellin (New York: Norton, 1966), 867–92; Kepler, *The Harmonies of the World,* 1040, 1049.

dictation of the Holy Ghost manifested as a white dove). The truth
is that a great many chants already existed before he mounted the
papal throne and that he did not possess an effective means of
writing music. "Unless sounds are remembered by man," wrote
St. Isidore, whose time on this earth overlapped the great pope's,
"they perish, for they cannot be written down."[6]

Until the last generations of the first Christian millennium,
Europeans performed liturgical music from memory. The variety
of texts and performances must have been great, considering faulty
recall, regional differences, and individual tastes. Consider, for
instance, Brother Caedmon of the monastery of Streanaeshalch in
England, who, after a vision, took all that he knew of God and of
history from Creation to Doomsday and, "like one of the clean
animals chewing the cud," turned it into Anglo-Saxon verse set to
his own music or perhaps to melodies in circulation at the time.
Surely there was paganism in his poetry and a great deal that
was – we can probably use the word *tribal* – in his melody
and rhythm.[7]

On the other hand, there was a countertendency of conver-
gence and conformity to one tradition. Upwardly mobile rustics
were apt to believe that there was one and only one way to do
things right, especially if told so by visitors from the metropolis in
surplices. Eddi, known as Steven, the first singing master in the
Northumbrian churches, "was a most skilled exponent of the
Roman chant, which he had learnt from pupils of the blessed Pope
Gregory."[8] It was that tendency, personified by Eddi and amplified

[6] Giulio Cattin, *Music of the Middle Ages,* trans. Steven Botterill (Cambridge
University Press, 1984), 1: 48–53; *Source Readings in Music History,* 1:
Antiquity and the Middle Ages, ed. Oliver Strunk (New York: Norton,
1965), 93.
[7] Bede, *A History of the English Church and People,* trans. Leo Sherley-Price
(Harmondsworth: Penguin Books, 1968), 250–2.
[8] Ibid., 206–7.

by the Carolingian Renaissance, which drove the gathering and codification of what we call Gregorian chant and which motivated churchmen to evolve a kind of musical notation.

Gregorian chant is a sung version of the Roman Catholic liturgy. It is monophonic and without dramatic contrasts in pitch or loudness and softness. The characteristic of chant that strikes twentieth century ears as most distinctive is its lack of meter (or even, to the lowbrow ear, any pulse at all). Gregorian chant is as immaculately nonmensural as any music most of us are ever to hear. The structure of its musical line is dictated by the varying flow of the Latin, the meaning of the given line in the liturgy, and the otherworldly quality of worship.[9]

It is *not* quantified sound. In syllabic chant, for example, each syllable has one note, which is sung for as long as that particular syllable requires. That note is not necessarily an exact multiple or division of any other note; it is as long as it needs to be.[10] Gregorian chant provides as clear an example of time measured solely by its contents as we are likely to find. (In Chapter 9 on painting we will come upon a kind of space whose dimensions are also dictated by what it contains.)

---

[9] Donald Jay Grout with Claude V. Palisca, *A History of Western Music,* 3d ed. (New York: Norton, 1980), 36, 45; "Gregorian Chant," in *New Catholic Encyclopedia* (Washington, D.C.: The Catholic University of America, 1967), 6: 760; John A. Emerson, "Gregorian Chant," in *The Dictionary of the Middle Ages,* ed. Joseph R. Strayer (New York: Scribner's, 1985), 13: 661–4. In the fourteenth century Jacques de Liège railed that some singers were distorting Gregorian chant by reducing it to mensural music, which suggests that our widespread assessment of it as unmensural is accurate. See F. Joseph Smith, *Iacobi Leodiensis Speculum Musicae,* 1: *A Commentary* (Brooklyn: Institute of Mediaevel Music, 1966), 30. See also Curt Sachs, *Rhythm and Tempo: A Study in Music History* (New York: Norton, 1953), 147.

[10] Cattin, *Music of the Middle Ages,* 1: 69, 74.

By the last century or so of the first Christian millennium the accumulation of chants to be memorized had grown so large that ten years of apprenticeship were insufficient to master this special art. "If at any time the memory of a singer," wrote a contemporary, "even an experienced singer, were to fail, there was nothing he could do to recover it except to become a listener again."[11] And what was he to do if there was no one with a better memory than his own to listen to?

Western monotheists, struggling in the early Middle Ages to establish monotheism among polytheistic and animistic believers, were sure there was only one right way to do things and only one right version of every chant: they needed a means of writing music down. The monks produced neumatic notation. It was for generations little more than a collection of marks derived from the classical Greek and Roman antecedents to our acute, grave, and circumflex accents of written language, pertaining not so much to time as to relative pitch. What we would call an acute accent indicated a rise in pitch, a grave a drop, and a circumflex a rise and fall. These, with dots and curlicues indicating subtler variations – surges, hoverings, trills – were called *neumes,* a word derived from the Greek for either sign or, more likely, breath. They pertained not necessarily to single notes, but to a syllable of the text.[12] Neumes were to notes as words are to phonemes; that is, sometimes the relationship was 1 to 1 (as in the word and phoneme *a*) and sometimes 1 to 2, 5, or what have you (as in the

---

[11] Gregory Murray, *Gregorian Chant According to the Manuscripts* (London: L. J. Cary, 1963), 5.

[12] Cattin, *Music of the Middle Ages,* 1: 56–8; John Stevens, *Words and Music in the Middle Ages* (Cambridge University Press, 1986), 45, 272–7; Higini Anglés, "Gregorian Chant," in *The New Oxford History of Music,* eds. Richard Crocker and David Hiley (Oxford: Oxford University Press, 1954–90), 2: *Early Medieval Music Up to 1300,* ed. Dom Anselm

word *appreciate,* with its many phonemes) or, in accordance with the musical effect required, to any fractional division of these. Neumatic notation was *not* quantitative.

Let us consider the matter of notational pitch first, as did the monks, before we go on to our central interest, note duration or time. Neumes at first and often thereafter were written *in campo aperto,* "in the open field," that is, without staff lines. Their position, high or low, offered a hint as to whether a given note or phrase was higher or lower than the one preceding or following. After a while the monks lightly traced one and then two and more horizontal lines across the page to make the highs and lows easier to recognize. They were on their way to the musical staff, originally four and then five horizontal lines. The lines and the spaces between them, with a few additional markings, enabled the scribe to indicate and the performer to read all legitimate pitches in relation to each other.[13]

The musical staff was Europe's first graph. It measures the passage of time from left to right, and pitch according to position from top to bottom. The Schoolmen and the majority of everyone else who received formal education got, along with the alphabet and the abacus, this musical graph. Oresme's geometrical depiction of motion (see Figure 3, Chapter 3) just might be an adaptation of the staff. (Europeans, however, waited till the eighteenth

Hughes (Oxford: Oxford University Press, 1955), 106; Carl Parrish, *The Notation of Medieval Music* (London: Faber & Faber, 1957), 4–6; James McKinnon, "The Emergence of Gregorian Chant in the Carolingian Era," in *Antiquity and the Middle Ages: From Ancient Greece to the 15th Century,* ed. James McKinnon (Englewood Cliffs, N.J.: Prentice-Hall, 1990), 94; David Hiley, "Plainchant Transfigured: Innovation and Reformation through the Ages," in ibid., 123–4; *The Cambridge Encyclopedia of Language,* ed. David Crystal (Cambridge University Press, 1987), 404.
[13] Murray, *Gregorian Chant,* 6.

century to fully exploit this means of representing physical phenomena, a delay that one historian of mathematics has called
"incomprehensible" and even "inexcusable.")[14]

The invention of the staff is traditionally credited to an eleventh century Benedictine choirmaster, Guido of Arezzo, who la-
mented that in singing the divine offices "we often seem not to
praise God but to struggle among ourselves."[15] Neither he nor any
single individual invented the staff, but he does seem to have been
the first to standardize it and give it wide circulation. He and
others even color-coded the lines of the staff to minimize confusion
about intervals.[16]

A singer with a good ear could be trained to identify specific
intervals with a monochord by sliding the bridge back and forth
and lining it up with marks on the sounding board representing
the several pitches. That, however, took a long time and did not
always work. The resourceful Guido noticed that the ascending
tones represented on his staff matched, in order, those of the first
syllables of the phrases of one of the most familiar of hymns,
the 400-year-old "Ut queant laxis," sung for the feasts of John
the Baptist:

> *Ut* queant laxis *Re*sonare fibris
> *Mi*ra gestorum *Fa*muli tuorum
> *Sol*ve polluti *La*bii reatum
> Sancte Iohannes.

Anyone who knew the hymn melody would know the notes for
ut, re, mi, fa, sol, and *la* (in italics above), which meant that now

---

[14] Salomon Bochner, *The Role of Mathematics in the Rise of Science*
(Princeton, N.J.: Princeton University Press, 1966), 40.

[15] Charles M. Radding, *A World Made by Men: Cognition and Society,
400–1200* (Chapel Hill: University of North Carolina Press, 1985), 188.

[16] *Source Readings in Music History,* 1: 117, 118–19.

the mind's ear had something to match up with what the eye saw as it looked at music notation. Guido boasted that his methods reduced the time required to turn out a good singer of ecclesiastical chant from ten years to no more than one or two. He judged that he and his helpers had done so much for musicians that "from the gratitude of so many will come prayers for our souls."[17]

The history of the ultimate fate of his methods takes us far beyond the period to which this book is devoted, but the responsibility to tie up loose ends warrants a digression. Later generations replaced *ut* with *do* (probably because the former ends in an unsingable *t* and the latter with a singable vowel) and added *si* on the top, derived from the initials of the last two words, "Sancte Iohannes," of the Baptist hymn, completing the scale that hundreds of millions of us have memorized in our first days of formal acquaintance with music: *do, re, mi, fa, sol, la, si*.[18] (The latest alteration has been the change from *si* to *ti*, at least in the United States.)

There was need for new pedagogy in music by Guido's lifetime, and theory, too. Music at its best, he said, had to proceed on two feet, the foot of practice and the foot of reason or intellect.[19] The latter foot was lagging behind. Not only had the body of ecclesiastical music expanded in quantity beyond the capacity of memory, but it was changing in kind as well. By the ninth century the Gregorian chant was a sacrosanct whole, but interpolations and decorous additions at the ends of certain chants, as well as hymns separate from the chants, were allowed. As early as 860 someone added an interpolation *on top* of a traditional chant melody. At first such interpolations and the chant proceeded along

---

[17] Ibid., 121–4.

[18] Richard Rastall, *The Notation of Western Music* (New York: St. Martin's Press, 1982), 136–7.

[19] Cattin, *Music of the Middle Ages*, 1: 188.

at exactly the same pace, perfectly parallel and just a few notes apart, a minor innovation in itself but one that opened the flood-gates for others.[20] After a few generations the notes of the chant (restricted to the lower voice alone, the *tenor,* from the Latin *tenere,* to hold) stretched out until they filled the role, musically, if not liturgically, of a drone. The tenor was responsible for the foundation, the *cantus firmus* (firm song), originally always a chant, later sometimes a new and even secular melody. There, respect for tradition was taken care of, freeing the upper voice and then the upper voices to gambol and frisk.[21]

The first masters of this polyphony whose names we know, Leonin and Perotin, lived in the last years of the twelfth and first years of the next century. Their compositions are among the first examples of specifically *composed* (not evolved) music of which we have manuscript copies. The complexity of their music, the upper voices marching and countermarching above the massive and seemingly eternal foundation of the *cantus firmus,* was star-tling compared with the stolid monophony of Gregorian chant. These works brought Western music as far as it could go without radical advances in notation and theory.

The works of Leonin and Perotin were equivalent in innovation to the Gothic cathedrals. It is probable that they were first performed in one of the most magnificent of those cathedrals, Notre Dame of Paris. As Western music moved from Gregorian simplicity to polyphonic complexity, it also moved from the cloister and coun-tryside to the cathedral and the city, that is to say, into the realm of

[20] Manfred F. Bukofzer, "Speculative Thinking in Mediaeval Music," *Specu-lum,* 17 (Apr. 1942), 168–73; Cattin, *Music of the Middle Ages,* 1: 101–27.
[21] *The New Oxford Companion to Music,* ed. Denis Arnold (Oxford: Ox-ford University Press, 1983), 1: 312.

the university and marketplace. From the twelfth to the fourteenth century Paris was the center for the development of Western polyphony, as for so much else. There, where Abelard and Albert the Great and St. Thomas Aquinas taught, musicians were exposed to a sense of the possibility of change or at least reassessment and, at the same time, to a new and rigorous logic and sense of order. There in the urban swirl, musicians could stuff fingers and thumbs in their ears, but were still sure to hear the music of the ring and line dancers in the churchyards and streets. The popular *caroles* were so distracting that anyone who heard one and failed to tell his or her confessor automatically incurred eighteen days in Purgatory. Traces of popular melodies and rhythms began showing up in the upper voices of churchly polyphony early in the thirteenth century.[22]

In the city, musicians rubbed elbows with merchants and money changers, which had practical as well as intellectual effects. The rise of a cash economy meant that good singers of chant and polyphony in the cathedrals could exact fees, possibly even eke out a living as professional musicians. As they sang more and more, they improved their techniques and indulged themselves in what the traditionalists called "minstrelish and wanton music": that is, embellishments such as the *longa florata* and the *reverberatio,* even in the chants. Cistercian monks trimmed their chant until it was as unindividualistic as their robes, but others succumbed.[23] Then, as now, virtuosity in performance and composition was the accomplished musician's greatest temptation.

In Paris, at the epicenter of the Western cultural revolution, musicians strode forward on both of Guido's feet, first Leonin and Perotin – and then the theoreticians. If we intend to sing in unison,

---

[22] Christopher Page, *The Owl and the Nightingale: Musical Life and Ideas in France, 1100–1300* (London: J. M. Dent, 1989), 126, 152–3.
[23] Ibid., 135, 144–5, 148, 180.

then starting, singing, and stopping are not difficult. If we intend to sing polyphonically – that is, in several independent lines – then starting together will be easy, but everything from that instant on will tend to slide into anarchy. We need the guidance of sturdy forms and a temporal dictator; we need to know where we are going and the pace at which we are to march. To an extent the liturgy supplied the forms, but how long would these satisfy the young lions of polyphony? Leonin and Perotin and their anonymous colleagues (and just possibly the street minstrels) supplied what was lacking in chant, a time control, a rhythmic measure.

Music was a member of those four of the seven liberal arts called the quadrivium in which all advanced scholars were trained in the Middle Ages. It included arithmetic, geometry, and astronomy, which we can accept as mathematical, and music, which we may think of as being in odd company. But music, a matter of pitches and durations, is highly susceptible to mathematical analysis, as legions of theorists from Pythagoras to Arnold Schönberg have agreed. The significance of music in its influence on the general attitudes toward quantification and the relationship of mathematics to actuality is this: music was the only one of the four members of the quadrivium in which measurement had immediate practical application. The fourteenth century's reactionary Jacques de Liège scorned practical musicians as animals grinding out notes in ignorance of proportionality,[24] but his progressive colleagues paid attention to performance. They granted that practice could and should inform theory, even though the latter would always be mathematical at its core.[25] It is in music's twining of quantification and practice that its general intellectual significance lies.

[24] Smith, *Jacobi Leodiensis*, 2: 7–8.
[25] André Goddu, "Music as Art and Science in the Fourteenth Century," *Scientia und ars im Hock- und Spätmittelalter*, 22: *Miscellanea Mediaevalia* (Berlin: de Gruyter, 1994), 1038, 1039.

Medieval theorists had all read Anicius Manlius Boethius, arguably the West's most important source of knowledge about antique civilization from his time, circa 500, to the twelfth century's windfall of translations. He lasted longest as the primal authority on music in the schools. His *De institutione musica* contains little relating to musical practice and a great deal of mathematical analysis of harmonics, intervals, and proportions.[26] It has as little to do with the actual making of music as his work on number theory has to do with haggling about prices in the marketplace; but it was eminently respectable and intellectually rigorous – a solid, if narrow, base to build on.

At the beginning of the thirteenth century and continuing on into the fourteenth a pair of additional influences guided Western music into new paths. Polyphony, as we have already seen, challenged tradition, and translations of the Aristotelian corpus arrived, galvanizing a whole generation of philosophers into a reconsideration of nearly everything. Some of these philosophers were music theorists. They, utilizing the Scholastic techniques of definition and logic mentioned in Chapter 3, built the armature of formal music for Western civilization. They were Schoolmen in technique and most of them, perhaps all, were associated in one way or another with the University of Paris.

The period from 1260 to 1285 in Paris marked, one can reasonably claim, the moment and location of the acme of medieval civilization in the West. Kings Louis IX and Philip III ruled from Paris, France prospered, and a fresh translation of Aristotle by the Dominican William of Moerbeke appeared and became standard. St. Thomas Aquinas, St. Bonaventure, and Siger of Brabant, the radical Averröist, all taught at the University of Paris. In

---

[26] Claude V. Palisca, "Theory, Theorists," in *The New Grove Dictionary of Music and Musicians,* ed. Stanley Sadie (London: Macmillan, 1980), 18: 744.

those years Johannes de Garlandia, Lambertus, Franco of Cologne, and two gentlemen we know only as the Anonymous of 1279 and the Anonymous IV wrote about music. All five employed Scholastic concepts and terminology, and Scholastic dialectical analysis, specifically the *quaestio,* that is, a problematic statement, its possible clarifications, with citation of authorities, and then a solution.[27]

Johannes de Garlandia, for instance, divided and subdivided music into genres, these into species, and so on down to the specific. One of the genres was mensural music, which he divided into discant, copula, and organum, and so on. Having located in the characteristically Scholastic style his topics in relation to his subject as a totality, he submitted them to meticulous analysis, often mathematical. He devoted more consideration than any previous theorist to the rhythmical (time arrangement) problems that the *ars antiqua,* the music of Perotin and the others of the Notre Dame school, posed. He even introduced notations for rests of various lengths: rests were signs not for sounds, but for the *absences* of sound. It may be worth mentioning here that the zero, that eerie Hindu-Arabic sign indicating something that is not, was circulating in the West by this time.

Franco of Cologne (he and Johannes may have known each other) carried his reader through much the same process, and also codified and standardized a system of notation establishing time values for all notes and rests, even insisting on unequivocal time values for a slippery slur of notes called ligatures. He proclaimed, to give a sample of his practical contribution, that there were four single-note signs in music notation, called the double long, the long, the breve, and the semibreve. They were *exact* multiples

---

[27] *Music Theory and Its Sources: Antiquity to the Middle Ages,* ed. André Barbera (Notre Dame, Ind.: University of Notre Dame Press, 1990), 182–3; Page, *The Owl and the Nightingale,* 152.

or divisions of each other. The breve was either three tempora ("perfect") or two tempora ("imperfect") in duration.[28] (The breve three tempora long was "perfect" in large part because it echoed the Trinity.)[29] The sequence of the durations of the various notes was not like the organic and experiential succession of an inch (a thumb breadth), a foot (twelve thumb breadths or an actual human foot),[30] a yard (three feet), and a furlong (220 yards or a furrow long), but logical and abstract, a prefigurement of the metric system.

Theorists validated and systematized what practical musicians had invented in the years around 1200: not time as its contents, but time as a measuring stick of independent existence with which you could measure things or even their absence — abstract time. Franco of Cologne put it this way: "Time is the measure of actual sound as well as of the opposite, its omission."[31] Time measured its contents, not contents time. This time had units, like visible centimeters in a visible meter. The basic unit was called a *tempus* (plural, *tempora*). And how long was a tempus? Around 1300 Johannes de Grocheo (also spelled Grocheio) defined it pragmatically. The tempus, he said, was the "interval in which the smallest pitch or smallest note is fully presented or can be presented."[32]

---

[28] *Source Readings in Music History,* 1: 142.

[29] Nan Cooke Carpenter, *Music in the Medieval and Renaissance Universities* (New York: Da Capo Press, 1972), 58; Palisca, "Theory, Theorists," 748–9. This is a good deal more complicated than I have indicated. For a brief suggestion of just how much more, see Rebecca A. Baltzer, "Lambertus," in ibid., 10: 400–1.

[30] Ronald E. Zupko, *British Weights and Measures: A History from Antiquity to the Seventeenth Century* (Madison: University of Wisconsin Press, 1977), 10.

[31] *Source Readings in Music History,* 1: 140.

[32] *Johannes de Grocheo: Concerning Music,* trans. Albert Seay (Colorado Springs: Colorado College Music Press, 1967), 21, 22. See also F. Alberto Gallo, *Music of the Middle Ages* (Cambridge University Press, 1985), 2: 11–12.

The West had reached a turning of some sort: music theorists, who, with very few exceptions, most notably the pedagogue Guido, had written of music as if it were to be thought about rather than heard, were beginning to consult actual musicians as well as Aristotle and Boethius. For example, Johannes, just mentioned, scanted traditional authorities, mentioned secular composers, concerned himself with both secular monophony and sacred polyphony and with music as performed as well as music as mathematics.[33] One musicologist and historian has suggested that some medieval theorists were not really theorists, but "teacher-reporters."[34]

The musicians of the *ars antiqua* quantified sound and silence circa 1200, a half to a full century before the West's first mechanical clock. The theorists validated and systematized musical quantification within a few years, plus or minus, of that invention. The foundation they constructed in reverence both to mathematical proportion and to the actual effect of sound on the human ear underlies all formal Western music.[35]

Musicians took advantage of the disciplines of mensural music to exercise their wits. Sounds in abstract time – that is to say, sounds on parchment or paper – could be divided into pieces, turned backward and upside-down. Even the tenor, that beast of burden to the upper voices, could frolic. For instance, someone in the thirteenth century composed an organum in which the tenor proclaims monomaniacally the sacred word *Dominus,* but here the word is sung backward – *Nusmido* – and the sacred Gregorian melody proceeds aft to fore, stern to bow, as well.[36] A composer of even greater audacity wrote the motet (undated, unfortunately)

[33] Tom R. Ward, "Johannes de Grocheo," in *New Grove Dictionary of Music and Musicians,* 9: 662–3.
[34] Marion S. Gushee, "The Polyphonic Music of the Medieval Monastery, Cathedral, and University" in *Antiquity and the Middle Ages,* 152.
[35] Goddu, "Music as Art and Science in the Fourteenth Century."
[36] Bukofzer, "Speculative Thinking in Mediaeval Music," 176.

entitled *Dieus! comment porrai laisser la vie – O regina glorie*. Its
tenor sings a traditional chant, the middle voice glorifies the Virgin
Mary, and the upper proclaims:

> God! How could I leave life in Paris with my comrades?
> Never for good, they are so delightful. For when they are all
> gathered together, each one sets himself to laugh and play
> and sing.[37]

New attitudes toward self and the possibilities of accomplish-
ing more than hallowed predecessors surfaced, attitudes usually
associated only with the later and Italian Renaissance. Musicians
cultivated their egos and became progressive, self-consciously so –
unthinkable in the age of Guido, and even in that of Leonin and
Perotin. One of the leading composers and theorists was Philippe
de Vitry, born in Paris on 31 October 1291 and died there 9
June 1361. (Note the unmedieval precision about personal dates.)
Around 1320 a treatise appeared titled *Ars nova,* probably his, on
the new style of the same name. Johannes de Muris, mathematician and astronomer as well as musical theorist, wrote another
treatise just about this time, possibly even more influential than
Philippe's, with a nearly identical title, *Ars nove musice.* This
moment may have been the first in the history of music in which
musicians claimed and even publicized their claim that they were
making intentional changes, that music was moving ahead.[38]

---

[37] Gallo, *Music of the Middle Ages,* 2: 26.

[38] Ernest H. Sanders, "Vitry, Philippe de," in *New Grove Dictionary of
Music and Musicians,* 20: 22; "Philippe de Vitry's Ars Nova," trans.
Leon Plantinga, *Music Theory,* 5 (Nov. 1961), 204–20; Gallo, *Music of
the Middle Ages,* 2: 31; Daniel Leech-Wilkinson, "Ars Antiqua–Ars
Nova–Ars Subtilior," in *Antiquity and the Middle Ages,* 221. For the
original Latin and a French translation of Philippe de Vitry's treatise on
the new music, see Philippi de Vitriaco, *Ars Nova,* eds. Gilbert Reaney,
André Gilles, and Jean Maillard (n.c.: American Institute of Musicology,
1964).

Johannes Boen, writing circa 1355 about innovation in the performance of music, tossed off a profoundly unmedieval idea: the possibility of perpetual change as normal. Perhaps, he suggested, new sounds and techniques would "become audible through the use of new instruments and vocal skills." After all, before Pythagoras there had been "no such subtlety of singing as is used in our times." Historians usually date the rise of the concept of progress long after the fourteenth century, but it is not easy to put another name to what Boen wrote vis-à-vis *ars nova*.[39]

The musicians of the *ars nova* accepted duple, or "imperfect," meter as equal in status to triple, or "perfect," meter. Triple meter, with each breve composed of three tempora, had been so very right that duple, with each breve composed of two tempora, had been wrong, only two-thirds of something. *Ars nova* embraced duple meter and further offended traditionalists by creating notes of shorter durational value than had been formally recognized before. The *minim* was the shortest and most offensive. A musician could dash through eighty-one during just one *longissima*.[40] Daniel Leech-Wilkinson, the musicologist and historian, comments that "it is hard to think of any development in music which changed so much so quickly."[41] So much (again) for the old saw about the Middle Ages being stagnant.

The musicians of the *ars nova,* like other revolutionaries, scorned their elders,[42] but we can see at a distance of many centuries that they shared a great deal with them. The practitioners of *ars nova* were subject to the same Boethian yearnings for architec-

---

[39] Reinhard Strohm, *The Rise of European Music, 1380–1500* (Cambridge University Press, 1993), 38; J. B. Bury, *The Idea of Progress: An Inquiry into Its Origin and Growth* (New York: Dover, 1987).

[40] *Source Readings in Music History,* 1: 177.

[41] Leech-Wilkinson, "Ars Antiqua–Ars Nova–Ars Subtilior," 223.

[42] F. J. Smith, *Jacobi Leodiensis Speculum Musicae: A Commentary* (Brooklyn, N.Y.: Institute of Mediaeval Music, 1983), 3: 61.

ture in sound that had inspired the development of the organum and motet, and later the ricercar, fugue, and symphony. Philippe de Vitry and colleagues did not write rhapsodically – not even in monophony – but sculpted carefully proportioned jewels. In the larger forms they separated melody and rhythm, altered their paces, recombined the two (in vitro, so to speak), and set the hybrids going again, faster here, slower there. The effect could be delicious when the melodic and rhythmic patterns differed in duration and had to be repeated until they were synchronous again. These *isorhythmic* devices, which appeared and reappeared in the tenor and in various guises in the other voices, served two purposes: to bind large works together and to delight the West's first generation of musical cognoscenti.[43] "These procedures," wrote Johannes Boen in the fourteenth century, *"are more easily seen than heard"*[44] (my emphasis).

Between St. Isidore's rueful "Unless sounds are remembered by man, they perish," circa 600, and Boen's remark, circa 1355, Western music had changed more than it has between Boen and Igor Stravinsky and Arnold Schönberg.[45] Between the sixth and

[43] This matter of isorhythm can be easily explained with a piano, even to a nonmusician, but defies description in words. The least opaque explanation I have read is Albert Seay's on pages 132–6 of his *Music in the Medieval World*, 2d ed. (Englewood Cliffs, N.J.: Prentice-Hall, 1975).

[44] Gallo, *Music of the Middle Ages*, 2: 39.

[45] Grout, *History of Western Music*, 111, 118, 119–22; *Source Readings in Music History*, 1: 93, 175, 176; Gilbert Reaney, "Ars Nova," in *The Pelican History of Music*, 1: *Ancient Forms to Polyphony*, eds. Alec Robertson and Denis Stevens (Harmondsworth: Penguin Books, 1960), 273–4; Gallo, *Music of the Middle Ages*, 2: 36–9; Anselm Hughes, "The Motet and Allied Forms," in *New Oxford History of Music: Early Medieval Music up to 1300*, 2: 391; Rudolph von Ficker, "The Transition on the Continent," in *The New Oxford History of Music*, 3: *Ars Nova and the Renaissance, 1300–1540*, eds. Anselm Hughes and Gerald Abraham (Oxford: Oxford University Press, 1960), 145–6.

the fourteenth centuries something unique happened in Western Europe: the writer of music achieved control over the fine detail of sound, a physical phenomenon, moving through time.[46] The composer learned how to extract music from actual time, put it on parchment or paper, and make of it something that was satisfying as symbol as well as sound and vice versa. Deaf Beethoven writing his last quartets became a possibility.

Faith in absolute time, which the musicians who invented Western mensural notation were among the first to think about seriously, which thereafter a growing proportion of their fellows received as a self-apparent truth — such a faith altered perception of reality and promoted a reordering of the ways to understand it. Such a faith, for instance, enabled and emboldened Johannes Kepler, whose concern with music was as constant as his concern with the heavens, to recognize in the thicket of astronomical observations what we know as his second law of planetary motion, that a line drawn from any planet to the sun will always sweep equal areas in equal times.[47]

Not everyone admired the *ars nova*. In polyphony the text, which had once dictated every facet of the sung liturgy, was becoming unintelligible. As early as 1242 the Dominicans opposed elaborate polyphony in the divine service, and St. Thomas broadcast the opinion of his order on the matter. In the next century Jacques de Liège fumed that judicious people could not discern whether the language sung in the new motets was Hebrew, Greek, Latin, or some other. "Should," he asked, "the moderns be called subtle for introducing triplex longs, for joining duplex longs in ligature,

[46] John E. Kaemmer, *Music in Human Life: Anthropological Perspectives on Music* (Austin: University of Texas Press, 1993), 79.
[47] Arthur Koestler, *The Sleepwalkers: A History of Man's Changing Vision of the Universe* (Harmondsworth: Penguin Books, 1964), 332, 393–4.

for using duplex longs profusely, for using semibreves singly, for providing them with tails . . . ? Music was originally discreet, seemly, simple, masculine, and of good morals; have not the moderns rendered it lascivious beyond measure?"[48]

In 1322 Pope John XXII issued the first papal proclamation dealing exclusively with music, *Docta sanctorum patrum*. He raged that the music of the divine offices was "pestered" with semibreves and minims, and "depraved" with discant and secular melodies. Polyphonic voices "are incessantly running to and fro, intoxicating the ear, not soothing it," and "devotion, the true end of worship, is little thought of, and wantonness, which ought to be eschewed, increases." He particularly hated the hocket, a technique in which one voice sang one note while another voice rested, and then vice versa – rapidly. The word *hocket* comes from the French *hoquet* and the English *hiccup*.[49]

John XXII forbade perverse polyphony in church services, and the amount of new music sung in the cathedrals decreased, but music, old or new, did not have to be ecclesiastical. Anyway, there were places other than cathedrals to make music, sacred or secular. In Paris musical innovation shifted from Notre Dame to the king's end of the Ile de la Cité. Elsewhere the private chapels of the nobility and of cardinals and of Epicurean successors of John XXII in Avignon became laboratories for the *ars nova* and even further experimentation.[50] The next two centuries, the fifteenth and sixteenth, were the greatest in the history of vocal polyphony and perhaps all polyphony in the West – and of swift advances in

[48] *Source Readings in Music History,* 1: 184–5, 189, 190; Craig Wright, *Music and Ceremony at Notre Dame of Paris, 500–1550* (Cambridge University Press, 1989), 345.

[49] Gallo, *Music of the Middle Ages,* 2: 32; Goddu, "Music as Art and Science," 1031.

[50] *The Oxford History of Music,* 2d ed., eds. H. E. Wooldridge and Percy C. Buck, vol. 1: *The Polyphonic Period,* part 1: *Method of Musical Art, 330–1400* (Oxford: Oxford University Press, 1929), 294–5; Wright, *Music and Ceremony at Notre Dame,* 346–7.

other quantitative fields such as algebra, trigonometry, perspective painting, and cartography.

Granted, but does any of this have real significance vis-à-vis the core *mentalité* of the West? Are musicians central or peripheral to a given society? They were certainly close to the center during the scientific revolution of the late sixteenth and seventeenth centuries – Galileo, Descartes, Kepler, and Huyghens were all trained musicians who wrote on musical subjects, sometimes extensively[51] – but that might be a coincidence. What about the Middle Ages? Consider the specific example of Philippe de Vitry. He first appears as a probable contributor to the *Roman de Fauvel*, a scalding satire on court, church, and contemporary morality in general, consisting of thousands of lines of poetry, wildly impudent drawings, and 169 musical items, 34 of them polyphonic.[52] One of the latter, a motet entitled *In nova fert*, one of several attributed to Philippe, was inspired by the downfall and hanging of Enguerran de Marigny, minister to Philip IV. The tenor is a palindrome that ebbs and flows between comforting triple and discomforting duple meters. The rhythmic pattern repeats six times while the melody repeats twice and the upper voices clamor about a blind lion, treacherous cocks, cunning foxes, and victimized lambs and chickens.[53] The *désengagés* must have found it both musically and politically delicious.

[51] Claude V. Palisca, "Scientific Empiricism in Musical Thought," in *Seventeenth Century Science and the Arts*, ed. Hedley H. Rhys (Princeton, N.J.: Princeton University Press, 1961), 91–2.

[52] Leech-Wilkinson, "Ars Antiqua–Ars Nova–Ars Subtilior," 221–3; Ernest H. Sanders, "Fauvel, Roman de," in *New Grove Dictionary of Music and Musicians*, 429–33.

[53] Edward H. Roesner, "Philippe de Vitry: Motets and Chansons," Deutsche Harmonia Mundi (Compact Disk 77095-2-RC), 8, 22–3; *Le Roman de Fauvel in the Edition of Mesire Chaillou de Pesstain*, Introduction by Edward Roesner, François Avril, and Nancy Freeman Regalado (New York: Broude Brothers, 1990), 3, 6, 15, 24, 25, 30–8, 39, 41.

Such an exercise of musicianship in societies under authoritarian regimes today would land the composer in jail. The benign elites of more tolerant societies would identify and tag him, and exile him not to Siberia but to the bleak frontiers of the artistic avant-garde. But Philippe, a master of arts at the University of Paris, a mathematician, a student of ancient history and of moral philosophy, became secretary and adviser to kings of France. He led diplomatic missions to the papal court and became the bishop of Meaux. At his request, Levi ben Gerson, the Jewish mathematician and astronomer, wrote the treatise *De harmonicis numeris*. Nicole Oresme, the protoscientific genius of the age, dedicated his treatise *Algorismus proportionum* to Philippe, "whom I would call Pythagoras if it were possible to believe in the opinion about the return of souls." Francesco Petrarch, Philippe's friend and the intellectual doyen of Western Europe, called him "ever the keenest and most ardent seeker of truth" and "the unparalleled poet of France."[54]

If we could choose one and only one autobiography from the Western Middle Ages, our choice might well be that of Philippe de Vitry. If he thought in terms of a new kind of time, then that concept was not an eddy but a current in the mainstream of his society.

Generally speaking, nothing is more diagnostic of a society's reading of reality than its perception of time. The changes in medieval music in the thirteenth and fourteenth centuries entitled *ars antiqua* and *ars nova* are evidence of a major mutation in Western European culture. Victor Zuckerkandl, the author of *Sound and Symbol: Music and the External World,* declares that for most peoples and most eras musical time "is of the nature of poetic

---

[54] Ernest H. Sanders, "Vitry, Philippe de," in *New Grove Dictionary of Music and Musicians,* 20: 22–3; "Part 1 of Nicole Oresme's *Algorismus proportionum,*" trans. Edward Grant, *Isis,* 56 (Fall 1965), 328.

rhythm: free rhythm, in the sense that it is not constrained to keep time." Except for the special case of dance music, which is self-explanatory, only Western music of the second millennium A.D. "has imposed the shackles of time, of meter, upon itself."[55] The mechanical metronome was not invented for centuries more, but Europe's mental metronome began to tick in the era of Leonin and Perotin nearly a century before Europe's first mechanical clock.

Let us bring this chapter to a close with a musical artifact of the fourteenth century not by Philippe de Vitry — little of his music has survived — but by the greatest composer of the *ars nova*, Guillaume de Machaut (c. 1300–77) (Figure 4). Most of Machaut's contemporaries considered him a greater poet than Philippe, and posterity considers him a greater composer. Machaut, in his self-esteem a prefigure of the Italian Renaissance, would have agreed in both cases. We have more of his work to examine and enjoy than of any other musician before the age of music printing, for the very simple fact that he wanted us to. At the end of his productive life he gathered together all of his work and supervised its reproduction in several large and beautifully illustrated volumes.[56] He is an early and striking example of the convention, stronger in the West than elsewhere, according to which the composer is the most significant of all musicians.[57]

He gloried in the manipulation of time, in rhythm, the forte of

---

[55] Victor Zuckerkandl, *Sound and Symbol: Music and the External World*, trans. Willard R. Trask (New York: Pantheon Books, 1956), 159; G. Rochberg, "The Structure of Time in Music," in *The Study of Time*, 2: 143.

[56] William Calin, *A Poet at the Fountain: Essays on the Narrative Verse of Guillaume de Machaut* (Lexington: University Press of Kentucky, 1974), 15, 245; Sarah J. M. Williams, "Machaut's Self-Awareness as Author and Producer," in *Machaut's World: Science and Art in the Fourteenth Century*, eds. Madeleine P. Cosman and Bruce Chandler (New York: Annals of the New York Academy of Science, 1978), 189.

[57] Strohm, *Rise of European Music*, 2.

Figure 4. Guillaume de Machaut, "Ma fin est mon commencement –
Rondeau." Guillaume de Machaut, *Musikalische Werke: Balladen, Rondeaux und Virelais* (Leipzig: Breitkopf & Hartel Muskivetag, 1926),
63–4.

ars nova, utilizing $\frac{2}{4}$, $\frac{4}{4}$, $\frac{6}{8}$, $\frac{9}{8}$ time and the hocket (which Jacques de
Liège thought sounded like dogs barking).[58] He made easy use of
the difficult isorhythmic technique. Such music was possible only
because a clock was ticking in the composer's mind, the same

[58] Smith, *Jacobi Leodiensis*, 3: 127.

clock that was ticking in the performers' and listeners' minds.[59]

Machaut's "Ma fin est mon commencement" (Figure 4) is one of his rondeaux, which, Robert Craft writes, "both demand our respect and are, in truth, too sophisticated for us."[60] It has three voices. Two of the three have the same melody, one in forward motion and the other in retrograde, that is, one from A to Z, so to speak, and the other, simultaneously, from Z to A. The third voice, which has its own melody, reverses direction halfway through (goes from its A to its M and back to A).[61] No ear can fully comprehend such complexity in time, only the eye.

---

[59] Grout, *History of Western Music*, 113, 122–7. See also Armand Macha-bey, *Guillaume de Machault, 130?–1377: La vie et l'oeuvre musical*, 2 vols. (Paris: Richard-Masse, 1955); Gilbert Reaney, *Guillaume de Ma-chaut* (Oxford: Oxford University Press, 1971).

[60] Robert Craft, "Musical Rx for a Political Season," *New York Review of Books* (15 July 1976), 39.

[61] Gustave Reese, *Music in the Middle Ages* (New York: Norton, 1940), 350–2.

CHAPTER NINE

Painting

Among all the studies of natural causes and reasoning Light chiefly delights the beholder; and among the great features of mathematics the certainty of its demonstrations is what preeminently tends to elevate the mind of the investigator. Perspective, therefore, must be preferred to all the discourses and systems of human learning.

Leonardo da Vinci (1497–9)[1]

Humans invented picture making in order to manipulate light, line, and area[2] for purposes of intellectual and emotional satisfaction, economic gain, and political, social, and religious

Most of what is valuable in this chapter is drawn from two works of Samuel Y. Edgerton, Jr., *The Renaissance Rediscovery of Linear Perspective* (New York: Basic Books, 1975) and *The Heritage of Giotto's Geometry: Art and Science on the Eve of the Scientific Revolution* (Ithaca, N.Y.: Cornell University Press, 1991).

[1] *The Literary Works of Leonardo da Vinci,* trans. and ed. Jean P. Richter (London: Phaidon, 1970), 1: 112, 177.

[2] For the sake of brevity and clarity, I omit color and texture, just as I slighted pitch and ignored timbre in the chapter on music.

intent. As these incentives changed, so did the perception of light, extension, space, and proper representation of three-dimensional scenes on two-dimensional surfaces. In fourteenth century France portraits that actually looked like specific people, rather than generalized types, became fashionable as book illustrations, and we have a number of such of Charles V, the king who ordered Paris to accept the dictates of one clock (his) and who patronized *ars nova*. The manuscripts of Machaut included depictions of the composer himself as well as such innovations as differentiated foregrounds and backgrounds, landscapes, and naturalistic details (Figure 5).[3] These illustrations were sparks of a revolutionary development in picture making, possibly blown over the Alps from Italy, where an aristocracy of wealth was rising that craved aesthetic glorification for their God, their cities, and themselves.

Before we approach the artistic eruption they fueled with their patronage, we should familiarize ourselves with the way pictures had been made. Let us begin with the "now" of medieval pictures. A single illumination or fresco might include several clearly differentiated "nows." In one picture St. Paul's ship may go aground, he may struggle to shore and then preach to the pagans. That equals three "nows" and may well confuse us.

Even a single medieval "now" can be confusing. Today we usually think of pictures as depictions of what existed and was happening in a knife-edge instant; that is, the "now" of a sixteenth century fresco of the Holy Family's flight to Egypt or of a twenti-

---

[3]   Marcel Thomas, "French Illumination in the Time of Guillaume de Machaut," in *Machaut's World: Science and Art in the Fourteenth Century*, eds. Madeleine P. Cosman and Bruce Chandler (New York: New York Academy of Science, 1978), 144–65; John White, *The Birth and Rebirth of Pictorial Space* (Boston: Boston Book and Art Shop, 1967), 219–35; A. C. Crombie, *Medieval and Early Modern Science* (New York: Doubleday, 1959), 2: plate 1.

Figure 5. Miniature from the *Works of Guillaume de Machaut*, c. 1370. "The composer receives Love, who brings him Sweet Thoughts, Calm Enjoyment, and Hope," fourteenth century. Bibliothèque Nationale, Paris. Courtesy Giraudon / Art Resource, New York.

eth century photograph of a family picnic are essentially the same. The medieval "now" was closer to the kind described by the American pragmatist William James, that is to say, not a "knife-edge, but a saddle-back, with a certain breadth of its own on which we sit perched, and from which we look in two directions into time."[4] For example, as we pass a cubical building, we perceive it not in a durationless instant in which we can never see more than two walls, but *as we move,* and so we can, sometimes, catch sight of three walls in one "now."

The picture makers of the medieval West not only watched the world from William James's saddle, but got down and walked around to get a better look. If looking at an object from two or more points of view at once would help to convey information they thought was important, then they went right ahead and did it. They were no more reluctant to do so than Shakespeare was, later, to halt action while a protagonist thinks aloud in a soliloquy. If medieval picture makers wanted observers to have a good look at the dishes and food on a table, they tipped the table up like the lid of a trunk — and nothing slid off.

Medieval artists were sure that the rank of their subjects was more important than the actual shapes of their faces, the color of their eyes, or the way their arms set into their shoulders. Artists often indicated significance by the most obvious means: by size, making the protagonists — Christ, the Virgin Mary, emperors — relatively large and locating them at dead center. Unimportant people and things were small and fitted in along the edges or wherever there was an open patch. The artist, probably the monk, who drew *St. Dunstan at the Feet of Christ* some time before 956[5]

---

[4] *The Human Experience of Time: The Development of Its Philosophical Meaning,* ed. Charles M. Sherover (New York: New York University Press, 1975), 371.

[5] David M. Wilson, *Anglo-Saxon Art from the Seventh Century to the Norman Conquest* (Woodstock, N.Y.: Overlook Press, 1984), 179.

Figure 6. *St. Dunstan at the Feet of Christ,* tenth century. David M. Wilson, *Anglo-Saxon Art from the Seventh Century to the Norman Conquest* (Woodstock, N.Y.: Overlook Press, 1984), plate 224.

(Figure 6) was an accurate reproducer of *theological* reality, as well as a master of line.

The most distinctive characteristic of medieval art to the modern eye, however, is not the manipulation of size (Renaissance artists occasionally played that game, too, as we do), but the treatment of empty space, the three-dimensional vacancy around

Figure 7. Anonymous, panorama of Florence, detail from the Madonna della Misericordia fresco, fourteenth century. Loggia del Begallo, Florence. Courtesy Alinari / Art Resource, New York.

the subject or among the subjects. For us today, things exist in space like vegetables in an aspic salad. The vegetables may be the chief items of interest, but the aspic is undeniably *there* occupying the area among the items of interest. We do not deny the aspic because it is transparent, and we rarely ignore space even if it is empty.

The Florence painted around 1350 by an unknown artist in the medieval style (Figure 7) would not satisfy a twentieth century surveyor, but it is an accurate picture of what the city (a collection of buildings, *not* the nothing between them) looked like to perambulating visitors with medieval eyes as they passed through its narrow, twisting streets. Medieval space was what it contained, just as time was what happened. Vacancy had no authenticity or autonomy for a people who rejected vacuum as a possibility.

But by 1300 a change in the perception of space was under way in Italy. From the east came examples of Byzantine art, which was somewhat more representational than Western art. From the north came the influence of the sculptors whose three-dimensional statues and reliefs, more naturalistic than anything since the heyday of the Roman Empire, lent pious charm to the cathedral at Chartres. From under native earth came examples of the often naturalistic art of ancient Rome.[6]

There was also the West's growing obsession with optics and geometry, clearly in evidence by the turn of the fourteenth century. Jean de Meun, one of the authors of *The Romance of the Rose*, the nearest thing to a potboiler at that time, even managed to bring optics into this poem on courtly and sometimes rather uncourtly love. If Mars and Venus, he offers, had examined their bed of lust with magnifying mirrors or lenses, they would have seen the nets that her husband had placed there to catch them, "and cruel Vulcan, burning with jealousy and anger, would have never proved their adultery."[7]

Geometry, absent from Dante's *Inferno* and *Purgatorio,* shows up in *Paradiso,* where all is well ordered. In its thirteenth canto St. Thomas Aquinas refers to attempts to disprove one of Euclid's statements about triangles within circles. In the seventeenth canto there is an individual who can see the future "even as earthly

---

[6] Miriam S. Bunim, *Space in Medieval Painting and the Forerunners of Perspective* (New York: AMS Press, 1940), 127–35; John White, *Art and Architecture in Italy, 1250–1400* (Harmondsworth: Penguin Books, 1987), 19, 143–4, 161; John Beckwith, *Early Christian and Byzantine Art* (Harmondsworth: Penguin Books, 1979), 241–85.

[7] Guillaume de Lorris and Jean de Meun, *The Romance of the Rose,* trans. Charles Dahlberg (Hanover, N.H.: University Press of New England, 1986), 300–1.

minds see that two obtuse angles cannot be contained in a triangle." In the thirty-third and last canto Dante, facing God, the Light Eternal, compares his inability to fathom the relationship between the Deity and humanity to a geometer's inability to square the circle.[8]

"Geometry," Dante wrote elsewhere, "is most white in so far as it is without stain of error, and is most certain in itself, and in its handmaiden who is called perspective."[9] Perspective, then the division of geometry pertaining to light, included within its jurisdiction the making of accurate pictures.[10] What could be more perfect for the transmission of God's wishes? By means of pictures, wrote Roger Bacon, "the literal truth might be evident to the eye, and as a consequence the spiritual truth also."[11]

All this might have led to nothing more than words and more words, but as poets and philosophers were speculating, painters were painting – and they, like musicians, had to produce actualities for assessment. After 1250 the space in Italian paintings began to assert itself; the aspic was starting to stiffen. The Virgin's knee that supported the Christ child began to nudge forward in a shy display of a third dimension. The parallels of walls, ceilings, steps, and moldings of buildings, rooms, and altars announced their relief by easing away from their traditional positioning parallel to

[8] Dante Alighieri, *The Divine Comedy: Paradiso,* trans. Charles S. Singleton (Princeton, N.J.: Princeton University Press, 1975), 146–7, 186–7, 376–9.

[9] *Dante's Convivio,* trans. William W. Jackson (Oxford: Clarendon Press, 1909), 111.

[10] David C. Lindberg, "Roger Bacon and the Origins of *Perspectiva* in the West," in *Mathematics and Its Applications to Science and Natural Philosophy in the Middle Ages,* eds. Edward Grant and John E. Murdoch (Cambridge University Press, 1987), 250–3, 258–9; Vasco Ronchi, "Optics and Vision," in *Dictionary of the History of Ideas,* ed. Philip P. Wiener (New York: Charles Scribner's, 1968–74), 3: 410.

[11] *The Opus Majus of Roger Bacon,* trans. Robert B. Burke (New York: Russell & Russell, 1962), 1: 238–42.

the picture plane, and began converging toward some vague area in the back of the picture. These innovations were especially apparent in the frescoes of the basilica in Assisi dedicated to the founder of the Franciscan order.[12]

Some art historians have speculated that Giotto di Bondone (1267 or 1277–1337) was one of the artists of the Assisi frescoes. There is no contemporary evidence to that effect, but it is tempting to accept the hypothesis because soon after the completion of the Assisi series he painted frescoes that unquestionably utilized and advanced perspective. Be that as it may, Giotto was unquestionably the master of the new art in the early fourteenth century.

Like Machaut, he was one of the first individuals in his field of art about whom we know much at all, and, again like the Frenchman, he was famous in his lifetime. Dante, who may have known him (our most familiar portrait of the poet may be by Giotto), praised him in *The Divine Comedy*.[13] Petrarch called him "the prince of painters" and owned one of his paintings: "The ignorant do not understand the beauty of this panel but the masters of art are stunned by it." Boccaccio said of him that he had "brought back to light an art which had been buried for centuries beneath the blunders of those who, in their paintings, aimed to bring visual delight to the ignorant rather than intellectual satisfaction to the wise."[14]

[12] White, *Art and Architecture in Italy*, 143–224.

[13] Giovanni Boccaccio, *The Decameron*, trans. G. H. McWilliam (Harmondsworth: Penguin Books, 1972), 494; Dante, *Paradiso*, canto 11, lines 94–6; Giorgio Vasari, *Lives of the Artists*, trans. George Bull (Harmondsworth: Penguin Books, 1965), 68; Thomas C. Chubb, *Dante and His World* (Boston: Little, Brown, 1966), 505–7; Patrick Boyde, *Dante Philomythes and Philosopher: Man in the Cosmos* (Cambridge University Press, 1981), 350.

[14] Chubb, *Dante and His World*, 505–7; Boccaccio, *The Decameron*, 493–5; Theodor E. Mommsen, *Medieval and Renaissance Studies*, ed. Eugene F. Rice, Jr. (Westport, Conn.: Greenwood Press, 1966), 212.

Figure 8. Giotto di Bondone, *Adoration of the Magi,* 1306. The Scrovegni Chapel, Padua, Italy. Courtesy Alinari / Art Resource, New York.

Giotto's contemporaries were impressed by the strong organization of his paintings, their combination of high emotion and utter dignity, and the indications of a third dimension (Figure 8). To our eye his paintings are sealed in by walls and rocky hills that crowd in on the central figures, but to the medieval eye, accustomed to pictures being as flat as blueprints, they seemed deep enough to step into. He positioned buildings and other rectangular structures at an angle to the viewer, with one corner thrusting forward, and walls and edges sweeping from that corner into the background. Some found such radicalism disturbing, and Petrarch,

taking on a curmudgeonly persona for a turn, complained of this
new kind of picture with its

> images bursting from their frames, and the lineaments of
> breathing faces, so that you expect shortly to hear the sound
> of their voices. It is here in that the danger lies, for great
> minds are greatly taken with this.[15]

Giotto usually painted his frescoes as if each were a scene
viewed by a single observer at a single moment, and in the Arena
Chapel at Padua he painted a series of frescoes as if the viewer
were looking at all of them from the middle of the chapel, much
as one might stand in a city square and, turning, look left and
right.[16] (The growth of cities constantly presented scenes to the
eye – long lines of market stalls, towers so tall they seemed to rear
back from the viewer – to stimulate curiosity about perspective. It
cannot be completely accidental that so many of the age's greatest
painters, from Brunelleschi to Michelangelo, were also architects
and several of them city planners.)

Giotto was a genius, but empirically, not scientifically, so.
He would have had little to add to Cennino d'Andrea Cennini's
suggestion to artists at the end of the fourteenth century that they
paint buildings so that "the moldings which you make at the top
of the building should start downward from the edge next to the
roof; the molding in the middle of the building, halfway up the
face, must be level and even; the molding at the base of the
building underneath must slant upward."[17]

One is usually sure in a Giotto painting which figure is closer

[15] John Larner, *Culture and Society in Italy, 1290–1420* (New York:
Scribner's, 1971), 268.

[16] Edgerton, *Heritage of Giotto's Geometry*, 76.

[17] Cennino d'Andrea Cennini, *Il Libro del' Arte: The Craftsman's Hand-
book*, trans. Daniel V. Thompson, Jr. (New Haven, Conn.: Yale University Press, 1933), 57.

to the picture plane than another, but unsure as to how far apart, forward to back, the figures are. His frescoes remind us of *porto-lani,* maps that indicated directions more accurately than distances, the first of which may have been drawn in his lifetime.[18] Attempts to draw accurate floor plans of Giotto's scenes would be futile, and when he felt that departures from single-viewer perspective would be helpful, he made them. In the Arena Chapel he painted two scenes of the bedroom of Anna, mother of Mary. The position of the observer appears to be identical for both scenes, but Giotto depicted the bed from two different angles. In the first fresco, in which an angel announces to Anna that she will be Mary's mother, the bed, behind the kneeling Anna and at the moment quite unimportant, is painted in what we would call proper perspective. In the second, Anna gives birth to Mary, and now the sacred bed is tilted up at an "absurd" angle so that we may see it better.[19]

Giotto and his contemporaries made a brave start at perspective, but their successors made little progress during the rest of the fourteenth century. The problem of "seeing" geometrically was more difficult than we, on this side of their revolution, understand. Taddeo Gaddi, Giotto's student and, in the opinion of some, his successor as the most prominent Italian artist of the century, stuffed *The Presentation of the Virgin* (Figure 9) with architecture to indicate the relative position of its many people, but his technique does not fulfill the purpose. If one lived in a world that looked like that, throwing a ball accurately to anybody more than a step or so away would be a matter of pure luck. Even two hundred years later, after the problems of perspective had supposedly been solved, Jacopo da Pontormo wisecracked that God had

[18] Edgerton, *Renaissance Rediscovery of Linear Perspective,* 97.
[19] White, *Art and Architecture in Italy,* 317–19.

Figure 9. Taddeo Gaddi, *The Presentation of the Virgin,* 1332–8. St. Croce, Florence. Courtesy Alinari / Art Resource, New York.

created man not in two but in three dimensions because thus it is "much easier to give life to a figure."[20]

We might blame the lack of further progress toward geometrical perspective on the general horror of the Black Death, but it was more likely due to the fact that Giotto and his school were trying to forge ahead on the basis of no more than artistic instinct.

---

[20] *Pontormo's Diary,* trans. Rosemary Mayer (New York: Out of London Press, 1982), 59.

They produced masterpieces – but not geometrically accurate depictions of space. That required something supplemental to artistic genius: theory.

Plato and Aristotle remained influential throughout the Middle Ages and Renaissance, one more than another at a given time, never one alone. In St. Thomas's and Oresme's time Aristotelianism surged forward, along with confidence in the trustworthiness of the immediate experience and of meticulous logic. Yet Platonism, with its penchant for intuition and for mathematics as manifestations of ultimate reality, survived, and resurged as Scholasticism began its slow slide into nit-picking.

In the fifteenth century the West gained access to the original sources of Platonic thought through translations of Platonic dialogues into Latin, the work of scholars of northern Italy.[21] That region, like France, had its universities and Aristotelian philosophers, but the centers of its intellectual and aesthetic vitality were its courts – Venetian, Milanese, Roman, and, above all, Florentine – and in these Plato restaked his claim to the patriarchy of Western intellectual tradition.

To illustrate: the Medici (originally bankers, we should note), who figured so prominently in the affairs of Florence for so long, craved possession not only of power, but of the best of ancient civilization that could be retrieved. Marsilio Ficino (a Christian, who managed the considerable feat of accepting Zoroaster as one of the Magi)[22] labored to guide and to answer Medician tastes. He provided translations of Plato and ancient Platonists, with commentaries, plus his own Neoplatonic treatises. He founded a

[21] James Hankins, *Plato in the Italian Renaissance* (Leiden: Brill, 1990), 1: 3–10.
[22] Ibid., 2: 461.

Platonic Academy through which he propagated his theories that the soul's path to the highest reality led, successively, through moral, natural, and finally mathematical philosophy. Among those who visited his academy or who otherwise participated in the Neoplatonic surge that swept the Italian intelligentsia in the fifteenth century were Nicholas of Cusa, whom we met in Chapter 5, who tried to find God by squaring the circle; and Leon Battista Alberti and Piero della Francesca, of whom we will hear more in this chapter.[23]

Fincino, his colleagues, and their like across Italy provided the intellectual milieu for a revival of the Platonic faith that numbers "have the power of leading us toward reality" and that "geometry is knowledge of the eternally existent."[24] In 1504 the young Raphael gave artistic expression to that faith in *Sposalizio,* a painting of the wedding of the Virgin Mary in which nearly every line leads back to a building that is either irrelevant (impossible!) or the perfectly symmetrical architectural emanation of the perfect God (Figure 10).

In the fifteenth century the distance between theory and practice vis-à-vis space proved to be shorter than it had been vis-à-vis time in the thirteenth and fourteenth centuries, because now Westerners

---

[23] Paul L. Rose, *The Italian Renaissance of Mathematics* (Geneva: Libraire Droz, 1975), 5, 9, 119–20; E. A. Burtt, *The Metaphysical Foundations of Modern Science* (Garden City, N.Y.: Doubleday, 1954), 53–5; Paul O. Kristeller, *Renaissance Thought and Its Sources* (New York: Columbia University Press, 1979), 58, 62–3, 151; Nesca A. Robb, *Neoplatonism of the Italian Renaissance* (New York: Octagon Books, 1968), 60, 61, 69; *Nicholas of Cusa on Learned Ignorance,* trans. Jasper Hopkins (Minneapolis: Arthur J. Banning Press, 1981), 52, 116–17; Hankins, *Plato in the Italian Renaissance,* 1: 344.

[24] *The Republic of Plato,* trans. Francis M. Cornford (New York: Oxford University Press, 1945), 241, 244.

Figure 10. Raphael, *Marriage of the Virgin*, 1503. Pinacoteca di Brere, Milan. Courtesy Alinari / Art Resource, New York.

could take a shortcut through ancient Greece. As already mentioned, there appeared in Florence in 1400 a manuscript of Ptolemy's 1,300-year-old *Geographia*.[25] Ptolemy, building on what Euclid had taught about the behavior of light and how people see, provided rules for depicting with geometric rigor a curved surface (that of the globe) on a flat surface (a map) via a gridwork (of latitudes and longitudes). The group upon whom, arguably, these rules had the earliest effect was not cartographers but painters.

The identity of the hero or heroes who first actually quantified pictorial art, that is to say, applied Ptolemaic techniques to making naturalistic, two-dimensional representations of three-dimensional scenes as seen by a single observer at a single moment, is not entirely clear. He or they were surely Florentine.

The hero, if there was but one, was Filippo Brunelleschi,[26] a prime example of the Renaissance man – clock maker, goldsmith, military engineer, and archaeologist, among other things. Like Nicholas of Cusa, he was a fanatical measurer, and unlike Nicholas, he actually measured a great deal. When he studied the monuments of ancient Rome, he measured and recorded their dimensions as multiples of a basic quantum, not with an unsegmented piece of string or a stick, as was common practice. His ambition was to be so great an architect that his name would be as durable as Giotto's as a painter. This he achieved by designing and directing the construction of the amazing dome of his city's Cathedral of Santa Maria del Fiore. (We should note, lest we forget that music continued on after *ars nova*, that Guillaume Dufay composed for the dedication of this cathedral in 1436 a motet, *Nuper rosarum flores,* whose isorhythmic proportions, 6:4:2:3, corre-

[25] Edgerton, *Renaissance Rediscovery of Linear Perspective*, 93–7.
[26] Martin Kemp, *The Science of Art: Optical Themes in Western Art from Brunelleschi to Seurat* (New Haven, Conn.: Yale University Press, 1990), 9, 12–14.

spond to the proportions of the nave, the crossing, the apse, and the height of the dome of the church.)[27]

We can be sure, with that dome as evidence, that Brunelleschi knew enough geometry to understand the problems of perspective. He may also have come upon examples of perspective in ancient Roman wall paintings and mosaics, and he certainly had access to Euclid and Ptolemy. But, like Giotto, he left no autobiography or explanations of his techniques, and the only testimonies to his accomplishment as a perspective painter were written after the fact.[28]

According to Michael Kubovy, the laurel wreath for discovering Renaissance perspective should go to Leon Battista Alberti, who invented it – and here Kubovy picks his words carefully – "as a communicable set of practical procedures that can be used by artists."[29] Alberti, illegitimate offspring of an old Florentine mercantile and banking family, was another Renaissance man, a prominent architect, city planner, archaeologist, humanist scholar, natural scientist, cartographer, mathematician, champion of the Italian vernacular, cryptographer, and, like Brunelleschi, inveterate measurer. He offered, if allowed to take precise mea-

---

[27] Vasari, *Lives of the Artists,* 139–40; Giorgio de Santillana, "The Role of Art in the Scientific Renaissance," in *Critical Problems in the History of Science,* ed. Marshall Clagett (Madison: University of Wisconsin Press, 1959), 49; Charles W. Warren, "Brunelleschi's Dome and Dufay's Motet," *Musical Quarterly,* 59 (Jan. 1973), 92–105.

[28] Vasari, *Lives of the Artists,* 135–6; Antonio di Tuccio Manetti, *The Life of Brunelleschi,* trans. Catherine Enggass (University Park: Pennsylvania State University Press, 1970), 42–6; Edgerton, *Renaissance Rediscovery of Linear Perspective,* 143–52; Lawrence Wright, *Perspective in Perspective* (London: Routledge & Kegan Paul, 1983), 55–9; Eugenio Battisti, *Filippo Brunelleschi: The Complete Work,* trans. Robert E. Wolf (New York: Rizzolli, 1981), 102–11; Michael Kubovy, *The Psychology of Perspective in Renaissance Art* (Cambridge University Press, 1986), 32–9.

[29] Ibid., 32–8.

surements, to make an exact facsimile in any scale of any statue of whatever quality or size, even as big as Mount Caucasus, even if in two halves in two places, one on the Aegean island of Paros, the other in Lunigiani in northern Italy.[30] He wrote in the 1430s an instructive little book on perspective, a milestone in the history of art.

Alberti was a beneficiary of the best education available and a member of a class that produced books. He, unlike most of his class, was familiar with the practical problems of making pictures – indeed, may have dabbled in painting himself – and was well qualified to explain theories of perspective to the world.[31]

The Albertian theory of perspective was based on ancient Greek optical theory, interpreted, expanded, and publicized by the Arabs, Grosseteste, Bacon, and others. "Seeing" was a matter of information being acquired by the eye through a cone (or, as it was often called, a pyramid) of light extending out from the eye. An accurate picture was a slice of that cone, vertical to its central axis, made at whatever distance from the eye the picture maker selected. That slice would be identical to what we could produce by sliding a photographic plate across the cone at right angles. Renaissance artists sometimes actually did place a pane of glass across the cone and painted directly on the glass. This would not do for frescoes on walls, but Alberti produced rules that would.

Alberti informed his reader that the first step in producing a picture in proper perspective was to orient the cone or pyramid of the artist's seeing. Its "centric line" would be the shortest possible line from the eye to the center of the scene one wanted to picture.

[30] Leon Battista Alberti, *On Painting and On Sculpture,* trans. Cecil Grayson (London: Phaidon Press, 1972), 125.
[31] Vasari, *Lives of the Artists,* 208–9; Joan Gadol, *Leon Battista Alberti, Universal Man of the Early Renaissance* (Chicago: University of Chicago Press, 1969), 3–7; Jacob Burckhardt, *The Civilization of the Renaissance in Italy* (New York: Harper & Row, 1958), 1: 149.

Then, Alberti advised, one should resort to a crude kind of spatial quantification by setting up a veil between oneself and the subject to be painted, a "thin veil, finely woven, dyed whatever color pleases you and with larger threads [marking out] as many parallels as you prefer." (You will remember that Ptolemy's *Geographia*, with gridwork of latitudes and longitudes, was currently de rigueur.) The reality beyond the veil's network should be observed only through the veil, presumably with the head and eye always in exactly the same position. The veil was the picture plane, the slice through the visual cone. One was to paint or draw not what one *knew* to be true about the scene — for instance, with parallel lines always the same distance apart — but strictly what one *saw*. What one saw was parallel lines angling toward each other the farther they extended away from the observer. One could measure how much they converged in appearance by gazing at them through the veil and counting threads. Then one would transfer *that* to a flat surface on which one had carefully drawn lines equivalent to the veil's threads. The veil enabled the painter to quantify not reality, but something more subtle: the *perception* of reality.

Veils and networks proved to be very helpful, but it was hard to "see" only what one actually saw. Some of the early attempts at Renaissance perspective have some very odd features. Structures lean sideways . . . or do they extend back from the picture plane? One cannot be sure which. (See the strange lean-to at the left side of the building in *The Nativity of the Virgin*, Figure 11.) Painters needed, in addition to the veil, geometrical technique.

Alberti supplied that, too. First establish the picture plane, the "window" through which the painter sees what he or she wants to picture. Then draw a person in the foreground, with feet at the bottom of the picture. The head is at the eye level of the artist because it and the artist's head are presumably about the same distance above ground, and it is also at the horizon level because

Figure 11. Master of the Barberini Panels, *The Birth of the Virgin*, fifteenth century. Courtesy the Metropolitan Museum of Art, Rogers and Gwynne Andrews Funds, 1935 (35.121), New York.

we always see level horizons – oceans, steppes – as level with our eyes. Next divide the height of the person in the foreground into three equal units. These will be the basic units, the quanta, of the picture. Then divide the baseline of the picture into these units. Select a point, the centric point of the visual cone, in the middle of the horizon line. Draw lines from the quanta markers at the base of the picture to this point, which is the "vanishing point" at which all lines at right angles to the picture plane (orthogonals) meet. (Think of orthogonals as railroad tracks extending straight out from the bottom of the picture, which of course do appear to converge at the horizon.) As these lines converge, so should objects decrease in height and size on the surface of the painting as they recede back from the painter's eye.

Draw horizontal lines across the converging orthogonals. The distances separating the horizontals should diminish at the same rate as the orthogonals converge (this in accordance with one of Alberti's most felicitous inventions, but one too complicated to describe here).[32] Thus we have the chessboard floor typical of so many examples of Renaissance art. (Alberti called the horizontal grid the *pavimento,* the name of the tile floors of houses of his day.)[33] This network, as drawn lines or grooves, can be detected beneath the paint of Masaccio's *Trinity,* painted about 1425, as well as many of the greatest masterpieces of Western art for generations after Alberti. The new perspective, called the *costruzione legittima,* is right out in the open to be seen as tiled floors in scores, perhaps hundreds, of paintings by Leonardo, Raphael, and

---

[32] Alberti, *On Painting,* 43–56. For those who want to proceed further, I recommend Samuel Y. Edgerton, Jr.'s *The Renaissance Rediscovery of Linear Perspective,* Lawrence Wright's *Perspective in Perspective,* Michael Kubovy's *The Psychology of Perspective and Renaissance Art,* and, of course, Leon Battista Alberti's *On Painting.*

[33] Edgerton, *Heritage of Giotto's Geometry,* 156; Edgerton, *Renaissance Rediscovery of Linear Perspective,* 45.

dozens of lesser artists. These lesser artists, in their innocence, sometimes stood St. John the Baptist on a patch of tiled paving in the wilderness and provided the stable in Bethlehem with similar flooring.[34]

Perspective joined the exalted company of the liberal arts. In 1493 Antonio Pollaiuolo included an allegorical figure of *Prospectiva* as one of the Liberal Arts grouped around the tomb of Pope Sixtus IV.[35] The sculptor's contemporary, Leonardo da Vinci, proclaimed that painting was more deserving of a place among the liberal arts than music "because it does not fade away as soon as it is born, as is the fate of unhappy music."[36]

The sagging tent of medieval space, which had collapsed and billowed in the wind of every influence but Ptolemy's, stiffened and became something to contend with. It had become homogeneous, equal, and preemptory in all its qualities in every vicinity, in all directions, and in all times. Renaissance artists, asked if the laws of optics beyond the moon were necessarily the same as those beneath, might have said no, but even so they obeyed the dictates of *costruzione legittima* in their paintings of heaven.[37]

The intellectuals of the Middle Ages respected mathematics in the abstract and tended to veer away from it in practice. Those of the Renaissance respected mathematics, especially geometry, and utilized it extravagantly in practice. Paolo Uccello's portrait (that

[34] Wright, *Perspective in Perspective*, 82.

[35] Edgerton, *Renaissance Rediscovery of Linear Perspective*, 91–2.

[36] *The Literary Works of Leonardo da Vinci*, 1: 76, 117.

[37] William M. Ivins, Jr., *On the Rationalization of Sight* (New York: Da Capo Press, 1973), 7–10, and Samuel Y. Edgerton, Jr., "The Art of Renaissance Picture-Making and the Great Western Age of Discovery," in *Essays Presented to Myron P. Gilmore*, eds. Sergio Bertelli and Gloria Romalus (Florence: La Nuora Italia, 1978), 2: 144; Edgerton, *Heritage of Giotto's Geometry*, 107.

Figure 12. Albrecht Dürer, *Draftsman Drawing a Reclining Nude*, 1538. Courtesy the Museum of Fine Arts, Horatio G. Curtis Fund, Boston.

is the name it deserves) of a smoothly rounded chalice as hundreds of tiny rectangular surfaces seen at different angles; Albrecht Dürer's print of an artist trying to solve the most intractable problems of foreshortening by glaring through an Albertian veil at a supine nude endwise from the toes up (Figure 12); Carlo Crivelli's almost vertiginous *Annunication* (Figure 13) – these and dozens of other examples impress us with the fact that the artists of the Renaissance avant-garde, who were often architects, engineers, artisans, and mathematicians as well as painters, were obsessed with space-as-geometry. Uccello, a painter who cared little about color – or about food and drink, for that matter – would, when his wife called him to bed, answer from his study, "Oh, what a lovely thing this perspective is!"[38]

There was also the matter of confidence in contemporary achievement, even in what we can call progress, a sort of faith in short supply among the early medieval intelligentsia and increasingly abundant among the artistic and protoscientific avant-garde in following centuries. Giorgio Vasari, the sixteenth century artist and biographer of artists, praised the painting of his age like an

[38] Vasari, *Lives of the Artists*, 95–104.

Figure 13. Carlo Crivelli, *Annunciation*, 1486. National Gallery, London. Courtesy Foto Marburg / Art Resource, New York.

operatic tenor singing of his inamorata. Once upon a time, he said, there had been classical Greek and Roman art, which was very good, and then medieval Western and Byzantine art (with saints "staring as if possessed, with outstretched hands, on the tips of their toes"), which was very bad. Then came Giotto and the rebirth of painting: he and his successors painted in direct imitation of nature. The greatest of them, according to Vasari, was his own contemporary, Michelangelo, who "surpasses not only those whose work can be said to be superior to nature but also the artists of the ancient world." The only obstacle preventing artists from producing even greater works than they already had, said Vasari, was that they were not paid enough.[39]

We pay Renaissance perspective our highest respect: we call it realistic. That, of course, leads to the question, what do we mean by realistic? We do not mean *truly* realistic, because it is rare indeed that we mistake a picture for the real thing. Vasari recorded the story of a painting of a horse by Bramantino so true to life that a real horse kicked it repeatedly, but, as you might expect, Vasari himself had never seen the picture.[40] What we mean by realistic is geometrically accurate; that is to say, you could use a picture constructed according to the principles of *costruzione legittima* as you can use a good map. In contrast, traditional Muslim pictures are exquisitely decorated surfaces without an illusion of real depth; and Chinese landscape paintings, which do offer an impression of great depth, do not have a fixed point of view.[41] Only a boor would not find these beautiful, but you would

---

[39] Ibid., 36–8, 45–7, 89, 93, 253–4.   [40] Ibid., 193.

[41] Wright, *Perspective in Perspective,* 305; Edgerton, "The Art of Renaissance Picture-Making," 2: 135; Yi-Fu Tuan, "Space, Time, Place: A Humanistic Frame," in *Making Sense of Time,* eds. Tommy Carlstein, Don Parkes, and Nigel Thrift (New York: Wiley, 1978), 7–16.

not want to make your way across even a room, much less a landscape, carrying a tray of full glasses with these pictures as your only guide.

In order to paint pictures that would be realistic by Western Renaissance standards, the practitioners of *costruzione legittima* were obliged to make choices as arbitrary as any made by Islamic or Chinese artists. To cite a few examples, Westerners depicted scenes, they thought, as if viewed in a single instant by a single eye. Most of us have two, which produces stereoscopic vision, but no matter. The eye can focus in a single instant on only the center of a scene, but no matter again. Giotto, Alberti, and company drew and painted scenes as they appeared to be at a single instant – and then took the time to move up and down, back and forth, in order to focus on their several parts.[42] Helpful, useful, justifiable, but in its way as arbitrary as showing St. Paul in a foundering ship and ashore and preaching to the heathen within one frame.

The Renaissance perspective masters chose to obey the laws of optical perspective as they apply to parallel lines stretching out in front of an observer, which appear to converge, but to ignore the fact that parallel lines that stretch out laterally appear to converge, as well. For the artist to draw these as he or she actually sees them would be to draw parallel lines that converge toward *two* different vanishing points, left and right. That would mean these straight lines would have to appear to *bend*. The only twentieth century artists who consistently obey this optical truth are, oddly enough, comic book artists seeking exaggerated effects.

After the quattrocento the stream of creativity that originated with Giotto, Brunelleschi, Masaccio, and Alberti split and ran off in two directions. One led to more art, eventually to the tortured

---

[42] Wright, *Perspective in Perspective*, 1–32; *Dante's Convivio*, 98; Graham Nerlich, *The Shape of Space* (Cambridge University Press, 1976), 63–4.

perspectives of the sixteenth century mannerist painters. The other led to more mathematics: projective geometry, invented by Girard Desargues (1593–1662), advanced by Blaise Pascal (1623–62), and today one of the principal branches of mathematics. Renaissance picture making may be the only art ever to have led to the creation of a kind of mathematics.[43] That validates it, for all its arbitrariness, as consonant in considerable part either with optical reality or at least with the way the human mind constructs reality.

Picture making veered close to mathematics, even melded with it, in the fifteenth century, more so than music had in the preceding century or two. The career of Piero della Francesca, who was born about the time when *costruzione legittima* was invented, and who died the year that Columbus set sail for what turned out to be America, provides evidence in support of that statement. Of Renaissance painters none was a greater master of mathematics, and of Renaissance mathematicians none was a greater painter.[44] Like Machaut, he came from an undistinguished family; yet somehow he became an apprentice to Domenico Veneziano, an expert in the new perspective and a colleague of Brunelleschi, Alberti, Masaccio, and Donatello. Among such men, according to Kenneth Clark, Piero "breathed the air of mathematical proportion."[45]

Piero wrote three treatises pertaining to arithmetic, geometry, and painting. The simplest of them instructed merchants and arti-

---

[43] Morris Kline, *Mathematics for the Nonmathematician* (New York: Dover, 1985), 232–41.

[44] Vasari, *Lives of the Artists,* 191; E. Emmett Taylor, *No Royal Road: Luca Pacioli and His Times* (Chapel Hill: University of North Carolina Press, 1942), 191; Kenneth Clark, *Piero della Francesca* (London: Phaidon, 1969), 70; Marilyn A. Lavin, *Piero della Francesca* (London: Allen Lane, 1972), 12.

[45] Clark, *Piero,* 10–16.

sans in the use of the counting board and in commercial procedures. For example, this is how to gauge the volume of a barrel:

> There is a barrel, each of its ends being 2 bracci in diameter;
> the diameter at its bung is 2 and ¼ bracci and halfway be-
> tween bung and end it is 2 and ⅔ bracci. The barrel is 2 bracci
> long. What is its cubic measure?

The answer, obtained after a flurry of calculation, is 7 and 23600/
54432 bracci,[46] a calculation and answer that show how deeply at
least some of the Renaissance Neoplatonists were acquainted with
practical quantification (and also illustrate how much Renaissance
mathematicians needed decimals!).

Piero's other two books, among the most important scientific
texts of the fifteenth century, were technical treatises on the making of pictures and geometry. Though a master of the subtle use of
colors, he ignored color in *De prospectiva pingendi,* a work refining the Albertian principles of picture making. Color was secondary, geometry primary. He devoted the third and last of his major
writings (which appeared posthumously in Luca Pacioli's *Divina
proportione,* of which more in Chapter 10) to the five regular
bodies of geometry. These, the tetrahedron, cube, octahedron,
icosahedron, and dodecahedron, had fascinated Plato and would
obsess Kepler a century later.[47]

Piero's devotion to Neoplatonism, mathematics, and his art is
nowhere more apparent than in his enigmatic masterpiece, *Flagellation* (Figure 14). Its Albertian vanishing point is rigidly certain,

---

[46] Michael Baxandall, *Painting and Experience in Fifteenth-Century Italy,*
2d ed. (Oxford: Oxford University Press, 1988), 86.
[47] Clark, *Piero,* 70–4; Arthur Koestler, *The Sleepwalkers: A History of
Man's Changing Vision of the Universe* (Harmondsworth: Penguin Books,
1964), 251–4.

Figure 14. Piero della Francesca, *Flagellation of Christ,* 1450s. Galleria Nazionale delle Marche, Urbino, Italy. Courtesy Alinari / Art Resource, New York.

but where is the center of interest? Is it the three men to the right in the foreground who stand together but seem to be ignoring one another? Or is it the party of men in the background centering on Christ (Christ in a background?), who is being whipped in a scene as bereft of direct emotional expression as a still life of a bowl of fruit?

The *Flagellation* is not a modern painting. It does not exemplify patriotic, class, ethnic, or even painterly values so much as piety. It is full of symbols of a Platonized and personal Christianity, and we do not and probably never will understand most of them, but (and this is the painting's special significance for us) they are almost entirely quantitative and geometrical. In their meanings, whatever they may be, they urge the viewer toward

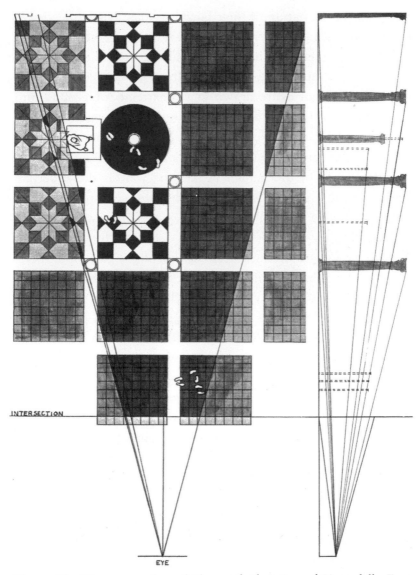

Figure 15. "Reconstruction of Plan and Elevation of Piero della Francesca's *Flagellation of Christ.*" R. Wittkower and B. A. R. Carter, "Perspective of Piero della Francesca's 'Flagellation,'" *Journal of Warburg and Courtauld Institutes,* 16 (July–Dec. 1953), plate 44.

mysticism. In the nature of their language, they hustle the viewer toward a mathematical perception of reality.

Painter-mathematicians of the quattrocento painted with a picture unit, a quantum, in mind. Alberti favored dividing the height of a human figure drawn in the extreme foreground into thirds, and used that third as his quantum.[48] The quantum Piero chose for *Flagellation* seems to have been the distance on the surface of the painting between the floor and the point at which the level glance of the painter strikes the wall at the Albertian vanishing point behind the man with the whip. Most of the floor of the visible area is taken up by large squares of brown tiles, each square eight tiles in width and eight in depth. Each of the tiles in the extreme foreground measures two quanta by two, and, therefore, each large brown square measures sixteen by sixteen of the quanta. The square at the center of which Jesus stands is composed of differently colored tiles in a complex geometrical pattern, but the whole square appears also to be sixteen by sixteen quanta. The distance between the centers of the two columns close to the picture plane is nineteen quanta. It is thirty-eight quanta, twice nineteen, from the group in the front to the closest of the figures in the group in the rear, the turbaned figure seen from the back. From him to Christ is another nineteen quanta. Christ's column, including the statue on top, is nineteen quanta high. The distance from the painter's eye to the plane of the picture, which can be calculated geometrically, is thirty-one and a half quanta; Christ's column is sixty-three quanta, twice times thirty-one and a half, behind the picture plane. All the main features of the painting – the foreground group, the nearest column, the turbaned figure, the man with the whip – all are at distances from the observing eye that can be expressed in multiples of the quantum times the forever

[48] Edgerton, *Renaisssance Rediscovery of Linear Perspective*, 42–3, 195.

mystical π. And on and on and on into the mazes of mystical mathematics.[49]

If you were a Neoplatonist Christian, you could consult Piero's *Flagellation* as a guide to the ultimate reality. If you were a crass secularist, you could confidently use it to buy and cut carpet and wallpaper for the whole scene[50] (Figure 15). Perhaps more than any other Renaissance masterpiece this painting confirms the judgment of the premier historian of Renaissance art, Erwin Panofsky, that perspective was the bellwether of the age: "Perspective, more than any other method, satisfied the new craving for exactness and predictability."[51]

[49] R. Wittkower and B. A. R. Carter, "Perspective of Piero della Francesca's 'Flagellation,' " *Journal of Warburg and Courtauld Institutes,* 16 (July – Dec. 1953), 293–302. For further quantitative analysis of this painting, see Kemp, *Science of Art,* 30–2. See also Marilyn A. Lavin, *Piero della Francesca: "The Flagellation"* (London: Allen Lane, 1972).

[50] Wittkower and Carter, "Perspective of Piero della Francesca's 'Flagellation,' " plate 44.

[51] Erwin Panofsky, *The Life and Art of Albrecht Dürer* (Princeton, N.J.: Princeton University Press, 1955), 1: 261. See also Suzi Gablik, *Progress in Art* (London: Thames & Hudson, 1976), 70.

CHAPTER TEN

Bookkeeping

We shall ever give ground to honor. It will stand to us like a public accountant, just, practical, and prudent in measuring, weighing, considering, evaluating, and assessing everything we do, achieve, think and desire.

Leon Battista Alberti (1440)[1]

Money, which represents the prose of life, and which is hardly spoken of in parlors without an apology, is, in its effects and laws, as beautiful as roses.

Ralph Waldo Emerson (1844)[2]

Inasmuch as all things in the world have been made with a certain order, in like manner they must be managed," wrote the merchant Benedetto de Cotrugli in the fifteenth century. Order was particularly necessary in matters "of the greatest importance,

[1] Leon Battista Alberti, *The Family in Renaissance Florence (1440)*, trans. Renée Watkins (Columbia: University of South Carolina Press, 1969), 150.
[2] Ralph Waldo Emerson, "Nominalist and Realist," in *Essays and Lectures* (New York: Literary Classics of the United States, 1983), 578.

such as the business of merchants, which . . . is ordered for the preservation of the human race."[3]

It is to be expected that merchants, who were herding the West into capitalism, patronizing practitioners of *costruzione legittima,* and marrying into the aristocracy, would think that in rationalizing their affairs they were doing humanity a favor. They may have been right, not perhaps exactly as they thought, but insofar as they were teaching humanity how to be businesslike.

The dictionary defines *businesslike* as efficient, concise, direct, systematic, and thorough. Nothing about courageous or elegant or pious, terms the noble and priestly classes might claim for themselves. *Businesslike* means careful and meticulous and, in practice, is a matter of numbers. It was one of the trails that led to science and technology insofar as its practitioners were quantitative in their perception and manipulation of as much of experience as could be described in terms of quanta. In their case the quanta were money – florins, ducats, livres, pounds, and so on. "Money," as Paul Bohannan has put it, "is one of the shatteringly simplifying ideas of all time, and like any other new and compelling idea, it creates its own revolution."[4]

Benedetto's or any other merchant's business – with merchants, with bankers, with providers of raw materials, with laborers, with customers – was complicated. There was the defensive tactic of hedging your bets: "My ventures are not in one bottom trusted," said Antonio in *The Merchant of Venice,* "nor in one place; nor is my whole estate upon the fortune of this present year." And there was the torrent of transactions. No merchant, Benedetto advised, should trust his memory "unless he were like King Cyrus, who could call by name every person in his entire

---

[3] *Medieval Trade in the Mediterranean World,* eds. Robert S. Lopez and Irving W. Raymond (New York: Columbia University Press, 1955), 413.

[4] Paul Bohannan, "The Impact of Money on an African Subsistence Economy," *Journal of Economic History,* 19 (Dec. 1959), 503.

army."[5] Musicians and artists conceivably might have clung to the skirts of their ancient muses and rejected quantification, but merchants, by definition, quantified their affairs and, in order to survive, made them visible on parchment and paper.

Consider, for instance, one short chapter in the career of Francesco di Marco Datini, the merchant of Prato who liked to begin his ledgers with "In the name of God and of profit." On 15 November 1394 he transmitted an order for wool to a branch of his company in Mallorca in the Balearic Isles. In May of the following year the sheep were shorn. Storms ensued, and so it was not until midsummer that his agent dispatched twenty-nine sacks of wool to Datini, via Peniscola and Barcelona in Catalonia, and thence to Porto Pisa on the coast of Italy. From there the wool traveled to Pisa by boat. There the wool was divided into thirty-nine bales, of which twenty-one went to a customer in Florence and eighteen to Datini's warehouse in Prato. The eighteen arrived on 14 January 1396. In the next half year his Mallorcan wool was beaten, picked, greased, washed, combed, carded, spun, then woven, dried, teaseled and shorn, dyed blue, napped and shorn again, and pressed and folded. These tasks were done by different groups of workers, the spinning, for instance, by ninety-six women in their homes. At the end of July of 1396, two and a half years after Datini had ordered his Mallorcan wool, it was six cloths of about thirty-six yards each and ready for sale. The cloths were dispatched via mule over the Apennines to Venice for shipping and sale back in Mallorca. The market there was dull, so they were sent on to Valencia and Barbary. Some sold there, and some were returned to Mallorca for final disposal in 1398, three and a half years after Francesco had ordered the wool.[6]

---

[5] *Medieval Trade in the Mediterranean*, 375; William Shakespeare, *The Merchant of Venice*, act 1, scene 1, lines 43–5; act I, scene 3, lines 17–20.

[6] Iris Origo, *The Merchant of Prato: Francesco di Marco Datini, 1335–1410* (Boston: David R. Godine, 1986), 61–2.

We may wonder at his patience, but – think a moment – how more wondrous was his ability to keep track of his business affairs, of which this matter of the Mallorcan wool was but one small part. How did this man even know whether he was a success or a bankrupt? Merchants like Datini were driven to invent bookkeeping just as physicists were later driven to take up calculus. It was their only hope of knowing what was going on.

Merchants of the West's late Middle Ages and Renaissance lived in a blizzard of transactions. Barges, ships, and mule trains connected the biggest cities and ultimately every European city with every other one in Europe and a number more in Asia, Africa, and America in the sixteenth century. Bills of exchange, the various kinds of promissory paper, and the practice of credit in general scrambled the normal sequence of events: production always preceded delivery, but payment might precede delivery or even production. And payment was a matter that must be called undulatory, with currencies and bills of exchange billowing and plunging in value in relation to one another.

The merchant struggling to make sense of his accounts was a stock figure in medieval stories. When the time came for one of that brotherhood in Chaucer's "Shipman's Tale" to reckon whether he "encreased were or noon," he collected his books and moneybags, laid them out on the counting board, ordered that no one disturb him, and left his wife with a lusty young monk. A virtuous woman, she knocked and cried,

> How longe tyme wol ye rekene and caste
> Youre sommes, and youre bookes, and youre thynges?
> The devel have part on alle swiche rekenynges!

He answered that he was busy, that commerce was a perilous business, that merchants "stonde in drede of hap and fortune," and sent her away – with predictable results. A neat and rational system of accountancy might have saved the merchant a great deal of "rekenygnes" — and even more.[7]

How does one keep track of a blizzard? A meteorologist does by keeping exact records, quantitatively, if at all possible. Merchants were obliged to do the same. Some were lazy and tried to hold the numbers in their memory. Datini complained that they were "like the carriers who reckon up their accounts twenty times along the road. . . . And God knows how they do! For four out of six of them have neither book nor ink well, and those who have ink have no pen." Others tried to write down everything. Cotrugli proclaimed that a merchant for whom the pen was a burden was no merchant. Benedetto Alberti, one of the patriarchs of the Leon Battista Alberti house, advised that the trademark of the good merchant was ink-stained fingers. Once, in 1395, Datini wrote so much he made himself sick. "Yestereve I was ailing, by reason of all the writing I have done in the last two days, without sleeping either by day or night, and eating in these two days barely one loaf."[8]

By keeping good books the good merchant saved himself from "a chaos, a confusion of Babel."[9] The key technique in achieving that end proved to be double-entry bookkeeping. Matthäus Schwartz, accountant to the Fuggers in the sixteenth century, called it a magic mirror in which the adept sees both himself and others.[10] Before we examine the mirror directly (in which I think we will see ourselves), we must go back several centuries before

[7] Geoffrey Chaucer, "The Shipman's Tale," *The Canterbury Tales*, in *The Complete Poetry and Prose of Geoffrey Chaucer*, ed. John H. Fisher (New York: Holt, Rinehart & Winston, 1989), 235–41.

[8] Origo, *Merchant of Prato*, 109, 185; *Medieval Trade in the Mediterranean*, 375; Alberti, *The Family*, 197.

[9] *Medieval Trade in the Mediterranean*, 377.

[10] Michael Baxandall, *The Limewood Sculptors of Renaissance Germany* (New Haven, Conn.: Yale University Press, 1980), 136, 231.

the Fuggers became great bankers. There were no accounts receivable or payable, very little loaning of money, and no accountants. There were no *companies,* no *firms,* no economic entities apart from the actual person or persons involved. One could not be a cog in a machine of a purely economic nature, because there were no such machines. The manor was economic, yes, but also familial, social, religious, and political. The monastery was often economically efficient, with platoons of laborers in its fields and tending its mills, but it was first and foremost religious.

The merchant of the early Middle Ages in many cases, especially in Northern Europe, was not much more than a peddler. He did not balance his books, because there were no such books. He did not balance his accounts any more than we do when, in the course of our lives, we discover on a Wednesday that the money we put in our pocket as we left for work on Monday ("walking-around money" in American vernacular) is nearly gone. Modern bookkeeping probably began with a sort of diary of the course of an individual businessman's life, a chronicle mixing notices of commercial transactions, military defeats and victories, and social events, all cheek and jowl with no more than a punctuation mark between – if that. The Italians called this a *ricordanza,* and that is all well and good, but how does one balance a diary?[11]

After the tenth century commerce increased in quantity, value, and the variety of goods involved. Merchants began to form partnerships in order to pool capital and expertise, and to hedge against failure, that is, to divide and distribute risk, to dismantle the single possible disaster into a number of individually survivable misfortunes. They discovered that partnerships had a perplexing nature: they often had shorter lives than the partners, but

[11] Edward Peragallo, *Origin and Evolution of Double Entry Bookkeeping* (New York: American Institute, 1938), 18–19. See also Origo, *Merchant of Prato,* 109.

sometimes outlived one or more of them. A partnership's debits and credits could also take on a quality of immortality: they almost seemed to be owed to and by the partnership rather than by the actual partners.

Then there was the matter of interest on debts and loans, which mounted with delay and could make confusion very expensive. There was the aggravation of doing business via representatives. As commerce increased, the great merchants stayed home from even the biggest fairs and operated by mail through partners and lieutenants permanently stationed in the chief trading cities. These obviously should report to their master, but exactly how should that be done? What should be reported and how? The slovenly way that a reeve of a manor reported to his lord would not do. It was too easy to shave the master's profits, as did the reeve in *The Canterbury Tales:*

> His lord well koude he pleson subtilly,
> To yeve [give] and lene hym of his owene good,
> And have many a thank, and yet a cote and hood.[12]

Even the most honest accountancy, if inexact, led to misunderstandings, misunderstandings to losses, and losses to anger. "You cannot see a crow in a bowlful of milk!" wrote the great Datini to one agent; and to another, "You have not the mind of a cat! You would lose your way from your nose to your mouth!"[13]

Records, concise and precise, were becoming a necessity. By 1366 Hindu-Arabic numerals began to appear in some parts of Datini's account books. That was an improvement, or at least the start of one, but for years afterward he and his accountants continued to use the narrative form, though the clearer and more abstract double-entry system was available. We have a continuous

---

[12] Chaucer, "General Prologue," *Canterbury Tales,* lines 610–12.
[13] Origo, *Merchant of Prato,* 98.

set of the books of Datini from 1366 to 1410, and they are all in
narrative form before 1383. A reader or auditor can learn a good
deal about the Datini business from them prior to 1383. But the
most important bit of information – was the business, at a particular moment, solvent or not? – is difficult to discern. Income and
outgo, what was owed to Datini and what he owed, are all woven
together in a single fabric. That is to say, reading Datini's pre-
1383 books is as confusing as life: it is easy to lose track of where
you are and of what you are trying to do. Then in 1383 he and his
agents and employees began to use a new method that at last made
bookkeeping clearer than life.[14]

About 1300, in that wondrous era of eyeglasses, clocks, *ars
nova,* and Giotto, some Italian accountants began using what we
call double-entry bookkeeping. Possibly, in its origins, it had some
relationship with algebra (from the Arabic *al-jabr,* and not by
accident), which also divides the grist that comes to its mill into
two categories, insisting that what is plus in one column can be
only minus in the other, and vice versa.[15] What we do know is
that at the beginning of the fourteenth century Rinieri Fini, agent
of a Florentine banking house at the fairs in Champagne, and
Tuscan merchants working out of Nîmes in the south of France
were keeping their books with assets and liabilities posted separately. This was just a beginning; yet to come were a number of
features of technical language, abbreviation, and form that we
consider characteristic of and even essential to bookkeeping. For
instance, in the fourteenth century many merchants recorded re-
ceipts in the front sections of their books and expenditures in the
rear and left it at that, making it hard to compare the two. Not
until 1366 did money changers in Bruges use the modern arrange-

---

[14] Peragallo, *Origin and Evolution of Double Entry Bookkeeping,* 22, 25.
[15] R. Emmett Taylor, *No Royal Road: Luca Pacioli and His Times* (New
York: Arno Press, 1980), 61.

ment with assets and liabilities in parallel columns on the same page or on facing pages, an arrangement they probably copied from Italian examples. In Tuscany it was known as *alla veneziana*, the Venetian manner. Datini's firm began experimenting with the new method about fifteen years later.[16]

An early example of double-entry technique, not yet fully realized but already single-mindedly *double*, might be useful here. On 7 March 1340 the Commune of Genoa bought 80 lots of pepper of 100 pounds each at 24 libbre and 5 soldi per lot. This expense – that is, outgo – was posted on the left side of the ledger. Over the next few days there were additional expenses for labor, weighing, taxes, and other things connected with the pepper, which also went down on the left side. Several sales of the pepper, all in March, were posted on the right side. Then the accountant, as far as the ledger indicated, turned his attention elsewhere for months. But double-entry bookkeeping has one commandment (many rules, but only one commandment) and that is that all accounts must be balanced, even if dishonestly, with a final admission of profit or loss. When the accountant of the Genoese Commune obeyed the precept of his profession and struck the balance the following November, he found that the expenses – purchase cost, taxes, and all – amounted to 2,073 libbre and 4 soldi. When he added up all income from the pepper, the sum fell 149 libbre and 12 soldi short of the expenses. That fact had to be recognized

---

[16] R. de Roover, "The Organization of Trade," in *Economic Organization and Policies in the Middle Ages,* eds. M. M. Postan, E. E. Rich, and Edward Miller, The Cambridge Economic History of Europe (Cambridge University Press, 1963), 91–2; Peragallo, *Origin and Evolution of Double Entry Bookkeeping,* 25; Geoffrey A. Lee, "The Coming of Age of Double Entry: The Giovanni Farolfi Ledger of 1299–1300," *Accounting Historians Journal,* 4 (Fall 1977), 79–95. See also the first ninety or so pages of *The Development of Double Entry, Selected Essays,* ed. Christopher Nobes (New York: Garland, 1984).

and acknowledged and the account balanced by writing 149 libbre and 12 soldi of undeniable loss at the bottom of the income column, which was the only proper way to bring that total up to the required 2,073 libbre and 4 soldi. If the shortfall had appeared at the bottom of the other column, that is to say, if the excess 149 libbre and 12 soldi were income, that would have been the profit, which the accountant would also have dutifully acknowledged. (The commune's bookkeeper, by the way, wrote the crucial amount, 2,073 libbre, in Roman numerals: IILXXIII. The initial "II" meant two of what you would expect to find at the beginning of such a big number, thousands.)[17]

Perhaps I should pause here to admit that double-entry bookkeeping guaranteed clarity, but not honesty. The commune's flyer in pepper appears to have been a flop, but it may have been something more subtle. Perhaps the commune was buying on credit and selling for cash to raise real money fast, or perhaps the whole deal was some sort of fiction to conceal the paying of interest, which the Church condemned as usury.[18]

The immediate significance of double-entry bookkeeping was that it enabled European merchants, by means of precise and clearly arranged records kept in terms of quantity, to achieve comprehension and, thereby, control of the moiling multitude of details of their economic lives. The mechanical clock enabled them to measure time, and double-entry bookkeeping enabled them to stop it – on paper, at least.

---

[17] Peragallo, *Origin and Evolution of Double Entry Bookkeeping*, 7–9.

[18] Ibid., 7–9; Raymond de Roover, "The Development of Accounting Prior to Luca Pacioli According to the Account-books of Medieval Merchants," in *Studies in the History of Accounting*, eds. A. C. Littleton and B. S. Yamey (Homewood, Ill.: Irwin, 1956), 132 (for another printing of the same article, see *Business, Banking, and Economic Thought: Selected Studies by Raymond de Roover* [Chicago: University of Chicago Press, 1974], 119–82); Origo, *Merchant of Prato*, 156.

Balancing the books was not in the beginning the sacred ceremony it is today. In the fourteenth and fifteenth centuries Florentine merchants were often sloppy in their bookkeeping, double entry or not, and were satisfied with balances that did not quite balance. The proverbial "close enough" was acceptable. They did not usually balance their books at any regular and preordained moment. Sometimes a year or two or more passed before they took up that arduous task. Sometimes they simply waited until the last page of a given ledger was filled. We can see, however, portents of our veneration of fiscal precision (swindlers are especially careful to genuflect when passing in front its altar) in the practices of some of the old businesses. The partners who managed the Avignon branch of Datini's business produced a *bilancio* at the end of every fiscal year. In a city swirling with intrigue and reeking with corruption, in the midst of recurrent waves of Black Death, dynastic war, and informal pillaging, Franciescho and Toro balanced the books. A representative balance sheet follows:

Accounts and closings of the secret red book No. 139 of the Avignon branch, page 7. Below will be entered the closing of a fiscal period, began October 25, 1367, and ended September 1368.

On September 27, 1368, we have in our stores merchandise, furniture, and fixtures amounting to 3141 fiorini, 23 soldi, and 4 denari, as shown in the account book.

f. 3141, s. 23, d. 4.

Accounts receivable, as shown in the memorandum book B and in the yellow ledger A, amount to 6518 fiorini, 23 soldi, and 4 denari.

f. 6518, s. 23, d. 4.

Total of merchandise, fixtures, and receivables amount to 9660 fiorini, 22 soldi, and 8 denari.

f. 9660, s. 22, d. 8.

Total liabilities, as per ledger, including in said sum the capital of the two partners, i.e. Franciescho and Toro, taken

from page 7 of this ledger, amount to 7838 fiorini, 18
soldi, and 9 denari.

f. 7838, s. 18, d. 9.

The profit for the fiscal period, October 25, 1367, to September 17, 1368, the length of which is ten months 22 days,
amounts to 1822 fiorini, 3 soldi, and 11 denari.

f. 1822, s. 3, d. 11.

The profit is divided into two parts, i.e., one to Franciescho
and one to Toro:

Credit Franciescho, on page 6, for his half of the profit,
amounting to 911 fiorini and 2 soldi.

f. 911, s. 2.

Credit Toro on page 6, for his half of the profit, amounting
to 911 fiorini, 1 soldo, and 11 denari.

f. 911, s. 1, d. 11.

The two men had an odd number of soldi, and so perhaps flipped
the last one to see who would get it. Franciescho won and got the
final soldo, and Toro only eleven denari, one short of a soldo.[19]

Today's accountant would use fewer words and less space,
and would clarify matters with ruled columns, thereby making
comparisons between items and totals simpler. Even so, the above
is a medieval miracle of rationality and neatness.

Luca Pacioli, often called the father of double-entry bookkeeping,
was certainly not the inventor, because he lived about two centuries after the event. But he was indisputably the first accountant to
combine his knowledge with Johann Gutenberg's technology to
instruct the world on the subject in print.

Pacioli was fortunate in the timing and place of his birth. He
was born in the middle of Italy's most glorious age, the quattrocento, in the little town of Borgo San Sepolcro. It was small and

---

[19] Paragallo, *Origin and Evolution of Double Entry Bookkeeping*, 27–9.

sleepy in comparison with Venice or Florence, but it was the home of Piero della Francesca, who may have accepted Luca as a protégé. A boy with a talent for numbers could have found few better mentors in all of Europe, and Piero thought well enough of Luca to include him in one or more paintings.[20]

When Pacioli became his own man he left Borgo San Sepolcro for Venice, where he lived in the home of a wealthy merchant and tutored his sons. The city, the European center of innovation in commercial arithmetic and bookkeeping and probably the first municipality ever to endow public lectures on algebra, was one of the best places in the world to study mathematics. There Pacioli studied, as well as taught, and he also may have traveled abroad as a factor for the father of his pupils, which would have provided him with firsthand experience with the new business practices.[21]

Pacioli met Leon Battista Alberti, possibly through their mutual friend, Piero. Alberti took him into his home and introduced him to the circle of influential men around the pope. To exploit that introduction an odor of sanctity was necessary, and in the 1470s Pacioli became a Franciscan. He was pious in his way, admonishing businessmen to write the name of God at the beginning of every memorandum book, journal, and ledger; and he was mystical in his appreciation of mathematics, as befitted a Christian Neoplatonist.[22] But he was a very different Franciscan from those of the generation who had founded his order.

Pacioli became one of the leading mathematicians in Italy and

[20] S. A. Jayawardene, "Pacioli, Luca," in *The Dictionary of Scientific Biography,* ed. Charles C. Gillispie (New York: Scribner's, 1970–80), 10: 269; Taylor, *No Royal Road,* 9, 20, 23, 119.

[21] Taylor, *No Royal Road,* 48, 53, 55.

[22] Ibid., 90, 91, 117, 121, 124, 149, 176, 264–5; *Pacioli on Accounting,* trans. and eds. R. Gene Brown and Kenneth S. Johnston (New York: Garland, 1984), 27.

taught at universities in Florence, Milan, Perugia, Naples, and Rome. He produced a number of books, including one on chess, a collection of mathematical puzzles and games, and a painstaking translation of Euclid. He was not an innovator, but a translator and compiler of books that were popular, and as such he is valuable to a historian. We can use Pacioli as an indicator of what book buyers, the literate elite of his age, thought was important.[23]

His two most important books were, in order of publication, *Summa de arithmetica, geometria, proportioni et proportionalita* (1494) and *Divina proportione* (1509). The first was a practical book written for anyone who could read and wanted to learn mathematics, both pure and commercial. As such, it is the most important of his works. The second was written for a narrower market, the courts of Renaissance Italy, with their dilettante nobles and attendant intellectuals. They all aspired to knowledge higher than basic arithmetic or geometry. The author of *Divina proportione* is the Luca Pacioli of Jacopo de Barbari's portrait, now in the National Museum in Naples (Figure 16). In it Pacioli is austere and pompous, one hand on an open volume of Euclid, the other holding a pointer resting on a figure of plane geometry. There is a geometrical solid to his left, a glass prism suspended in air to his right, and a noble patron in the near background staring at us to see if we are paying attention. *Divina proportione* was, like Piero's *Flagellation,* a product of the avant-garde intellectual fashion of the Italian quattrocento.

Pacioli completed the first part of the book in 1497 while he was a member of the duke of Sforza's brilliant court in Milan. There Pacioli had as a companion and an adviser Leonardo da Vinci, who must have found it easy to agree with a man who

---

[23] Jayawardene, "Pacioli," 270–1.

Figure 16. Jacopo de Barbari, *Portrait of Fra' Luca Pacioli,* c. 1500, Museo Nazionale de Capodimonte, Naples. Courtesy Alinari / Art Resource, New York.

wrote that seeing is the most noble sense and "that the eye is the entrance portal through which the intellect perceives."[24] It was Leonardo who supplied the geometrical illustrations for *Divina proportione.*

The book was Neoplatonic and even Neopythagorean, as the author made clear in the title. The first part was devoted to the divine proportion or golden section, which per se need not concern

---

[24] Samuel Y. Edgerton, Jr., *The Heritage of Giotto's Geometry: Art and Science on the Eve of the Scientific Revolution* (Ithaca, N.Y.: Cornell University Press, 1991), 148.

us here. We might note, though, that it fascinated Johannes
Kepler, too. A century later he affirmed that it was of higher
worth than the Pythagorean theorem. The latter, he said, we may
compare to gold, the other "we may name a precious jewel."[25]

The middle chapters of Pacioli's *Divina proportione* deal with
architecture, and the last part consists of Piero della Francesca's
unpublished treatise on the five fascinating Platonic solids. Pacioli
does not make it clear that the author of this section was his old
mentor and for this and other uncited borrowings has been
roundly condemned, all the way from the sixteenth century in
Giorgio Vasari's *Lives of the Artists* to the present day. The matter
is complicated because in some cases Pacioli actually did cite Piero,
and it is conceivable that the mathematical friar was the original
source of some of the artist's work in mathematics. There is also a
strong possibility that the compiling friar, frustrated with genu-
flecting to minds better than his own, was trying for a little ersatz
originality.[26]

Pacioli's earlier work, *Summa de arithmetica, geometria, proportioni et proportionalita,* is one of the most important compila-
tions in the history of mathematics. It is, in its six hundred closely
printed pages, an encyclopedia of the varieties of mathematics. In
the introduction the author announced to the newly numerate
of Europe that astrology, architecture, sculpture, cosmography,
business, military tactics, dialectics, and even theology were mathematical. He also included perspective, which he wanted added to

[25] H. E. Huntley, *The Divine Proportion: A Study of Mathematical Beauty*
(New York: Dover, 1970), 23. Those who want to pursue the subject of
divine proportion, Platonic solids, and such will do well to read this book.

[26] Paul L. Rose, *The Italian Renaissance of Mathematics* (Geneva: Libraire
Droz, 1975), 144; Jayawardene, "Pacioli," 269–70; Taylor, *No Royal
Road,* 251, 253, 262, 264–5, 268–9, 274–5, 334–55; Giorgio Vasari,
The Lives of the Artists, trans. George Bull (Harmondsworth: Penguin
Books, 1971), 191, 196.

the quadrivium, and music, which he declared to be "as nothing else but proportion and proportionality."[27]

Algebra and geometry, stimulated by fifteenth century translations of Archimedes and the other Greek mathematicians, were moving forward, and now there was a book in the Italian vernacular laying out the old and the new in black and white. Commercial arithmetic had been improving in clarity and efficiency for two centuries, and here was a clear explication of it all, plus a whole section on money and money exchange. Nearly every number in the book was written in the new, convenient Hindu-Arabic numerals (and, lest we think that the modern age had already arrived, the book included a whole page illustrating how to count from 1 to 9,000 by the ancient finger system).

The *Summa* was published twice in its entirety, the first time in 1494 and the second in 1523. It provided the foundation for many of the advances in mathematics, especially in algebra, of the sixteenth century. Mathematicians Girolamo Cardano and Niccolò Tartaglia paid tribute to its influence, and Raffaele Bombelli said that Pacioli was the first man since the thirteenth century's Leonardo Fibonacci to throw a new light on the science of algebra. For a half century that light shone bright, and then faded as brighter lights snapped on in Italy and France.[28]

Pacioli exerted the most enduring influence not as a seer of Neoplatonism or as a teacher of mathematics, but as a bookkeeping instructor. He supplied, in print, a clear, simple explanation of the technique. The section of the *Summa* on bookkeeping, "De computis et scripturis," was published separately in Italian, Dutch, German, French, and English editions in the sixteenth century,

---

[27] Ann E. Moyer, *Musica Scientia: Musical Scholarship in the Italian Renaissance* (Ithaca, N.Y.: Cornell University Press, 1992), 127, 132, 133; Jayawardene, "Pacioli," 270; Taylor, *No Royal Road,* 183, 190–5, 197.

[28] Jayawardene, "Pacioli," 270, 271–2.

and was plagiarized widely. In the nineteenth century his pages on bookkeeping appeared in German and Russian translations, and instruction books on double-entry bookkeeping published in the United States referred to the technique as in "the true Italian form," a tribute to the Italian inventors of the method and, as well, to Pacioli, who published his instruction book on the subject only a year after Columbus returned from his first voyage to America.[29]

Pacioli compared the successful businessman to "a rooster which is the most alert animal that exists, for among other things, it keeps night vigils in winter and summer, never resting."[30] Pacioli mentioned, in his explanations, that a busy merchant might expect to be doing business with banks in Venice, Bruges, Antwerp, Barcelona, London, Rome, and Lyon, and with partners, agents, customers, and suppliers in Rome, Florence, Milan, Naples, Genoa, London, and Bruges. These cities had different standards of weights and measurements, different currencies, and different ways of doing business. "If you cannot be a good accountant," Pacioli chided, "you will grope your way forward like a blind man and may meet great losses."[31]

Good bookkeeping was vital to good partnerships: "Frequent accounting makes for lasting friendship." Good bookkeeping allowed the merchant to discern profits and losses (what a physician might call "the vital signs") at a glance. Good bookkeeping provided a means to determine the trends, short and long term.[32]

The first step toward an accurate set of books was to find out

---

[29] *Pacioli on Accounting*, 8; William Jackson, *Bookkeeping: In the True Italian Form of Debtor and Creditor by Way of Double Entry, or, Practical Bookkeeping* (Philadelphia, 1801, 1818).

[30] *Pacioli on Accounting*, 33, 55, 76–8, 79, 99.

[31] Ibid., 98.   [32] Ibid., 9, 87.

where one was to begin with, that is, to make an inventory.[33]
This, advised the friar, should be accomplished in one specific day
because one's affairs might change from day to day. The *in-
ventario* should begin as follows, to give an example: "In the name
of God, on the eighth day of November, 1493, in Venice. The
following is the inventory of myself, of Venice, Street of the Holy
Apostles." Then one should list the contents of one's home and
shop: cash, jewels, and gold, designating each item by weight;
next clothing, describing the style, color, and condition of each
piece; silverware, again with a complete description, including not
only the weight but the alloy; then linens – bedsheets, tableclothes,
and such – and featherbeds, and so on. Next one should go to the
warehouse and record, in precise weight, number, and measure,
everything there: the spices, dyewood, pelts, and so on. Then one
should record all one's real estate and money on deposit, with
every detail about the location, rentals, and interest and the full
circumstances of each item of both. Finally, one should lay out in
black and white one's credit situation: how much money was
loaned out and to whom, with full names and references to perti-
nent records, and with an attempt at assessment; how much was
loaned to those who would pay it back, and how much to dead-
beats; how much was owed and to whom, again in detail.[34]

   That done, the businessman could begin current bookkeeping.
The books he should keep on that subject were three in number,
the memorandum book, the journal, and the ledger, of which there
might be several volumes each. Each volume should be marked
with "that glorious sign from which all enemies of the spiritual

---

[33] The sources of the following description of Pacioli's bookkeeping techniques are a neat summary of same on pages 64–75 of Taylor's *No
Royal Road* and pages 25–109 of Gene Brown and Kenneth S. Johnston's
translation, *Pacioli on Accounting.*
[34] *Pacioli on Accounting*, 28–33.

flee, and before which all the infernal pack justly tremble: the Sign of the Holy Cross." The pages of the volumes should be numbered so as to frustrate any who would tear out pages to conceal facts for dishonest purposes.[35]

The memorandum book should include notations of every transaction, large and small, in whatever currency was being used and in as much detail as time and circumstance allowed. Some merchants included their inventory in their memorandum books, but Pacioli advised against this because this book lay out on the counter where anyone might read it, "and it is not wise to let people see and know what you possess." The memorandum book was a sprawling collection of raw data from which the other two shapelier books were to be made. The journal (likewise kept where only the merchant and those he authorized could see it) was a dated record of the transactions scribbled in the memorandum book, with extraneous details eliminated and order imposed on the chaos of the raw data. For instance, each completed transaction entered in the journal should be expressed in terms of a single currency chosen by the firm, "since it would not be proper to total different kinds." For his "money of account" (see Chapter 3, this volume) Pacioli preferred Venetian coinage, based on the gold ducat. The gist of the journal was a matter of income and outgo, which, Pacioli recommended, should be expressed by the expressions *Per* for debit (we would say "from") and *A* for credit (we would say "to").[36]

The journal was the source for the ledger, where the double-entry bookkeeping was done. It was in the ledger that the businessman could learn before anyone else whether he was a success or a failure. Here every journal entry would be entered twice, with page references to the journal, the asset entry on one side and the liability entry on the other. Every transaction was a matter of

---

[35] Ibid., 37.   [36] Ibid., 43–5, 47.

gaining something – goods, services, a loan – in return for something to be provided now or in the future. Every transaction was double, in-and-out like breathing. Because each entry was double, the ledger was longer than the journal, so Pacioli advised making an index for it, with creditors and debtors listed alphabetically. (The latter was a useful practice merchants probably picked up, not necessarily directly, from the Schoolmen; again, see Chapter 3.)

To balance the ledger, Pacioli advised, take a piece of paper (available in Italy since the thirteenth century)[37] and list on the left side the debit totals and on the right the credit totals. Add the two columns separately and compare them. If the total of all the debits, "even if there were ten thousand," equals the total of all the credits, except for acknowledged profit or loss, then the accounts are in all likelihood accurate. If the sums are unequal, there is a miscalculation, omission, or falsehood somewhere. You will have to look for this or these "diligently." Every accountant since Pacioli is familiar with the task, a labor arduous enough to test even a Neoplatonist's faith in the symmetries of creation.

If the income was greater than outgo, all was well. If the opposite were true, that would be as undeniable as wormwood on the tongue: "May God protect each of us who is really a good Christian from such a state of affairs."[38]

Double-entry bookkeeping did not change the world. It was not even essential for capitalism. For example, the Fugger family made a great deal of money in the fifteenth century without resorting to it.[39] It was not an intellectual masterpiece like Copernicus's model

[37] Arnold Pacey, *Technology in World Civilization: A Thousand-Year History* (Cambridge, Mass.: MIT Press, 1990), 42.

[38] *Pacioli on Accounting*, 97.

[39] Joseph R. Strayer, "Accounting in the Middle Ages, 500–1500," in *Accountancy in Transition*, ed. Richard P. Brief (New York: Garland, 1982), 20–1.

of a heliocentric universe, and literati and cognoscenti have scorned bookkeepers' ledgers as no more glorious than the sawdust and shavings on the floor of a carpenter's shop. We revere Montaigne in his tower, San Juan de la Cruz in his cell, Galileo with his telescope, but the thought of Luca Pacioli with his ledger elicits no sense of awe. Indeed, the thought of him in such company strikes most of us as mildly absurd – a dray horse among thoroughbreds. But our tastes affect the development of our cultures and our societies less than our practices do. Bookkeeping has had a massive and pervasive influence on the way we think.

Double-entry bookkeeping was and is a means of soaking up and holding in suspension and then arranging and making sense out of masses of data that previously had been spilled and lost. It played an important role in enabling Renaissance Europeans and their successors in commerce, industry, and government to launch and maintain control over their corporations and bureaucracies. Today computers compute faster than friar Pacioli would ever have dreamed possible, but they do so within the same framework (accounts payable, accounts receivable, and all) as he did. The efficient friar taught us how to oblige grocery stores and nations, which are always whizzing about like hyperactive children, to stand still and be measured.

The Venetian style, *alla veneziana,* encouraged us in our often useful and sometimes pernicious practice of dividing everything into black or white, good or evil, useful or useless, part of the problem or part of the solution – either this or that. When Western historians look for the founts of our enduring Manichaeism, they point to the Persian prophet Manes himself and to Aristotle and his concept of the "excluded middle." Let me suggest that the influence of these men has been less than that of money, which speaks to us so eloquently in balance sheets. Money is never middle-ish. Every time an accountant has divided everything within his or her purview into plus or minus, our inclination to categorize all experience as this or as that has gained validation.

In the past seven centuries bookkeeping has done more to shape the perceptions of more bright minds than any single innovation in philosophy or science. While a few people pondered the words of René Descartes and Immanuel Kant, millions of others of yeasty and industrious inclination wrote entries in neat books and then rationalized the world to fit their books. Precision, indispensable to our science, technology, economic and bureaucratic practice, was rare in the Middle Ages, and even more rarely quantitative. In the sixth century, for instance, Bishop Gregory of Tours toted up the number of years since Creation and, according to our manuscripts of his work, misadded by 271 years. Few medieval readers seem to have noticed or, if they did, to have cared.

In contrast to Gregory's imprecision, read the following, offered by Pacioli as a model entry for a memorandum book. It seems from another world, which in a manner of speaking it was.

> On this day, we have (or I have) bought from Filippo de Ruffoni of Brescia, twenty pieces of white Bresciani cloth. They are stored in Stefano Tagliapietra's vault and are of so many arm lengths apiece, as agreed upon. They cost twelve ducats each and are marked with a certain number. Mention if the cloth is made of triple warpcord, four to five arm lengths square, wide or narrow, fine or medium, whether Bergamene, Vicenzan, Veronese, Paduan, Florentine, or Mantuan. State whether the transaction was made entirely for cash, or part only for cash and part on time. State when the balance is due or whether payment was partly for cash and the remainder in goods.[40]

As Pacioli wrote, bourgeois Italian students, attending not cathedral schools or universities, but *abacco* schools (you might call them trade schools for merchants and their aides),[41] were honing their mathematical skills on such problems as this:

---

[40] *Pacioli on Accounting*, 40.

[41] Paul F. Grendler, *Schooling in Renaissance Italy: Literacy and Learning, 1300–1600* (Baltimore: Johns Hopkins Press, 1989), 22–3, 306–23.

> Three men, Tomasso, Domenego, and Nicolo, entered into partnership. Tomasso put in 760 ducats on the first day of January, 1472, and on the first day of April took out 200 ducats. Domenego put in 616 ducats on the first day of February, 1472, and on the first day of June took out 96 ducats. Nicolo put in 892 ducats on the first day of February, 1472, and on the first day of March took out 252 ducats. And on the first day of January, 1475, they found they had gained 3168 ducats, 13 grossi and $\frac{1}{2}$. Required is the share of each, so that no one shall be cheated.[42]

In 1200 St. Francis of Assisi, who lived in a world that seethed and smoked with mysterious and uncontrollable forces, achieved fulfillment by embracing poverty. Three hundred years later the Franciscan Luca Pacioli wrote a classic of reductionism, laying out the techniques for reducing the world to pluses and minuses, for reducing the world to something visual, quantitative, and, therefore, understandable and possibly controllable. He received from the pope a dispensation to own property, and seems to have bequeathed five hundred ducats to his heirs.[43]

Figure 17 illustrates the last one of Pacioli's pages on bookkeeping. The top third is a discussion of "Items That Require Recording by Businessmen," the bottom two-thirds "An Illustration of Ledger Postings." How odd to see Italian in black letter, now usually called Gothic script, which was common everywhere in the 1490s. Note Pacioli's use of Hindu-Arabic numerals except for the biggest number of all, the year. Like us, Pacioli reverted to Roman numerals for the large, the grand, the awesome effect. "Use the ancient letters in making this entry, if only for the sake of more beauty," he advised, though, he added, "it does not matter."[44]

[42] Frank J. Swetz, *Capitalism and Arithmetic: The New Math of the 15th Century* (La Salle, Ill.: Open Court, 1987), 139.

[43] Taylor, *No Royal Road*, 359, 370–3, 379, 381.

[44] *Pacioli on Accounting*, 51, 107–9.

Distinctio nona. Tractatus.xj°. De scripturis

Casi che acade mettere ale recordançe del mercante.

Utte lemasserizie di casa o di bottega che tu ti truoui. Ma vogliono essere per ordine. cioe tutte le cose di ferro da perse con spatio da potere agiongnere se bisognasse. E cosi da segnare in margine quelle che fussino perdute o vendute o donate o guaste. Ma non si intende masserizie minute dipoco valore. E fare ri cordo di tutte le cose dottone da perse comme e vetro. E simile tutte le cose distagno. E si mile tutte lecose dilengno. E cosi tutte le cose dirame. E cosi tutte le cose dariento e doro zc. Sempre con spatio di qualche carta da potere arrogere se bisognasse. e cosi vadare notan di quello che mancasse. Tutte lemalleuerie o obbrighi o promesse che promettessi per ql che amico. e chiarire bene che e comme. Tutte lemercantie o altre cose che ti fossero las sate i guardia o a serbo di pstança da qlche amico. e cosi tutte lecose ch tu pstassi'a altri tuoi amici. Tutti limercati conditionati cioe compre ovedite come p ereplo uno contrato cioe ch tu mi mandi con lepprossime galee che torneranno dinghilterra tanti cantara di lane velimi stri'a caso che le sieno buone e recipienti. Jo ti daro tanto del cantaro o del cento o verame te ti mandaro alincontro tanti cantara di cottoni. Tutte le case o possessioni o botteghe o gioie che tu affitassi a tanti duc.o a tante lire lanno. E quando tu riscoterai ilfitto aloza ql lidinari sanno a mettere al libro comme disopra ti dissi. Prestando qualche gioia o uasella menti dariento o doro a qualche tuo amico per otto o quidici giorni diqueste tale cose no si mettono al libro. ma sene fa ricordo ale ricordançe. perche fra pochi giorni lai bariauere. E cosi per contra se a te fossi pstato simili cose non li debbi mettere al libro. Ma farne me moria alericordançe perche presto lai a rendere.

Comme si scriuono lire e soldi e danari picioli e altre abreuiature.

Lire soldi danari picioli libbre once danarpesi grani carati ducati fiorin larghi.
℔   ℔   ᛞ   ℔   libbre   ℔   ℔ᵖ   g°.   ℞   duc.   fio.lar

Còme si debbe dettare le ptite de debitori.
Mcccc° Lxxxxiij°.

Lodouico dipiero forestan devare a di.xiiii.nouembre. 1493.℔.44.ʄ.1:ᛞ.8.porto contani in pstaça. posto cas sa auere. a car. 2

8   44 ʄ1 ᛞ8.

E a di.18.detto ℔.18.ʄ.11.ᛞ. 6.promettemo p lui a marti no dipiero foraboschi asuo piacer posto bere i qsto.a c.2.℔ 18 ʄ11 ᛞ6.

Cassa i mano di simone da lesso bobeni de dar adi.14. nouebre 1493. 8.62.ʄ.13. ᛞ.2.da francesco dantonio caualcanti in qsto a c.2

8   62 ʄ13 ᛞ6.

Martino di piero fora bo schi de dare a di.20.nouem bre.1493.℔.18.ʄ.11.ᛞ.6.por to luimedesimo contani po sto cassa a car. 2.

8   18 ʄ11 ᛞ6.

Francesco dantonio caual cati de dare a di.12.di noue bre.1493.℔.20.ʄ.4.ᛞ.2.cl.p misse anostro piacer p lodo uico di pieroforestan a c.2.

8   20 ʄ4 ᛞ2.

Còme si debbe dittare leptite di creditori.
Mcccc° Lxxxxiiij.

Lodouico dipiero forestan de hauere a di.22.nouebre 1493.℔.20.ʄ.4.ᛞ.2.sono p parte di pagamento. E per lnicelia promissi a nostro piacere fracescho datonio. caualcatn posto dare a c.2.℔

20 ʄ4 ᛞ2.

Cassa in mano di simone dalesso bobeni de hauere a di.14.nouebre.1493.℔.44. ʄ.1.ᛞ.8.alo douico di piero forestani in qsto. a car. 2. ℔

44 ʄ1 ᛞ8.

E a di.22.nouembre.1493 ℔.18.ʄ.11.ᛞ.6.a martino di piero foraboschi.a ca. 2. ℔

18 ʄ11 ᛞ6.

Martino di piero fora bo schidi hauere a di.18.noue bre.1493.℔.18.ʄ.11.ᛞ.6.gli pmettemo a suo piacere p lodouico di piero forestan posto obbi bere i qsto a c.2.℔

18 ʄ11 ᛞ6.

Francescho datonio caual canti de hauere a di.14.no uebre.1493.℔.62.ʄ.13.ᛞ.6. reco lui medesimo ptan po sto cassa dare a.car.2. ℔

62 ʄ13 ᛞ6.

Figure 17. A page from Luca Pacioli on bookkeeping, 1494. John B. Geijsbeek, *Ancient Double-Entry Bookkeeping* (Houston: Scholar's Book Co., 1974), 80.

PART THREE

Epilogue

For many parts of nature can neither be invented with sufficient subtilty nor demonstrated with sufficient perspicuity nor accomodated unto use with sufficient dexterity, without the aid and intervening of the Mathematics: of which sort are Perspective, Music, Astronomy, Cosmology, Architecture, Enginery, and divers others.

Francis Bacon (1605)

I often say that when you can measure what you are speaking about and express it in numbers you know something about it; but when you cannot measure it, when you cannot express it in numbers, your knowledge is of a meagre and unsatisfactory kind.

William Thompson, Lord Kelvin (1891)

CHAPTER ELEVEN

The New Model

Beginning in the miraculous decades around the turn of the fourteenth century (decades unmatched in their radical changes in perception until the era of Einstein and Picasso) and continuing on for generations, sometimes swiftly, sometimes sluggishly, sometimes in one terrain of *mentalité* and sometimes another, Western Europeans evolved a new way, more purely visual and quantitative than the old, of perceiving time, space, and material environment.

Vision was and is a martinet and an aggressor, encroaching on the realms of the other senses. Record events in chronological order on parchment or paper and you have a time machine. You can step back and observe beginnings and endings simultaneously. You can alter time's direction, and you can halt time so as to examine individual events. If you are an accountant, you can proceed backward to find a mistake; you can construct a balance sheet like a still photograph of the whistling storm of transactions.

You can compare in detail one sequence with another, or supplement the one with another or several others, all running at their own rates. Or you can begin with now and trigger a retrogression, or even a retrogression and a progression simultaneously.

Western composers pioneered such adventures in the thirteenth and fourteenth centuries, creating masterpieces to delight musicians and mathematicians alike to this day.

Vision empowered its aficionados to see and think of space geometrically. Awed by light that expanded, instantly, it seemed, in cones and globes of radiation, light that was the one discernible thing that behaved with the neatness of diagrams in a Euclidean text, they let vision guide them to Renaissance perspective and some of the greatest works of art of all the ages, and thence to a new astronomy.

The greatest advantage the aficionados of sight gained was simply its compatibility with measurement in terms of uniform quanta. St. Bonaventure, Schoolman and minister general of the Franciscans, proclaimed that "God is light in the most literal sense";[1] ipso facto, it functioned *uniformly* throughout time and space. The luminous-numinous implication was that a league, if measured precisely, would be found to be the same everywhere and at all times, and so would an hour. Westerners, monotheists fascinated with light, gloried in *pantometry*.

In practical terms, the new approach was simply this: reduce what you are trying to think about to the minimum required by its definition; visualize it on paper, or at least in your mind, be it the fluctuation of wool prices at the Champagne fairs or the course of Mars through the heavens, and divide it, either in fact or in imagination, into equal quanta. Then you can measure it, that is, count the quanta.

Then you possess a quantitative representation of your subject that is, however simplified, even in its errors and omissions, pre-

---

[1] Patrick Boyde, *Dante, Philomythes and Philosopher* (Cambridge University Press, 1981), 210. For a succinct statement of Bonaventure's theory of light, see David C. Lindberg, "The Genesis of Kepler's Theory of Light: Light Metaphysics from Plotinus to Kepler," *Osiris*, n.s., 2 (1986), 17.

cise. You can think about it rigorously. You can manipulate it and experiment with it, as we do today with computer models.[2] It possesses a sort of independence from you. It can do for you what verbal representation rarely does: contradict your fondest wishes and elbow you on to more efficacious speculation. It was quantification, not aesthetics, not logic per se, that parried Kepler's every effort to thrust the solar system into a cage of his beloved Platonic solids and goaded him on until he grudgingly devised his planetary laws.[3]

Visualization and quantification: together they snap the padlock − reality is fettered (at least tightly enough and for long enough to get some work out of it and possibly a law of nature or two).

Nature seemed to be agreeable to this approach (the greatest of miracles), and the human mind to be good at visualization and numbers: "These [numbers] alone we apprehend correctly," Kepler said four hundred years ago, "and if piety permits to say so, our comprehension is in this case of the same kind as God's, at least insofar as we are able to understand it in this mortal life."[4]

As early as 1444 Bessarion, the Byzantine ambassador and cardinal, wrote home that young Greeks should be sent secretly to Italy to learn craft skills.[5] Already Westerners were leading the world in the invention and utilization of machinery. At the end

[2] There are many sources for these last few paragraphs. Most important among them are the previously cited works of Walter J. Ong and Samuel Y. Edgerton, Jr. See also Bruno Latour, "Visualization and Cognition: Thinking with Eyes and Hands," *Knowledge and Society: Studies in the Sociology of Culture Past and Present, A Research Annual,* 6 (1986), 1−40.

[3] Arthur Koestler, *The Sleepwalkers: A History of Man's Changing Vision of the Universe* (Harmondsworth: Penguin Books, 1964), 276.

[4] Ibid., 535.

[5] A. G. Keller, "A Byzantine Admirer of 'Western' Progress: Cardinal Bessarion," *Cambridge Historical Journal,* 11, no. 3 (1955), 22−3.

of the century they were abreast or drawing ahead of others in cartography, navigation, astronomy, commercial and banking procedures, and practical and theoretical mathematics. By the end of the next century they had lengthened their old leads and had attained new ones.

The West's lead overall was not nearly as great as in the nineteenth century (when the gap became, so to speak, a matter of the steamboat versus the junk and dhow), and in some areas the West still lagged behind. For example, the Ottoman armies were better organized and trained and demonstrably superior to the West's: in 1529 the Turks were at the gates of Vienna. For another example, the Chinese version of the heavens, with no crystal spheres but celestial bodies floating in space, was closer to the truth than the West's. But Westerners' lead in the way they *perceived* reality and could, thereby, reason about and then manipulate it was enormous. They were cultivating what Eviatar Zerubavel calls the rationalistic character of modern culture: "precise, punctual, calculable, standard, bureaucratic, rigid, invariant, finely coordinated, and routine."[6] All, we might add, pertain to or at least smack of the visual and quantitative.

Printing amplified the prestige of visualization and accelerated the spread of quantification. The demand for more books had engendered *stationeries* (publishing houses, one might call them) around the universities, where scribes using the new Gothic script copied more books faster than ever before.[7] Then, in the 1450s, a metalworker in Mainz, Germany, Johann Gutenberg, began print-

---

[6] Eviatar Zerubavel, *Hidden Rhythms: Schedules and Calendars in Social Life* (Chicago: University of Chicago Press, 1967), xvi.

[7] Geo. Haven Putnam, *Books and Their Makers During the Middle Ages* (New York: Putnam's, 1896), 10–11, 184–6, 205; Curt F. Bühler, *The Fifteenth Century Book* (Philadelphia: University of Pennsylvania Press, 1960), 22.

ing books with movable type, specially formulated inks, and a printing press adapted from the ancient wine press. That event was far more significant than the contemporaneous fall of Constantinople to the Turks, though not a soul thought so at the time.

Printing (a single arbitrary title for a combination of inventions) spread faster than anything new and mechanical since the clock. By 1478 they were printing in London, Cracow, Budapest, Palermo, Valencia, and a number of cities in between. By the next century millions of books had been printed.[8] Unlike the societies of the East the West was hungry to learn by staring at standardized marks on paper.

The full range of effects of that hunger is too broad to consider here and already has been analyzed extensively and insightfully by Elizabeth L. Eisenstein.[9] We will content ourselves with one last archaeological trench, one cutting through strata directly subject to the seismic influence of printing.

Western scientific and engineering illustration reached an early and artistically unsurpassed peak in the 1400s and 1500s. In the half century before Europe's first printed book, Mariano di Jacopo, usually called Taccola, had utilized the pictorial devices of Giotto and Alberti (the perception of the picture as a window through which the viewer sees a visually realistic scene from a single point of view) to initiate modern engineering drawing. The

[8] Carlo M. Cipolla, *Before the Industrial Revolution: European Society and Economy, 1000–1700* (New York: Norton, 1980), 179; Elizabeth L. Eisenstein, *The Printing Revolution in Early Modern Europe* (Cambridge University Press, 1983), 13–16; Hermann Kellenbenz, "Technology in the Age of the Scientific Revolution, 1500–1799," in *The Fontana Economic History of Europe: The Sixteenth and Seventeenth Centuries,* ed. Carlo M. Cipolla (London: William Collins, 1974), 180; Fernand Braudel, *Civilization and Capitalism, 15th–18th Century,* 1: *The Structures of Everyday Life: The Limits of the Possible,* trans. Siân Reynolds (New York: Harper & Row, 1981), 400.

[9] Eisenstein, *The Printing Revolution.*

next generation or two of artists and artistic artisans invented many of the pictorial conventions — the cutaway view, the perspective section, the transparent view — by which the engineer, architect, anatomist, botanist, and others show the reader what would be impossible to describe clearly in words. Francesco di Giorgio Martini sketched for us the verbally indescribable double-reciprocal flap-valve pump, and Leonardo da Vinci displayed in one drawing the familiar exterior of the left side of the face of a skull and, in a cutaway view of the right side, the mysterious interior.[10]

With printing, the utility and significance of the precise technical illustration bounded ahead. Scribes might reproduce writing with no more than minor omission and error, but never complex or subtle illustrations. (Imagine asking poor students, scribbling in a stationery shop in order to earn enough money to pay their fees, to provide a hundred copies of Leonardo's depiction of the skull.) Printers, on the other hand, could produce perfect copy after copy of whatever plate, be it wood or metal or stone, they locked into their presses.

Luca Pacioli provided a print in perspective of the icosahedron that defined in a flash the twenty-sided solid for the confused geometry student. Cesare Cesariano provided a hybrid of picture and diagram to make clear both the actual operation and the geometric function of the lever. The trend climaxed in the middle decades of the sixteenth century with the publication of technical drawings in Georg Bauer Agricola's *De re metallica;* with the elegant illustrations in Agostino Ramelli's *Diverse et artificiose machine;* and with what are to this day the scientifically inspirational and artistically incomparable illustrations of human anat-

---

[10] Samuel Y. Edgerton, Jr., *The Heritage of Giotto's Geometry: Art and Science on the Eve of the Scientific Revolution* (Ithaca, N.Y.: Cornell University Press, 1991), 126, 129, 131, 136–7, 142.

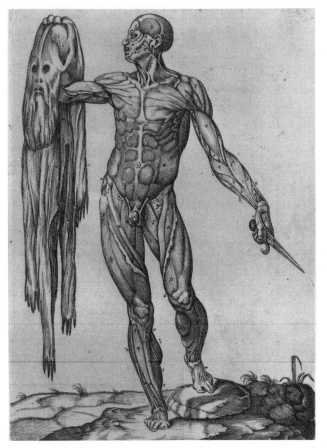

Figure 18. A page from Juan Valverde di Hamusco's *Anatomia del corpo humano*, 1560. Courtesy Harry Ranson Humanities Research Center, University of Texas, Austin.

omy in Andreas Vesalius's *De humani corporis fabrica*.[11] (See Figure 18 for a crib of Vesalius's style by a lesser artist and anatomist, Juan Valverde di Hamusco.) It is not easy to imagine the scientific revolution of the late sixteenth and seventeenth cen-

[11] Ibid., 168, 172, 181, 182, 188, 190.

turies, in which so much was visualized preparatory to and in the process of analysis, without the printed illustration.

Renaissance perspective gave Westerners the means not only to produce on flat surfaces accurate depictions of material reality, but also to play with them, to pull and stretch them in controlled and useful ways. Humans could play god, at least in two dimensions. Albrecht Dürer, building on what Alberti had taught, published a treatise in 1537 of advanced analysis and instruction about perspective. He illustrated how the human face, drawn on an Albertian grid, could be stretched this way and that, altering the shape of the whole but, surprisingly, never the proportions of the features (Figure 19).

Dürer's book circulated among cartographers, just as Ptolemy's had among artists. Abraham Ortelius, the great Dutch mapmaker, owned a copy, and it is likely that Gerardus Mercator was also familiar with Dürer on perspective.[12] It is likely that Dürer provided at least part of the inspiration for the greatest visual-cum-quantitative tour de force of the sixteenth century, that which we call to this day Mercator's projection.

The *portolani* charts, which were only a bit more sophisticated than freehand sketches of coastlines, sufficed for the closed seas of Europe, but on voyages into unknown waters the old maps and the old wisdom were useless. Sailors were obliged to bet the lives of their ships and themselves not only on the compass for direction, but on devices, new to them if not to astronomers, like the astrolabe, quadrant, and cross-staff, for judging position by the locations of heavenly bodies. When the North Star finally slid below the horizon of the Portuguese bound for southern Africa and India, they learned to reckon their north–south position by taking the altitude, the *altura,* of the sun at noon.

These devices and accumulating blue water experience helped

[12] Ibid., 173–8.

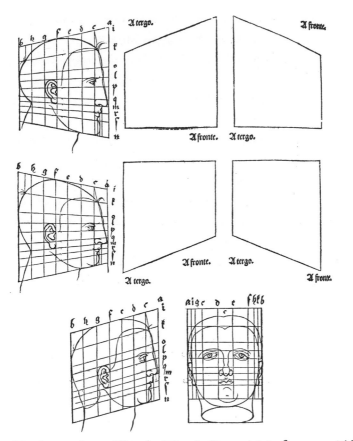

Figure 19. A page from Albrecht Dürer's *De varietate figurarum*, 1537. Owned by Abraham Ortelius. Courtesy Chapin Library of Rare Books, Williams College, Williamstown, Mass.

Western Europeans to cross oceans and find their way back, but there was still much guesswork. Navigators needed accurate charts in order to lay compass courses. Maps with equally spaced longitude and latitude lines drawn at right angles, as if the world were flat, were helpful on short voyages, but the world is round and on long voyages such maps were misleading, even dangerous. Maps drawn in accordance with the systems of cartographic projection inherited from Ptolemy were geometrically consistent and academically useful depictions of the earth's surface, but not helpful to the sailor who wanted to plot a course across not a sea but an ocean.[13]

Lines of latitude are called parallels because they are just that, parallel. Lines of longitude, meridians, are not: they are curves that meet at the poles. On a chart uniformly crosshatched like graph paper a course of constant bearing (a rhumb) is a straight line, but it is not that on the surface of the earth (unless the course is due north–south or east–west, which will seldom take you where you want to go). A rhumb cuts each curving meridian at a slightly different angle than the previous one and is itself a curve. A navigator needs a multiple paradox, a flat map of the round world on which he can draw a rhumb, a curved line in actuality, with a straightedge.

The Portuguese geographer Pedro Nuñez discovered that a line of constant bearing (again unless north–south or east–west) beginning at the equator is a long spiral ending at a pole. His spiraling rhumbs apparently fascinated Gerard Mercator, the Flemish cartographer, because he drew a set of them on his first terrestrial globe.[14] In the world map he printed in 1569, a "New and Improved Description of the Lands of the World, amended and intended for the Use of Navigators," he straightened the curved rhumbs by employing "a new proportion and a new arrangement of the meridians with reference to the parallels." He drew the meridians as parallel, an outrageous distortion enormously broadening poleward areas. He committed a further distortion by increasing the distances between the lines of latitude as

[13] Samuel Y. Edgerton, Jr., *The Renaissance Rediscovery of Linear Perspective* (New York: Basic Books, 1975), 99–110.

[14] E. G. R. Taylor, *The Haven-Finding Art: A History of Navigation from Odysseus to Captain Cook* (New York: Abelard-Schuman, 1957), 157–78.

they proceeded away from the equator in proportion to the artificial broadening of the distances between the meridians. The result was a map in which northern lands, Greenland, for instance, were enormously larger in proportion to the more southerly areas than in reality. But (a very useful but) sailors could plot compass courses as straight lines on maps drawn in accordance with Mercator's projection.[15] As with Dürer's distorted head, the consistency of a single characteristic was preserved, but at the expense of just about everything else.

Albertian perspective was the product of efforts to preserve as much of visualized spatial and directional accuracy as was compatible with reducing three dimensions to two. The sixteenth century Mannerist painters distorted Albertian perspective for the sake of dramatic effect. *Portolani* and Ptolemaic maps were the results of efforts to preserve a maximum of directional and spatial accuracy while depicting the earth's roundness on a flat surface. Mercator made a map grossly distorting size for the sake of one thing, sailorly convenience. It was a visual tour de force.

He left no explanation of the mathematics of his projection, perhaps because he, like Giotto, had proceeded on the basis of experience and guesswork rather than rigorous theory. An Englishman, Edward Wright, provided the mathematics in his 1599 book, *Certaine Errors of Navigation*. He may have utilized for the complicated calculations an early form of what was arguably the last gift of the Renaissance and the first gift of Scotland to mathematics, the system of logarithms being thought out by the eighth laird of Merchiston, John Napier.[16]

Napier was working on logarithms in the 1590s, but this

[15] John Noble Wilford, *The Mapmakers: The Story of the Great Pioneers in Cartography from Antiquity to the Space Age* (New York: Vintage Books, 1982), 73–7.

[16] Ibid., 76; Taylor, *The Haven-Finding Art*, 223, 226; Margaret E. Baron, "Napier, John," in *The Dictionary of Scientific Biography*, ed. Charles C. Gillispie (New York: Scribner's, 1970–80), 9: 610.

fanatic Calvinist was distracted by the religious broils of the day. He wrote a treatise on the Revelation of St. John the Divine, identifying Rome as "the mother of all spiritual whoredom," and planned giant mirrors to focus the sun's rays on enemy ships and destroy them "at whatever appointed distance." Common folk thought him a limb of the Devil, as they did many mathematicians. It was not until 1614 that he published his *Mirifici logarithmorum canonis descriptio* (*A Description of the Marvelous Rule of Logarithms*), with its pages and pages of columns, cascades, cataracts of numbers, numbers, numbers.[17]

The West in the sixteenth century was unique. It was advancing faster than any other large society in its ability to harness and control its environment. Few if any other societies equaled the West in its science and technology, its ability to project its power over long distances and to improvise new institutions and new commercial and bureaucratic techniques. The other side of that coin was the West's instability. It shook and rattled and fizzed as if about to blow itself to pieces, which it nearly did.

Montaigne, sane in an insane age, protested religious war and the random ravaging that followed on its heels, war "so malign and so destructive that it destroys itself along with everything else, tearing itself limb from limb in its frenzy." He condemned the witchcraft epidemic, commenting that "it is to place a very high value on your surmises to roast a man alive for them." The West sought pious certainty through massacre – for example, the obliteration of the Anabaptists of Münster – and burned and otherwise

---

[17] John Napier, *Construction of the Wonderful Canon of Logarithms* (London: Dawsons of Pall Mall, 1966), xv–xvi; Carl B. Boyer, *A History of Mathematics* (Princeton, N.J.: Princeton University Press, 1985), 342–3; "John Napier," in *The Dictionary of National Biography* (Oxford: Oxford University Press, reprint 1922–3), 14: 60–4.

rid the world of thousands of witches, warlocks, and were-wolves.[18]

The West fizzed and bucketed, but survived and eventually flourished. The New Model, visual and quantitative, was one of its antidotes for the nagging insufficiency of its traditional explanations for the mysteries of reality. The New Model offered a new way to examine reality and an armature around which to organize perceptions of that reality. It proved to be extraordinarily robust, providing humanity with unprecedented power and many humans with the comfort of a faith – it lasted for centuries – that they were capable of an intimate understanding of their universe.

Galileo Galilei, a skilled lutenist whose father, though driven to buying and selling wool by necessity, was a musician and one of the most prominent music theorists of the sixteenth century; Galileo Galilei, an amateur artist skilled in perspective, a member of Florence's Accademia del Disegno (Academy of Drawing), and a gushing admirer of Michelangelo, Raphael, and Titian;[19] Galileo, who was in himself a personification of the chief themes of

---

[18] Brian P. Levack, *The Witch-Hunt in Early Modern Europe* (London: Longman, 1987), 21.

[19] Claude V. Palisca, "Scientific Empiricism in Musical Thought," in *Seventeenth Century Science and the Arts,* ed. Hedley H. Rhys (Princeton, N.J.: Princeton University Press, 1961), 92; James Reston, Jr., *Galileo: A Life* (New York: HarperCollins, 1994), 6–10; Stillman Drake, *Galileo at Work: His Scientific Biography* (Chicago: University of Chicago Press, 1978), 15–17; Stillman Drake, *Galileo Studies: Personality, Tradition, and Revolution* (Ann Arbor: University of Michigan Press, 1970), 43; Edgerton, *Heritage of Giotto's Geometry,* 223–53; Galileo Galilei, *Dialogue Concerning the Two Chief World Systems,* trans. Stillman Drake (Berkeley: University of California Press, 1967), 104–5. For further information on the involvement of Descartes, Stevin, Kepler, and other contemporary scientists in music theory, see H. F. Cohen, *Quantifying Music: The Science of Music in the First Stage of the Scientific Revolution, 1580–1650* (Dordrecht: Reidel, 1984).

Bruegel's *Temperance* – Galileo expressed in one famous paragraph the visual and quantitative character of the New Model and, as well, the optimism it engendered:

> Philosophy is written in this grand book, the universe, which stands continually open to our gaze, but the book cannot be understood unless one first learns to comprehend the language and read the letters in which it is composed. It is written in the language of mathematics, and its characters are triangles, circles, and other geometric figures without which it is humanly impossible to understand a single word of it; without these, one wanders about in a dark labyrinth.[20]

[20] *Discoveries and Opinions of Galileo,* trans. Stillman Drake (Garden City, N.Y.: Doubleday, 1957), 237–8.

Index

241